D1747652

# *Kulturschätze in Deutschland*

## *Cultural Treasures in Germany*

Erhard Hehl
Rita Henß

# *Kulturschätze in Deutschland*

## Cultural Treasures in Germany

Englische Fassung:
Claudia Spinner

**SIGLOCH EDITION**

*Wer Weltkulturerbe hört, denkt sicher spontan an Bauwerke voller Pracht. Insofern kann ein Blick zum Altar der Wieskirche (Seite 2) im oberbayerischen Pfaffenwinkel richtig einstimmen. Meisterwerke sakraler und profaner Kunst sind eine sehr starke Fraktion in der zur Zeit mehr als 600 Objekte umfassenden Welterbe-Liste. Doch in ihr sind auch eine Reihe anderer Monumente vertreten: historische Industriekultur, beispielhafte Museen, großartige Landschaften – ob nun von Natur aus so vorhanden oder von Menschen mehr oder weniger stark gestaltet.*

# Inhalt

| | |
|---|---|
| **Vorwort** | 5 |
| **Kloster Maulbronn** | 7 |
| **Die Residenz Würzburg** | 13 |
| **Bamberg** | 19 |
| **Die Alte Völklinger Hütte** | 25 |
| **Die Quedlinburger Altstadt** | 29 |
| **Der Dom zu Aachen** | 35 |
| **Goslar und der Rammelsberg** | 41 |
| **Die Wieskirche** | 47 |
| **Grube Messel** | 53 |
| **Die Schlösser in Brühl** | 57 |
| **Trier** | 63 |
| **Hildesheim** | 69 |
| **Schlösser und Parks von Potsdam** | 75 |
| **Kloster Lorsch** | 85 |
| **Der Kölner Dom** | 91 |
| **Klassisches Weimar** | 97 |
| **Der Dom zu Speyer** | 103 |
| **Das Bauhaus in Dessau** | 109 |
| **Lübeck** | 115 |
| **Luthergedenkstätte Wittenberg** | 121 |
| **Die Wartburg** | 127 |
| **Die Berliner Museumsinsel** | 131 |
| **Register, Impressum** | 132 |

# Contents

| | |
|---|---|
| **Preface** | 5 |
| **Maulbronn Monastery** | 7 |
| **The Würzburg Royal Residence** | 13 |
| **Bamberg** | 19 |
| **The Old Ironworks at Völklingen** | 25 |
| **Quedlinburg Old Town** | 29 |
| **The Cathedral of Aachen** | 35 |
| **Goslar and the Rammelsberg Mountain** | 41 |
| **The Wieskirche Church** | 47 |
| **The Messel Pit** | 53 |
| **The Palaces at Brühl** | 57 |
| **Trier** | 63 |
| **Hildesheim** | 69 |
| **The Palaces and Parks of Potsdam** | 75 |
| **Lorsch Monastery** | 85 |
| **The Cathedral of Cologne** | 91 |
| **Classical Weimar** | 97 |
| **The Cathedral of Speyer** | 103 |
| **The Bauhaus at Dessau** | 109 |
| **Lübeck** | 115 |
| **The Wittenberg Luther Memorial** | 121 |
| **The Wartburg** | 127 |
| **The Berlin Museum Island** | 131 |
| **Index, Colophon** | 132 |

*More often than not, the term "world heritage" calls up a vision of splendid buildings. Thus, a view onto the Wieskirche altar (p. 2) in the Upper Bavarian Pfaffenwinkel may well set the right mood. Masterworks of sacral or profane art make up a large part of the UNESCO world heritage list of currently 600 objects, but a number of other sites are also included: historical industrial culture, exemplary museums, grandiose landscapes formed by nature or more or less man-made.*

## Vorwort

1959 bat Ägypten die UNESCO, die Sonderorganisation der Vereinten Nationen für Bildung, Wissenschaft, Kultur und Kommunikation, um Hilfe bei der Rettung von Abu Simbel zusammen mit dem gesamten Umfeld der vom Assuan-Staudamm bedrohten nubischen Tempel. Fünfzig Länder beteiligten sich an den Rettungsaktionen, darunter auch die Bundesrepublik Deutschland und die DDR. Aus diesem konkreten Projekt erwuchs eine neue, beispielhafte Idee: Die herausragenden Kultur- und Naturstätten der Welt gehören nicht allein den Staaten oder Völkern, auf deren Boden sie sich befinden, sondern sind Eigentum der gesamten Menschheit.

Das Welterbe-Programm der UNESCO ist eine weltweite Gemeinschaftsaktion der Regierungen und Fachorganisationen, über alle politischen und wirtschaftlichen Grenzen hinweg. Im Mittelpunkt steht die Selbstverpflichtung der jeweils verantwortlichen Regierungen. Das zwischenstaatliche UNESCO-Welterbe-Komitee nimmt nur solche Vorschläge zur Prüfung an, die zusammen mit konkreten Plänen und Garantien zur Erhaltung des kulturellen Erbes eingereicht werden. Erst dann treten die internationalen Gutachter in Aktion und untersuchen, wie einzigartig und international bedeutend das Objekt ist.

Die Annahme der Auszeichnung als Welterbe bedeutet zwar, auf ein Stück Souveränität zu Gunsten der internationalen Gemeinschaft zu verzichten, aber auch dauerhafte Garantie für internationale Wachsamkeit beim Schutz des Kulturerbes gegen kurzfristige wirtschaftliche Interessen.

Deutschland ist mit 22 Stätten auf der UNESCO-Welterbe-Liste vertreten. Daraus ergibt sich eine dreifache Verantwortung: Wir müssen alles Nötige auf uns nehmen, um dieses kulturelle Erbe authentisch zu bewahren. Wir müssen es in sinnvoller Weise allen zugänglich machen, die es kennen lernen möchten. Dieser schöne Band trägt dazu bei. Die Auszeichnung unserer eigenen Welterbe-Stätten weist uns jedoch auch auf eine noch wichtigere Aufgabe hin – dem Erbe aller Völker dieser Erde mit Interesse und Aufgeschlossenheit zu begegnen.

Bonn, im Dezember 1999
Dr. Traugott Schöfthaler,
Generalsekretär der Deutschen UNESCO-Kommission

## Preface

In 1959, Egypt asked UNESCO, the United Nations' organization responsible for education, research, culture and communications for help with saving Abu Simbel and the entire surroundings of the Nubian temple area, which were being threatened by the Assuan dam. Fifty countries participated in the rescue operations, among them the Federal Republic of Germany and the GDR. A new, exemplary idea then emerged from this particular project: Outstanding cultural and natural sites around the world not only belong to the states and nations whose soil they rest on, but should be considered the property of all humankind.

The UNESCO World Heritage Program is a joint action program by governments and organizations all over the world, transcending all political and economic borders. It is based on the voluntary commitment of the governments in charge. The crossnational UNESCO World Heritage Committee accepts proposals for consideration only if they are submitted together with concrete plans and guarantees for the preservation of the cultural heritage in question. If this is the case, international experts are appointed to evaluate the uniqueness and international significance of the respective object.

For a nation, the acceptance of the cultural heritage site distinction does entail the yielding of some of its sovereignty to the international community, but, in return, it is also a lasting guarantee for international attention to the protection of cultural heritage sites from short-term economic interests.

Germany is represented on the list of UNESCO World Heritage sites with no less than 22 entries, a fact that spells triple responsibility: We must endeavor, with all our might, to preserve our cultural heritage in an authentic state. We must make it accessible, and in a meaningful way, to all those who wish to benefit from it, an action to which this attractive book will contribute its fair share. And finally, our own World Heritage sites awards also point to another, even more important task: that we look at the heritage of all peoples around the globe with interest and an open mind.

Bonn, December 1999
Dr. Traugott Schöfthaler,
Secretary General of the UNESCO Commission in Germany

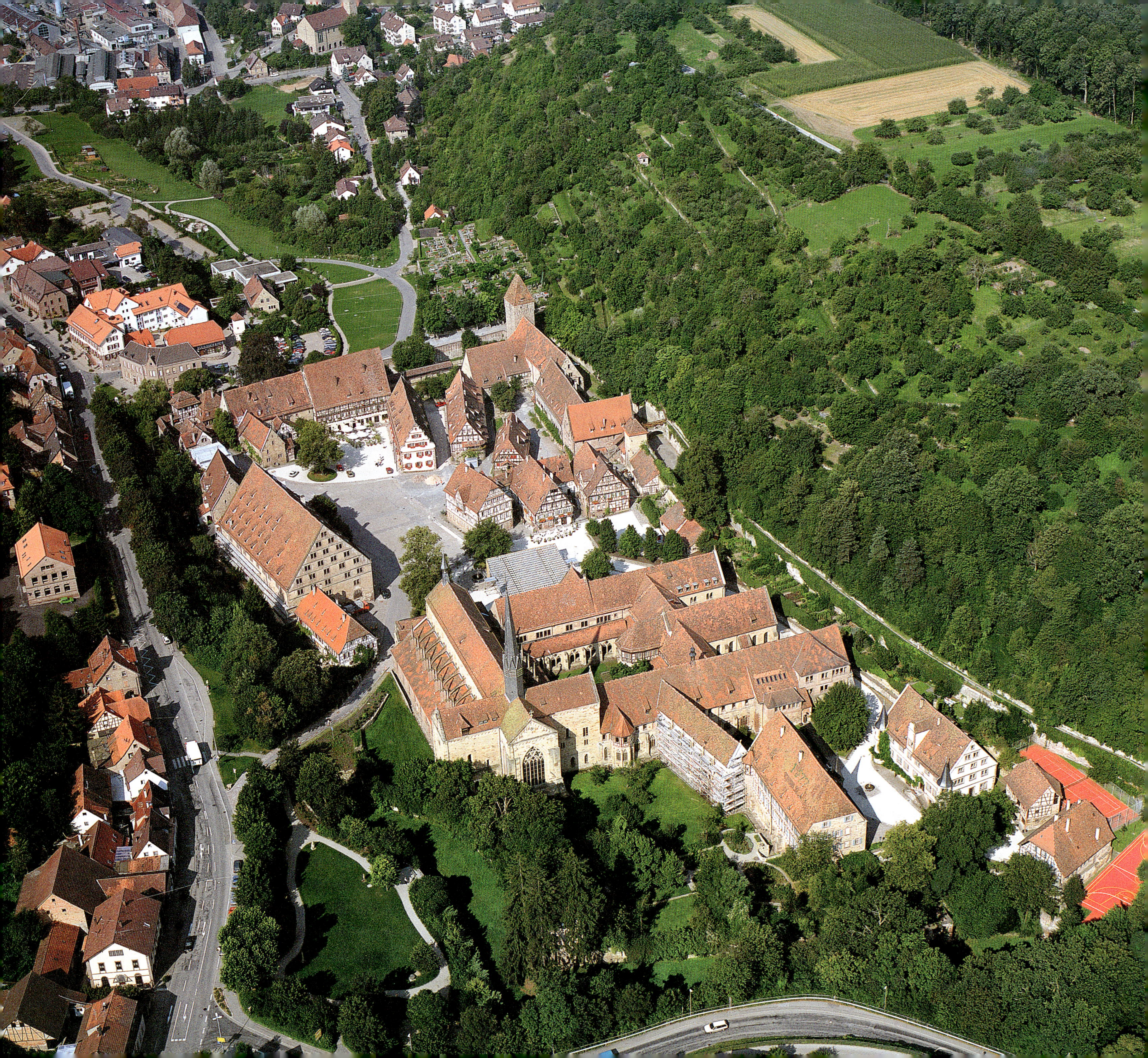

*Einzigartiges Architekturdenkmal inmitten intakter Natur: Das 1178 geweihte Zisterzienserkloster Maulbronn gilt als die am vollständigsten erhaltene Klosteranlage nördlich der Alpen (links und nächste Doppelseite). Neben Kirche, Krankenhaus und dem Konventbereich mit dem berühmten Speisesaal (auch Refektorium oder Remter genannt) der Chorherrenmönche umfasste sie zahlreiche Wirtschaftsbauten wie Haberkasten, Pfisterei (Bäckerei), Mühle, Bursarium (Finanzabteilung), Gesindehaus und Speisemeisterei.*

# Kloster Maulbronn

Wehrtürme, Krankenhaus, Mühle, Schmiede, Küferei und Wagnerei, ein Refektorium für die Laienbrüder und eines für die Herren – wie eine wehrhafte kleine Stadt errichteten die Zisterziensermönche aus dem elsässischen Neuburg jene Klosteranlage im lieblichen Salzachtal östlich von Karlsruhe: Maulbronn. Am 14. Mai 1178, nach 30-jähriger Bauzeit, weihte der päpstliche Legat und Erzbischof Arnold von Trier das romanische Grundensemble aus gelbem Keupersandstein. In den folgenden fast 300 Jahren wurde es immer wieder erweitert und verändert. Die französische Gotik mit ihren filigranen Wölbungen, Kreuzrippen, Pfeilern und Säulen brach die wuchtige bauliche Nüchternheit auf, die der asketischen Denkweise der reformerischen Zisterzienser entsprach; die Stile paarten und vermischten sich. Ein Glanzpunkt in der Baugeschichte Maulbronns ist das Refektorium, der Speisesaal der Chorherrenmönche: ein zweischiffiger Raum, höher, reicher, aufwendiger gebaut als alle anderen Klosterräume seiner Zeit. Und die Brunnenkapelle – ein wunderbarer Platz – wird oft gepriesen als Inbegriff Maulbronner Klosterarchitektur.

Um den Namen des Klosters rankt sich übrigens eine hübsche Legende: Da die Zisterziensermönche angeblich nicht wussten, an welcher Stelle des ihnen zugedachten Lehens sie ihr neues Refugium errichten sollten, ließen sie im Salzachtal ihr Maultier frei laufen. Dort, wo es stehen bleiben würde, so hatten sie beschlossen, würden sie das Kloster bauen. Das Muli verhielt seinen Schritt an einer Quelle. Dieser Bronn sprudelt noch heute auf dem Klostergelände.

Nach der Reformation wurde die wehrhafte Mönchsburg zur evangelischen Klosterschule für besonders begabte Schüler. Zu den Eleven zählte auch Johannes Kepler, der später als Astronom von sich reden machte. 1806 wandelte man die Schule um in ein evangelisch-theologisches Seminar. Friedrich Hölderlin erhielt hier sein Zertifikat für Poesie und auch Justinus Kerner gehörte zum Studentenkorps. Hermann Hesse büffelte ebenfalls in den Maulbronner Klostermauern. Er setzte der Anlage in seinen Werken „Unterm Rad" und „Glasperlenspiel" ein literarisches Denkmal.

# Maulbronn Monastery

Battlements, an infirmary, a mill, a smithy, a cooper's workshop and separate refectories for lay brethren and canons – Cistercian monks from Neuburg in Alsace built Maulbronn, the monastery complex in the pleasant Salzach valley east of Karlsruhe in the manner of a small fortified town. On May 14, 1178, after thirty years of construction, the Romanesque nucleus made of yellow sandstone was consecrated by the papal legate and archbishop Arnold of Trier. In the 300 years to follow, the building underwent numerous enlargements and changes. The sober, massive structure reflecting the asceticism of the reform-minded Cistercians was broken up by elements in the French Gothic style such as filigree arches, cross ribs, piers and columns; other styles merged and mixed. The refectory, i.e. the canons' dining-room, belongs among the highlights of Maulbronn's architectural history: a two-aisled hall, higher, richer and more elaborately built than any other monastic hall at the time. And the well chapel – a marvelous place – is often praised as the epitome of monastic architecture at Maulbronn.

Legend has it that the monastery owes its name to the following incident: Since the Cistercian monks were unsure as to the exact positioning of their new refuge on the newly granted fief, they let their mule run wild in the Salzach valley after having agreed to build the monastery wherever the mule came to a halt. The mule stopped at a spring, the spring that still wells up on the monastery grounds today.

After the reformation, the fortified monk's castle became a Protestant monastic school for gifted students. One of the students was Johannes Kepler, later a renowned astronomer. In 1806, the school was converted into a Protestant theological seminary. Friedrich Hölderlin received his diploma in poetry here, and Justinus Kerner, too, was among the students. Even Hermann Hesse applied himself to his books behind the Maulbronn monastery walls. The complex was immortalized in his works "Under the Wheel" and "Glass Pearl Game".

*A unique architectural site amidst unspoilt nature: The Cistercian monastery Maulbronn, consecrated in 1178, is the most intact monastery complex preserved north of the Alps (left and overleaf). It includes the church, an infirmary, the convent area with its famous canons' dining-room or refectory, as well as domestic buildings such as the oatcrib, mill, bakery, bursary, servants' quarters and larder.*

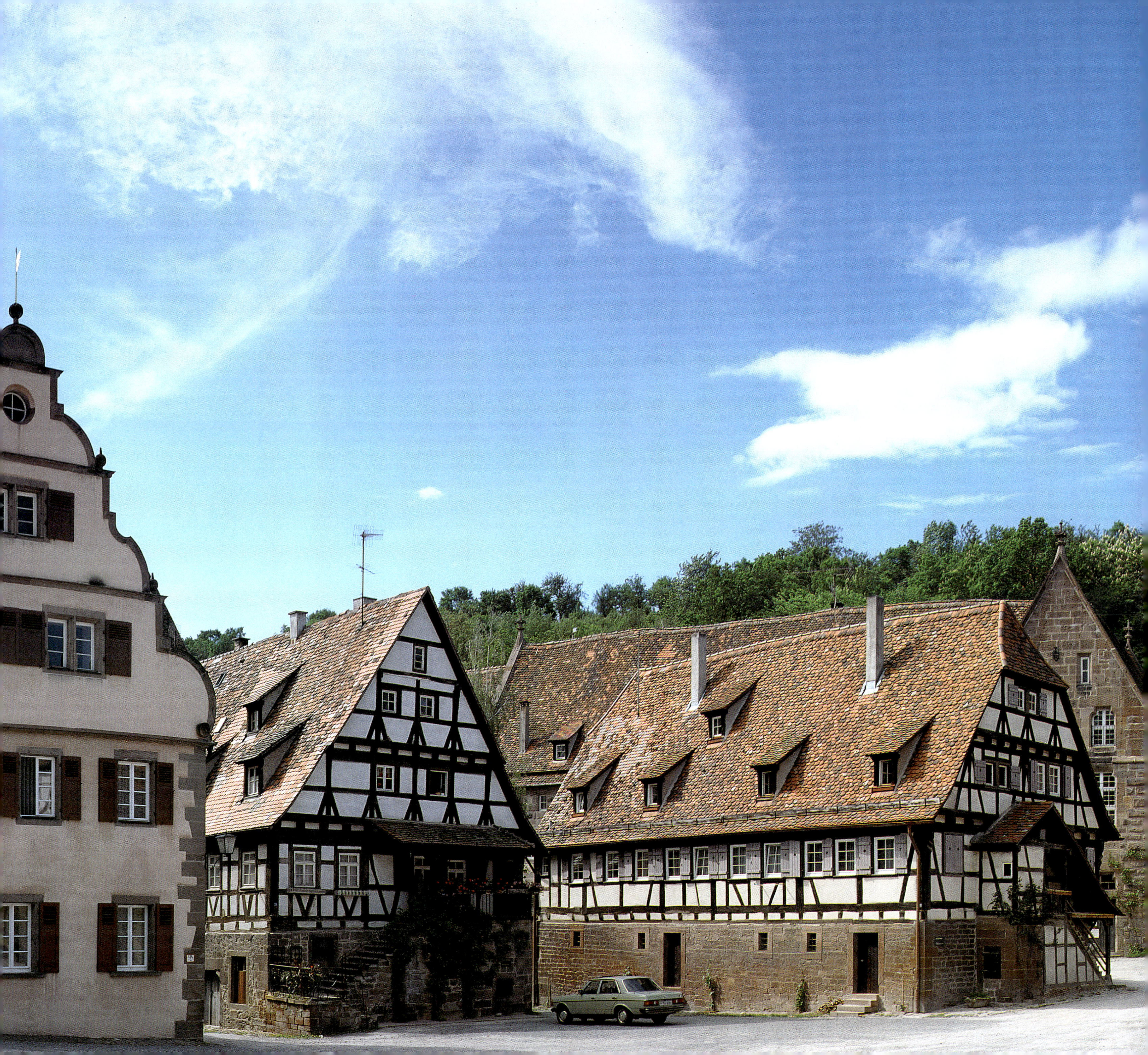

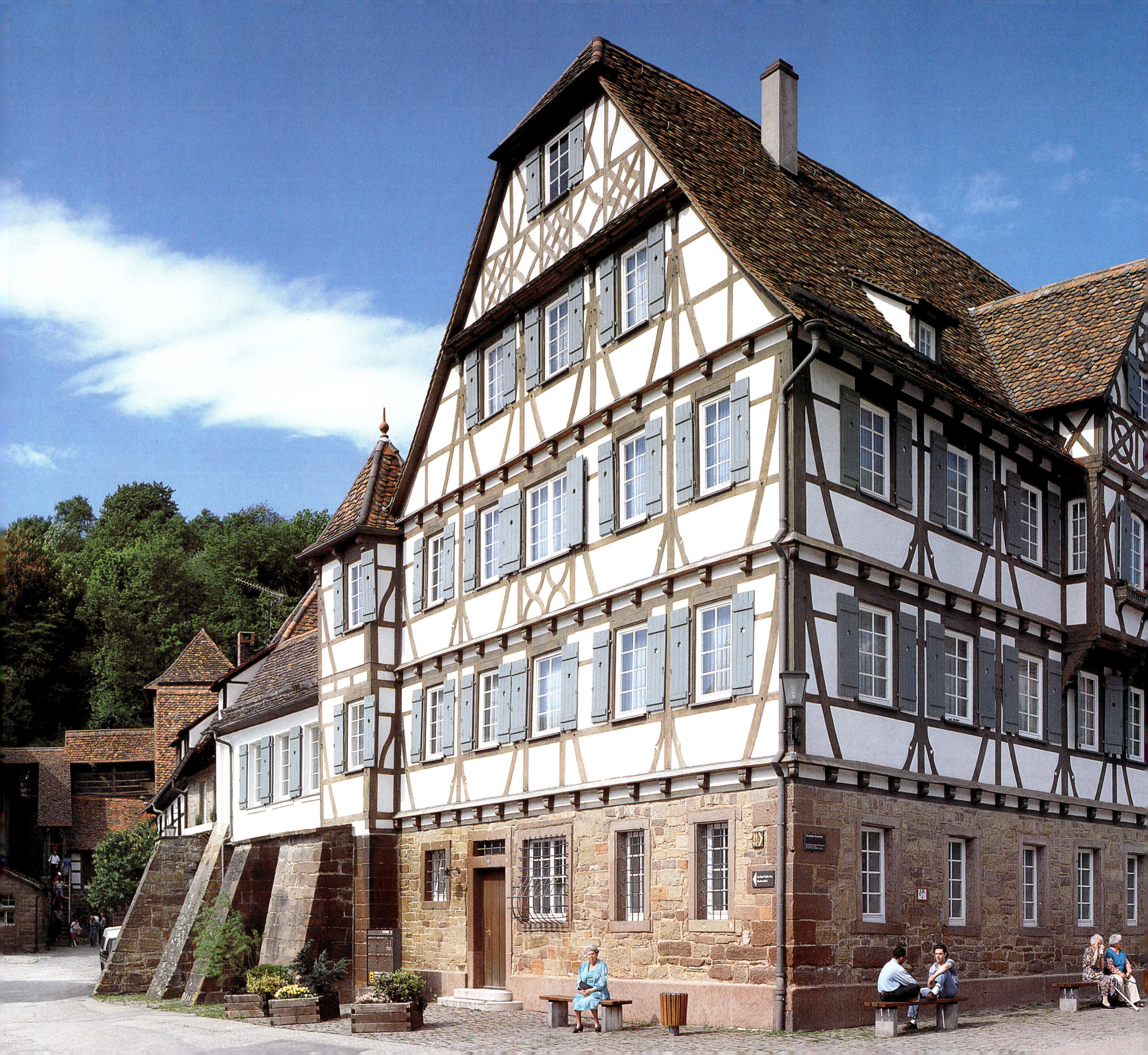

*Die Klosterkirche mit ihrer im Urzustand des 12. Jahrhunderts erhaltenen Chorschranke ist ein bedeutendes Beispiel der oberrheinischen Spätromanik.
Aus der Mitte des 14. Jahrhunderts stammt die Brunnenkapelle, dem Kreuzgang angegliedert. Mit ihrem dreischaligen Brunnen diente sie den Mönchen als Waschstätte; hier ließen sie sich auch die Tonsur scheren und den Bart schneiden.*

*The monastery church with its original 12th century chancel screen is an important example of the Upper Rhine Valley's late Romanesque style.
The well chapel off the cloister dates back to the 14th century. The monks used the well with its three basins as a grooming-place, including beard-trimming and the shaving of tonsures.*

*Das herzogliche Jagdschloss am Rande des Klosterareals – ein typischer Renaissancebau – wurde zeitweise von den Landesherren genutzt. Damals lebten in Maulbronn keine Mönche mehr und das Kloster war bereits zu einer evangelischen Klosterschule umgewandelt worden.*

*The ducal hunting-palace on the edge of the monastery grounds – a typical Renaissance structure – was occasionally frequented by the sovereign. At that time, Maulbronn was no longer inhabited by monks and had already become a Protestant monastic college.*

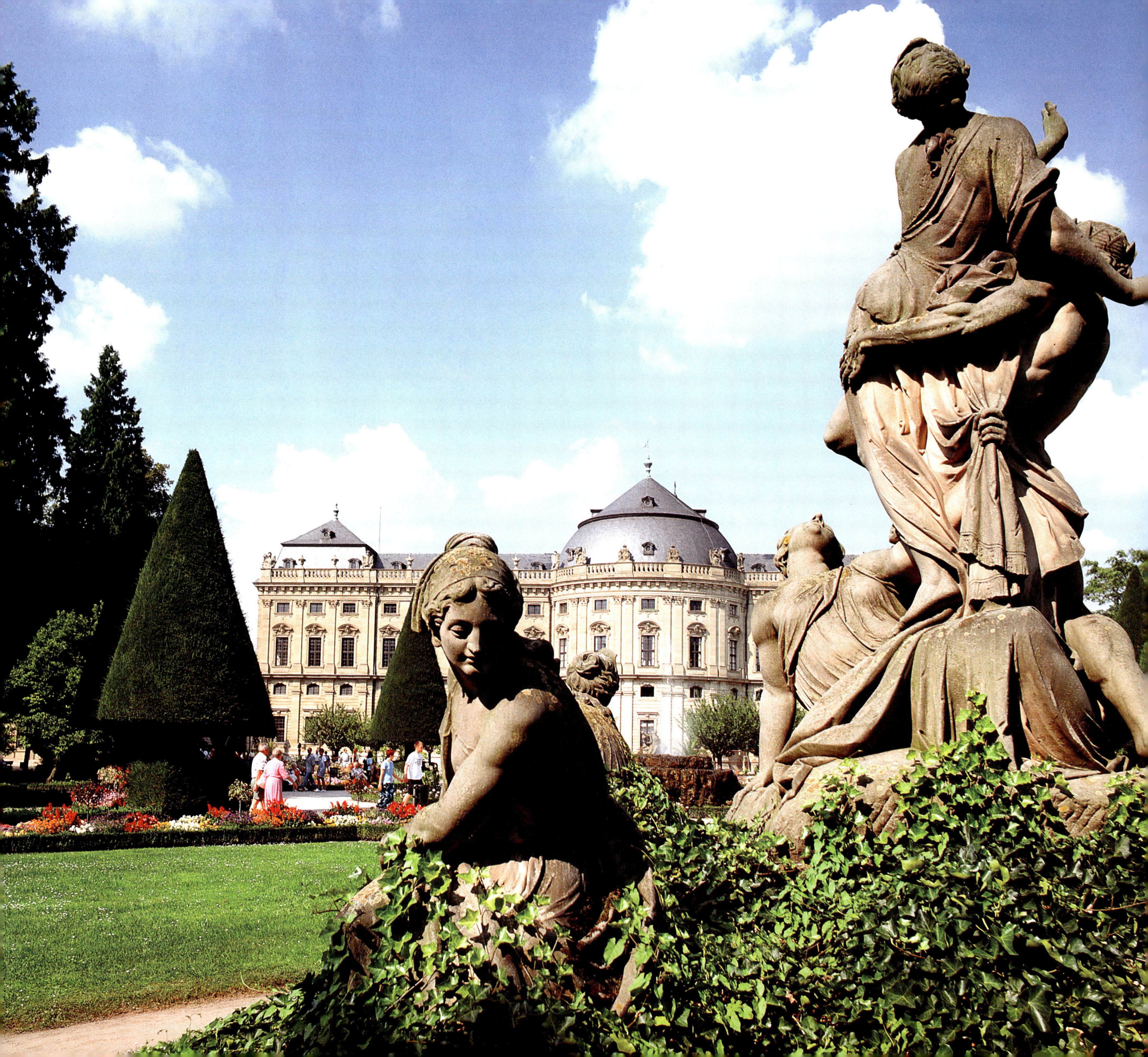

*Am Bau der Würzburger Residenz beteiligten sich die angesehensten Architekten, Kunsthandwerker und Künstler ihrer Zeit. Prunkstück des dreiflügeligen, von Gärten umgebenen Barockschlosses ist der von Balthasar Neumann, dem Hofbaumeister des Fürstbischofs, entworfene kühne Treppenhaussaal mit dem riesigen Deckengemälde von Giovanni Battista Tiepolo (nächste Doppelseite).*
*Mit der Anlage der prachtvollen Residenz-Gärten wurde erst begonnen, als die Bauten fertig waren. Seither wurden sie mehrfach umgestaltet.*

## Die Residenz Würzburg

Zu Recht wird sie mit den Schlössern von Versailles und Schönbrunn verglichen: die Würzburger Residenz, Paradebeispiel für ein Gesamtkunstwerk, bei dem Baukunst, Malerei, Plastik und Stuckaturen zu einer Einheit verschmelzen. Am 22. Mai 1720 legte Fürstbischof Johann Philipp Franz von Schönborn höchstpersönlich den Grundstein. Ein Monument des Ruhmes und der Kaisertreue seiner Familie wollte der Regent mit dem Schlossneubau geschaffen wissen und engagierte die Besten in der Branche. Johann Lucas von Hildebrandt aus Wien sowie die französischen Barock-Baumeister, Robert de Cotte und Germain Boffrand, steuerten Entwürfe bei; die Ausführungspläne jedoch zeichnete der junge Hofbaumeister des Fürstbischofs, Balthasar Neumann. Der sollte auch bis zur Vollendung des gewaltigen, dreiflügeligen Sandstein-Baus, der einen Ehrenhof und fünf Innenhöfe umschließt, die Oberhand über alle Arbeiten und Vorschläge behalten.

Wie wagemutig und genial der Würzburger Oberbaumeister arbeitete, zeigt sich vor allem im Mittelbau der Residenz. Hier gelang Neumann – als Einstimmung auf die prunkvollen Säle und Zimmerfluchten der Doppelanlage – ein gigantischer, lichter Treppenraum. Und dessen in etlichen Metern Höhe scheinbar schwebendes Muldengewölbe füllte Giovanni Battista Tiepolo mit einem einzigen herrlichen Fresko. Es zeigt die vier damals bekannten Erdteile und im darüber liegenden Himmel die Götter des Olymp. Neben Tiepolo, der auch den Kaisersaal mit Gemälden schmückte, prägten Antonio Bossi und Wolfgang van der Auwera die Innenausstattung der Würzburger Residenz. Gemeinsam schufen der italienische Stuckator und der flämische Bildhauer in den Jahren 1742 bis 1745 unter anderem das Spiegelkabinett. Es gilt als eines der vollkommensten Raumkunstwerke des Rokoko.

Beim Bombenangriff auf Würzburg am 16. März 1945 trotzte nur der Mittelbau mit der großartigen Raumfolge Balthasar Neumanns und den Fresken Tiepolos dem Inferno. Inzwischen wurde die gesamte Anlage restauriert. Neben den museal genutzten Prunkräumen birgt sie eine Reihe staatlicher Einrichtungen, darunter Hochschulinstitute und das Staatsarchiv.

## The Würzburg Royal Residence

The Würzburg Royal Residence has rightly been compared to Versailles and Schönbrunn – the classic example of a unified work of art where painting, sculpture and stucco art meld into a harmonious whole. On May 22, 1720, Prince Bishop Johann Philipp Franz von Schönborn personally laid the cornerstone. The sovereign's intention was to create a monument to his fame and his family's loyalty to the emperor, and he hired only the best in the field. The Vienna-born Johann Lucas von Hildebrandt as well as the two most renowned Baroque master builders, Robert de Cotte and German Boffrand, contributed designs; the final plans, however, were drawn by the prince bishop's young court master builder, Balthasar Neumann. It was he who oversaw all work executed or proposed until the completion of the massive three-winged sandstone structure which encompasses a court of honor and five inner courtyards.

The genius and innovativeness of the Würzburg master builder are especially evident in the center wing. Here, Neumann – anticipating the splendid chambers and suites of the twin structure – succeeded in creating a gigantic, airy staircase. Its lofty, seemingly floating vault construction, longer than wide, was decorated with a marvelous single fresco by Giovanni Battista Tiepolo. It shows the four continents known at the time and the Olympian Gods in the heavens above it. Apart from Tiepolo, who also painted the Imperial Hall, the interior decorations of the Würzburg Residence are the work of Antonio Bossi and Wolfgang van der Auwera. Between 1742 and 1745, the plasterer from Italy and the sculptor from Flanders crafted the mirror cabinet – considered one of the most ambitious rococo room designs –, among other things.

At the bombing of Würzburg on March 16, 1945, only the center building with its splendid suite of rooms by Balthasar Neumann and the frescoes by Tiepolo withstood the inferno. Meanwhile, the whole complex has been restored. Apart from the state rooms, now a museum, the complex includes a number of public institutions, university departments and the state archive among them.

*The Würzburg Royal Residence was built by the most renowned architects, craftsmen and artists of the time. The showpiece of the three-winged Baroque palace surrounded by gardens is the bold stairway designed by the royal master builder Balthasar Neumann, and its gigantic ceiling fresco by Giovanni Battista Tiepolo (overleaf).*
*The magnificent residence gardens were begun only after the buildings' completion and were redesigned a number of times.*

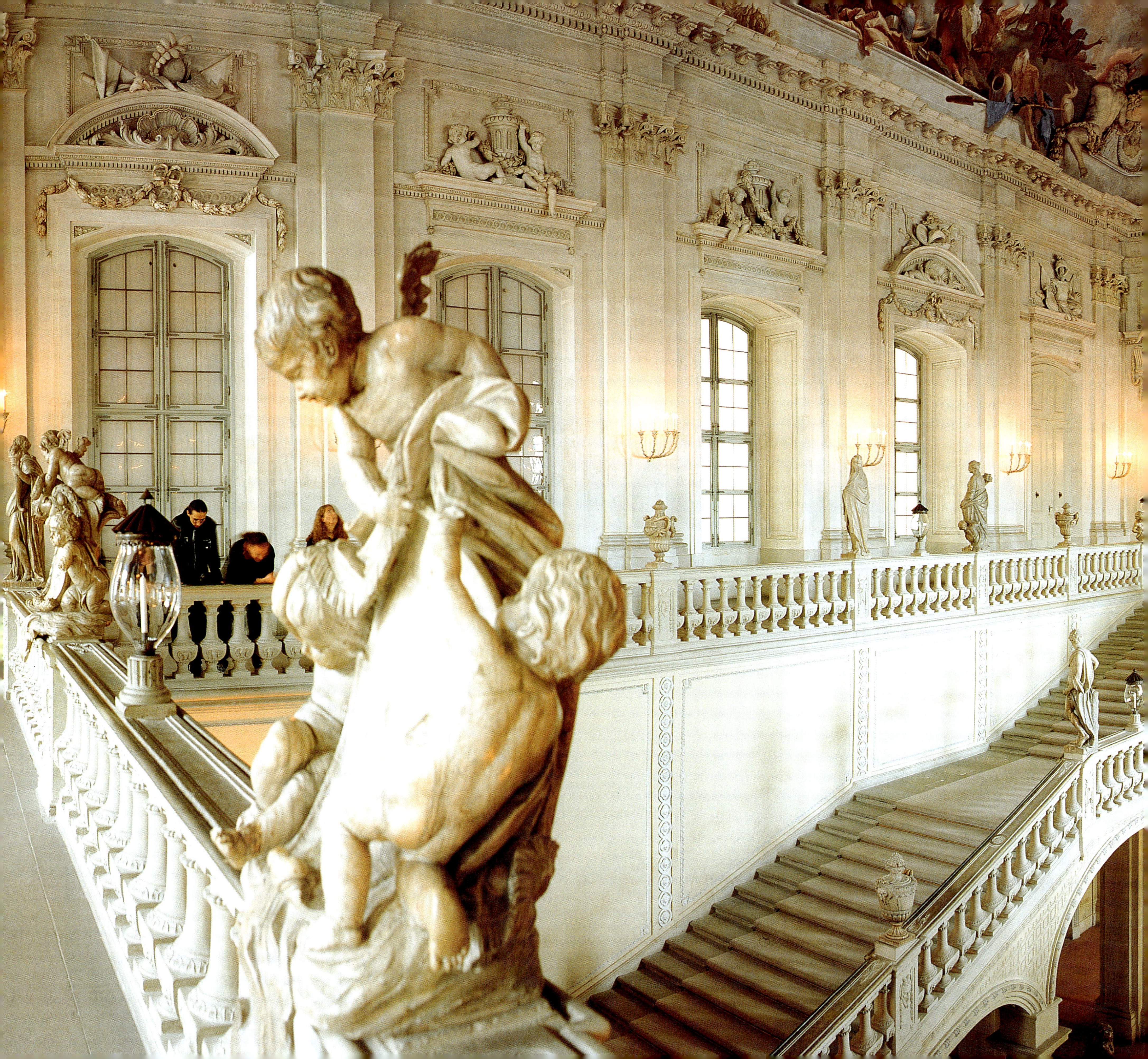

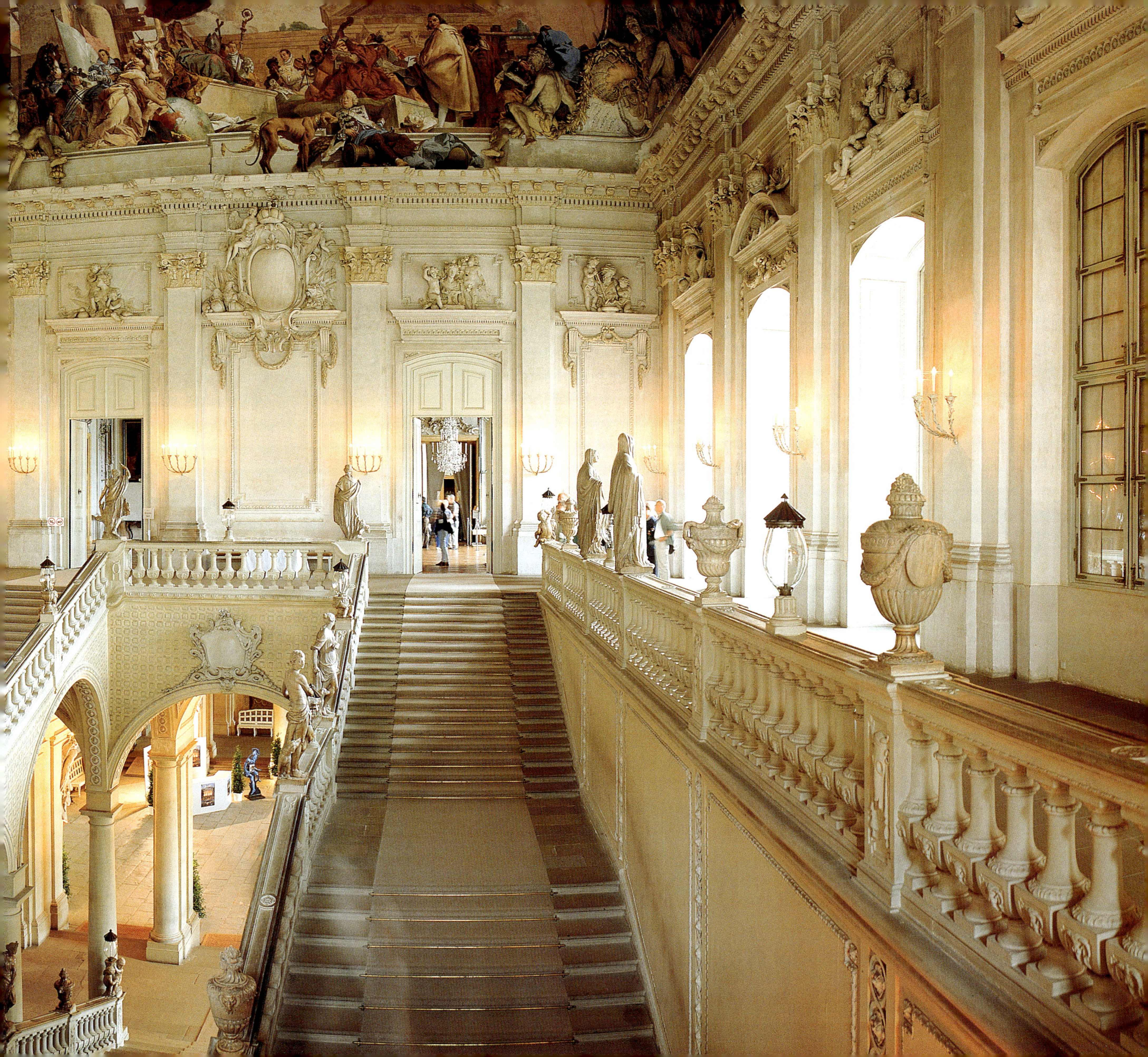

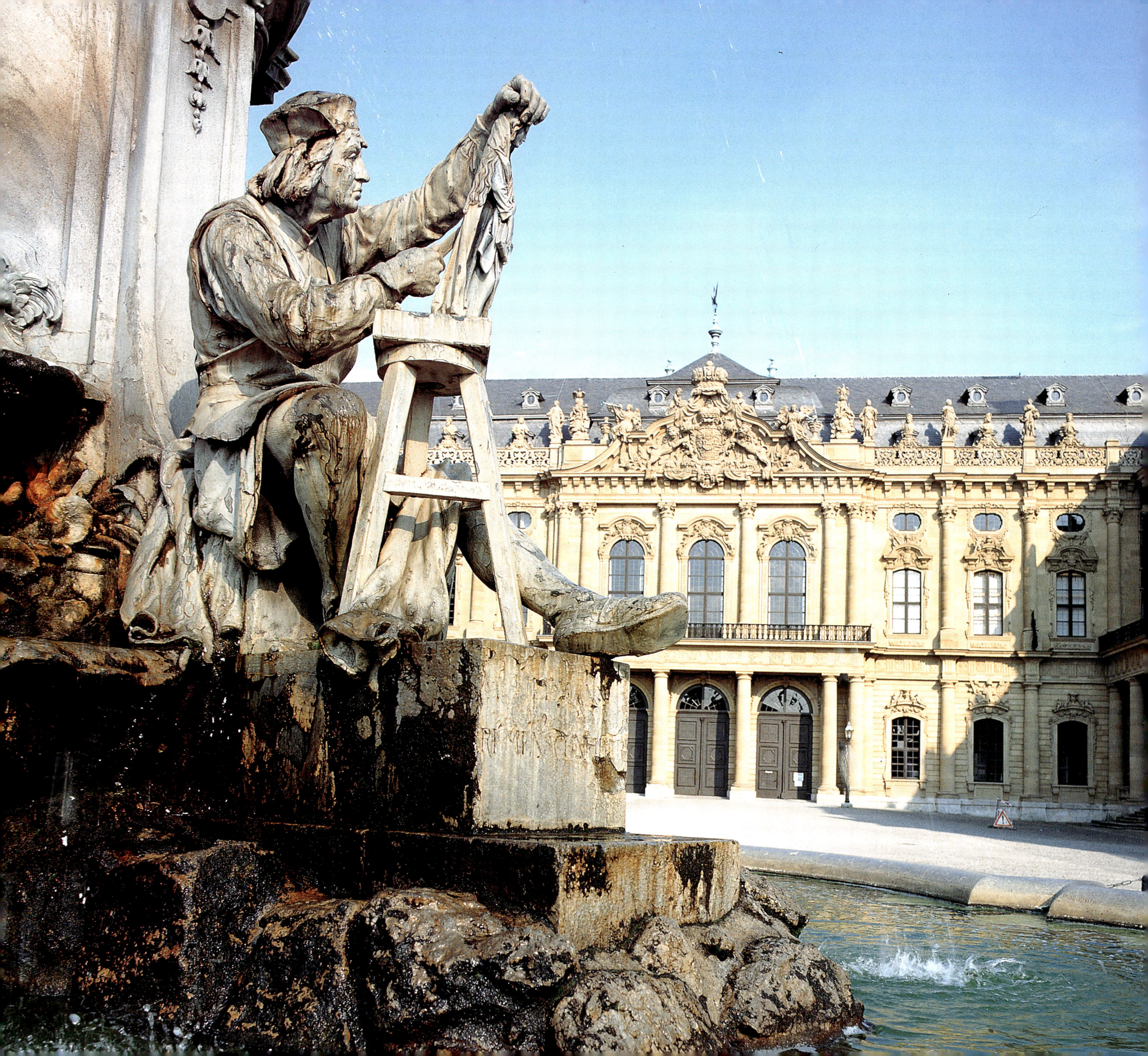

*Das Spiegelkabinett, das teilweise auch mit Hinterglasmalereien aufwartet, zählt zu den originellsten seiner Zeit in Europa. Die Plastiken und Skulpturengruppen für den Park (rechts) entwarf Peter Wagner. Eine der Figuren, die den Brunnen im Ehrenhof vor der Residenz säumen, stellt den großen Sohn Würzburgs dar, den Bildhauer und Schnitzer Tilman Riemenschneider (links).*

Die Komposition von Vestibül, Treppenhaus, Weißem Saal und Kaisersaal lässt das Wort von der Residenz Würzburg als einer einzigartigen „Synthese des Europäischen Barock" verständlich erscheinen. Insgesamt umfasst der mächtige Sandsteinbau mehr als 300 Gemächer. Die an den Toskana-Saal im Südflügel angrenzende Hofkirche gilt als der vollkommenste Sakralbau des 18. Jahrhunderts in Deutschland.

The harmonious unity of the vestibule, staircase, White Hall and Imperial Hall justifies the common description of the Würzburg Residence as a unique "synthesis of the European Baroque". Altogether, the massive sandstone structure includes more than 300 rooms. The royal chapel adjoining the Tuscany Hall in the southern wing is considered the most accomplished 18th century sacral structure in Germany.

*The mirror cabinet, which also features numerous glass paintings, is one of the most original in Europe of its time. The sculptural works and ensembles in the park (left) were designed by Peter Wagner.
One of the figures surrounding the well in the court of honor in front of the residence depicts Würzburg's great son, the sculptor and carver Tilman Riemenschneider (far left).*

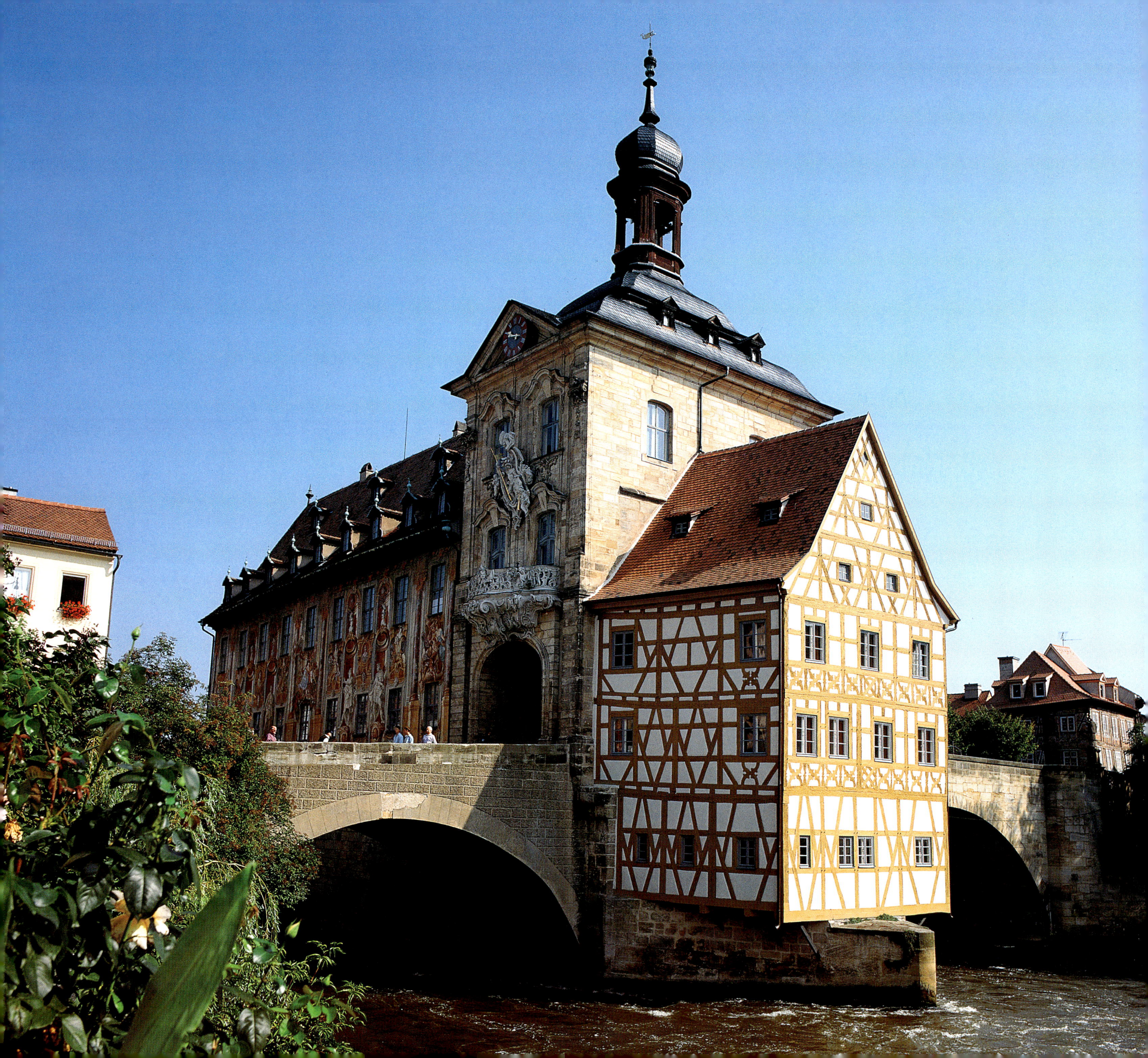

*Bambergs historisches Stadtbild vereint Bauwerke aus dem 11. bis 18. Jahrhundert. Mehr als tausend von ihnen stehen unter Denkmalschutz. Besonders eindrucksvoll ist das von der Regnitz umspülte, auf einer künstlichen Insel gelegene, zwischen 1744 und 1756 erbaute Alte Rathaus mit seinem viel älteren gotischen Brückenturm (links und nächste Doppelseite rechts der Mitte). Markante Punkte sind weiterhin (nächste Doppelseite von links): Ganz links am Horizont die Altenburg, im Mittelgrund das Karmeliterkloster, der viertürmige Dom, die Neue Residenz, die Spitzen der ehemaligen Benediktinerabtei St. Michael sowie die oft als „Klein-Venedig" bezeichneten Häuser der Gärtner und Fischer unten am Fluss.*

# Bamberg

Es sind wie in Rom sieben Hügel, über die sich Bamberg erstreckt. Zwar ist die Stadt an der Regnitz viel jünger, doch schon vor fast tausend Jahren wurden die Grundlagen des von Krieg und Zersiedelung weitgehend verschonten Stadtbilds geschaffen, genauer gesagt: links des Flusses die mittelalterliche Domstadt. Sie umspannt den Michaelisberg mit der gleichnamigen Benediktinerabtei sowie den Abts-, Jakobs-, Dom-, Stephans- und Kaulberg und den Altenburg-Hügel. Majestätisch ragt der spätromanisch-frühgotische, 1237 geweihte Kaiser-Dom auf, mit seinen vier Türmen und seinem weiträumigen Vorplatz, der von eindrucksvollen Gebäuden von der Gotik bis ins Rokoko gesäumt wird. Die Bildwerke im Dom zählen zu den hervorragendsten des 13. Jahrhunderts, das berühmteste ist zugleich Wahrzeichen der Stadt: der Bamberger Reiter.

Um die Neue Residenz, als mächtige vierflügelige Anlage von Leonhard Dientzenhofer erbaut und von einem wunderbaren Rosengarten umgeben, konzentrieren sich die architektonischen Zeugnisse des sowohl böhmisch wie italienisch inspirierten Barock. Und unten an den Ufern der Regnitz begegnet man der Bamberger Bürgerstadt mit ihren teils spätmittelalterlichen, teils barocken, teils aber auch jüngeren, typischen Gärtner- und Fischeranwesen. Zugleich als Grenze und Verbindungsglied zwischen der Bürgerstadt unten am Fluss und dem Sitz des Klerus über ihren Dächern fungierte das Alte Rathaus: als stolzer Ausdruck des im späten Mittelalter erstarkten bürgerlichen Selbstbewusstseins. Der gotisch gewölbte Durchgang seines Brückenturms ist noch original erhalten, heute birgt das an ein Schiff erinnernde Bauwerk unter anderem eine bedeutende Porzellan-Sammlung.

In Bambergs Judengasse bannt das „Böttingerhaus" sofort den Blick, Deutschlands – so heißt es – schönstes Barockpalais. Der strebsame Beamte Böttinger stand seinem Fürstbischof Lothar Franz von Schönborn offenbar in der Bauleidenschaft nicht nach, ja erhielt sogar Steuervorteile und Holz von höchster Stelle, damit er sein Anwesen sowie ein zweites, das „Palais Concordia" errichten lassen konnte. Hofarchitekt Dientzenhofer lieferte übrigens den Entwurf.

# Bamberg

Like Rome, Bamberg is built on seven hills. The town on the Regnitz river is much younger, of course, but its townscape – that of the medieval old town on the left bank of the river to be precise – was mostly spared by war and urban sprawl and dates back almost a thousand years. It includes Michaelisberg hill and the Benedictine abbey of the same name as well as the Abtsberg, Jakobsberg, Domberg, Stephansberg, Kaulberg and Altenburg hills. The Late Romanesque-Early Gothic imperial cathedral, a majestic structure aspiring to the heavens with four towers and a spacious forecourt enclosed by impressive buildings from all periods from the Gothic to the rococo, was consecrated in 1237. The works of art in the cathedral include some of the most magnificent 13th century pieces, with the most famous also being the hallmark of the town: the Bamberg Rider.

The architecture of the Neue Residenz, built as an impressive four wing complex by Leonhard Dientzenhofer and surrounded by a rose garden, is inspired by the Bohemian and Italian Baroque. The bourgeois part of town with its characteristic garden and fishing plots dating back to the Middle Ages, the Baroque or a later date is to be found further down, on the banks of the Regnitz. The old city hall functioned both as a border and a link between the citizens' quarters down at the river and the seat of the clergy high above: it is an impressive expression of a civic pride steadily growing since the Late Middle Ages. The Gothic vault of the bridgetower passageway is preserved in the original, and today the ship-like structure houses a fine collection of porcelain, among other things.

In Bamberg's Judengasse street, the eye is caught by the "Böttingerhaus", arguably Germany's most beautiful Baroque palace. The industrious civil servant Böttinger was evidently loath to take second place to his prince bishop Lothar Franz von Schönborn as far as his passion for building was concerned and even received tax advantages and timber from the highest authorities in order to build his estate and a second one, the "Palais Concordia". The royal architect Dientzenhofer supplied the plans.

*Bamberg's historical townscape includes buildings from the 11th to the 18th century. More than a thousand of these are protected sites. The impressive old city hall, washed by the waters of the Regnitz, situated on an artificial island, and its even older Gothic bridge tower (left and overleaf center right), was built between 1744 and 1756. Other interesting sights (overleaf, from the left) include: at the very left on the horizon the Altenburg, at the center the Carmelite monastery, the cathedral with its four towers, the Neue Residenz, the tops of the former Benedictine abbey St. Michael as well as some gardeners' and fishermen's plots down at the river, a quarter often referred to as "Little Venice".*

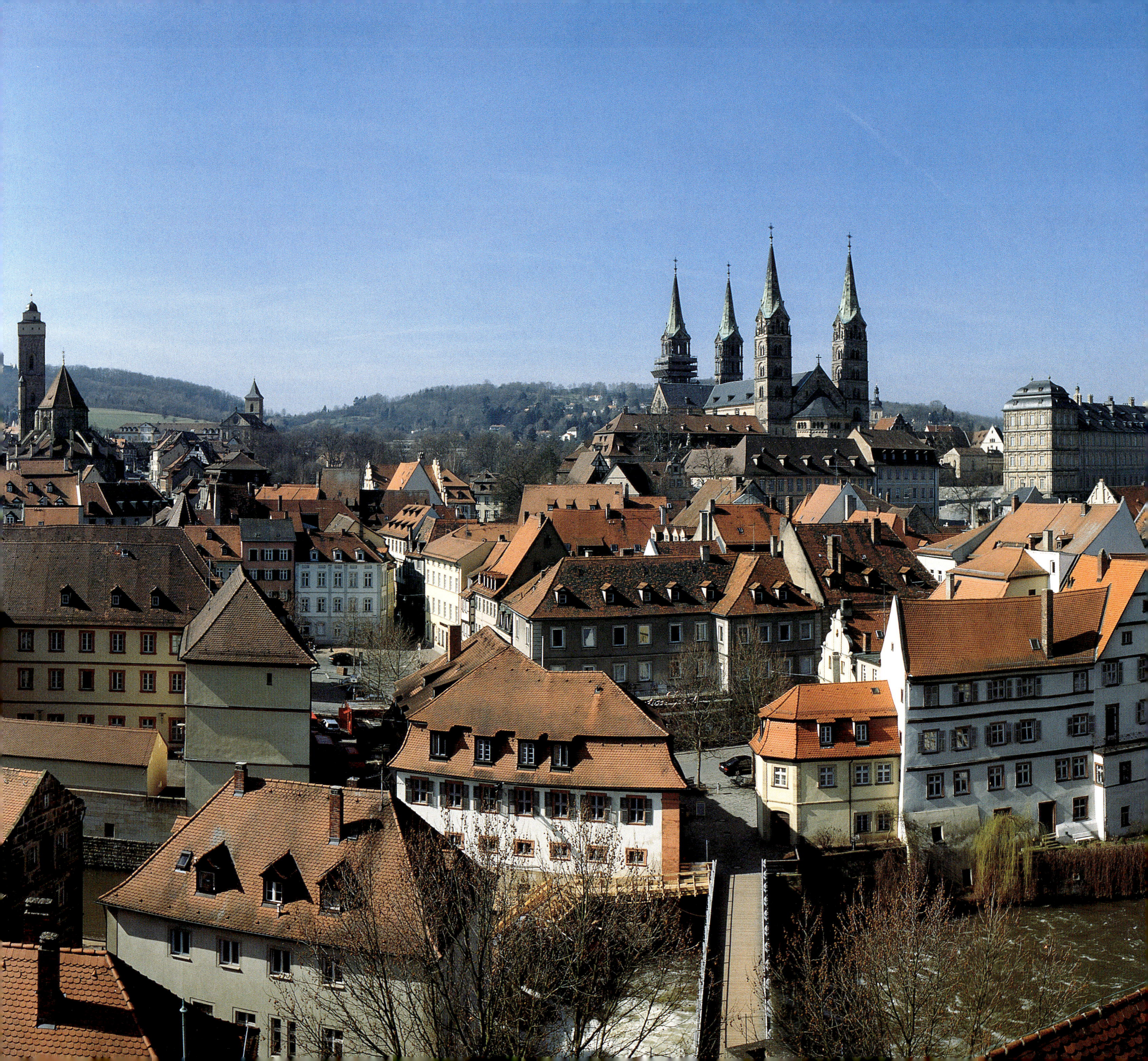

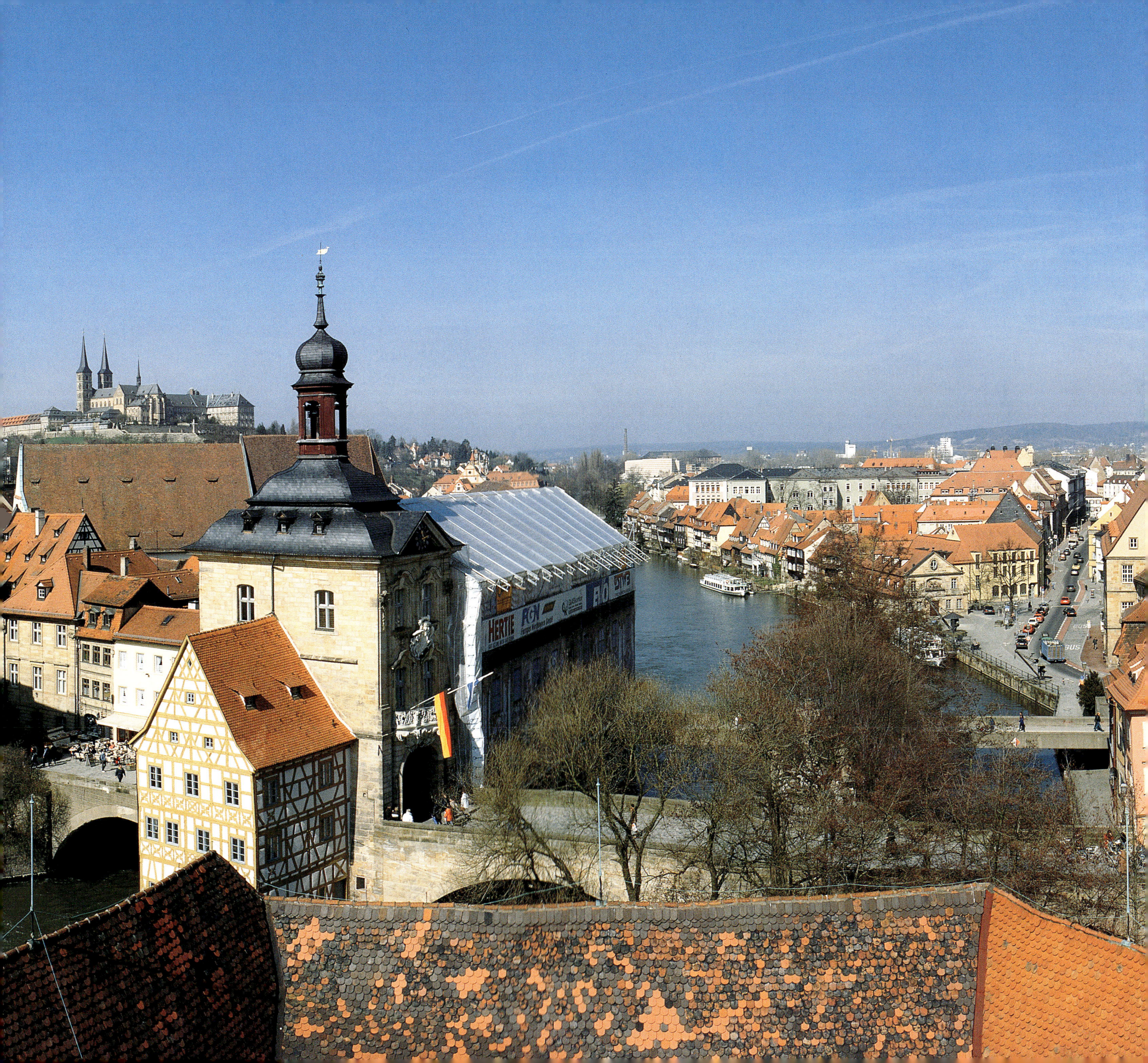
HERTIE

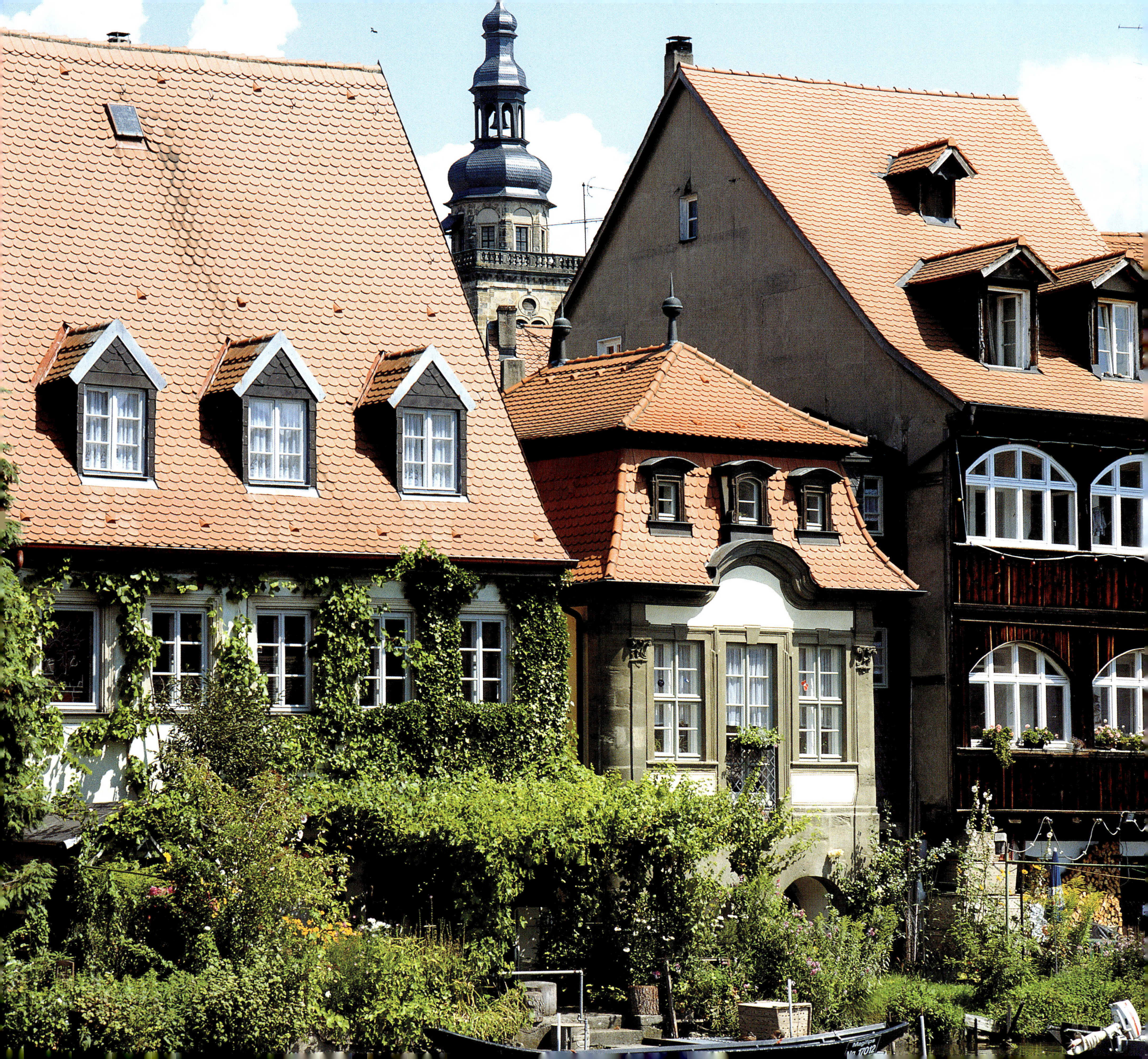

*Links noch einmal ein Detail aus „Klein-Venedig", den Häusern rechts der Regnitz.
Der Bamberger Reiter und das kunstvolle rechte Ostportal sind plastische Schätze des Domes. Reichen Steinbildschmuck zeigt auch die Pforte der Alten Hofhaltung, eines Renaissancebaus.
Mit dem Bau der Neuen Residenz (unten) wurde Anfang des 17. Jahrhunderts begonnen; Hofbaumeister Dientzenhofer schuf später An- und Ausbauten im Stil des römischen Barock.*

*Left, another detail from "Little Venice", the houses to the right of the Regnitz.
The Bamberg Rider and the ornate right eastern portal belong among the sculptural treasures of the cathedral. Richly carved stone ornaments are also found on the gate of the Alte Hofhaltung, a Renaissance building. Construction of the Neue Residenz (below) began at the beginning of the 17th century; the royal master builder Dientzenhofer later effected additions and changes in the Roman Baroque style.*

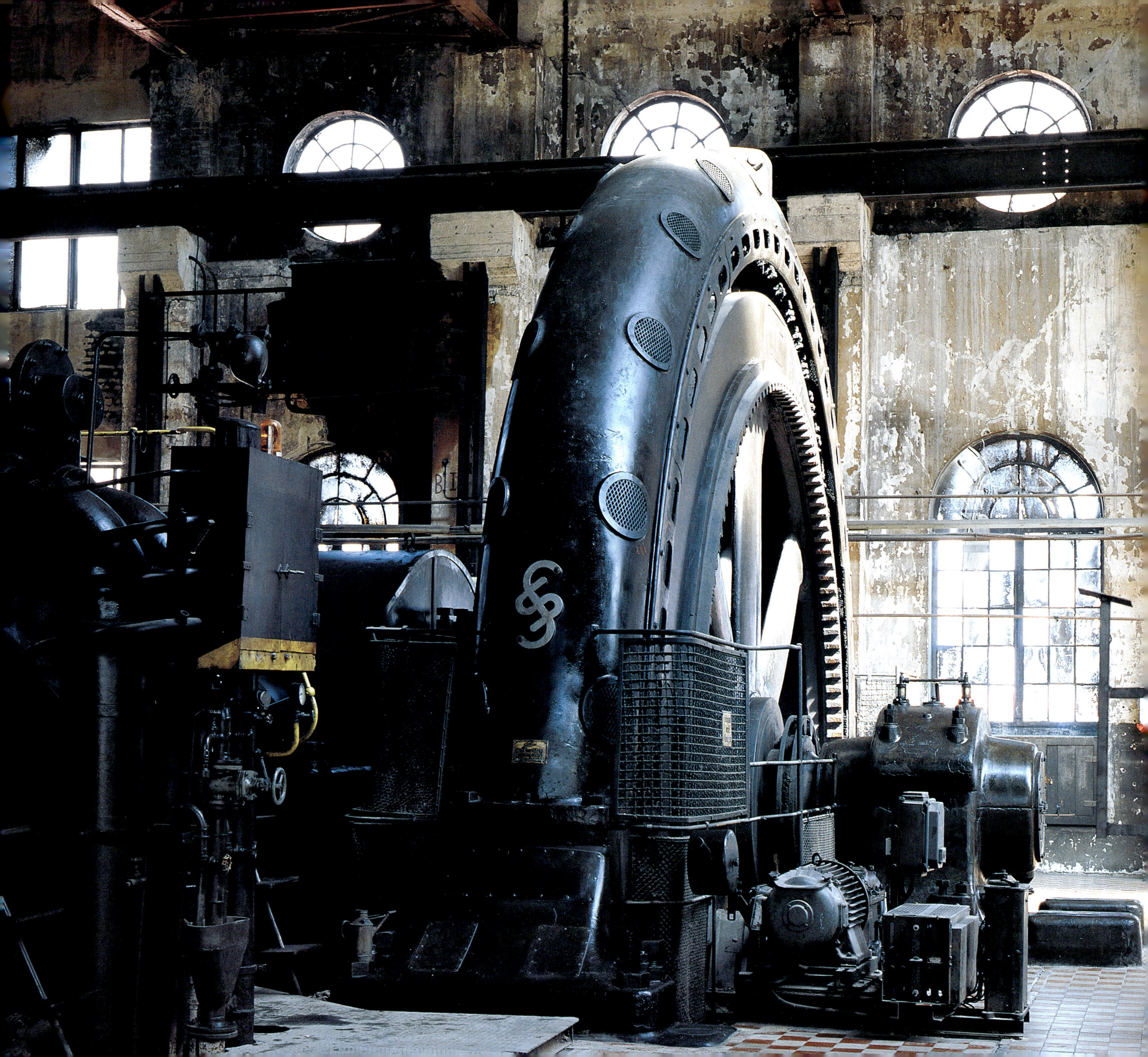

## Die Alte Völklinger Hütte

Außer Kirchen, Städten oder Landschaften zählen zum Weltkulturerbe auch historische Industrieanlagen. Von den im 19. und frühen 20. Jahrhundert in Westeuropa und Nordamerika errichteten Stahl- und Eisenhütten ist die Völklinger im Saarbogen westlich Saarbrücken die einzige, die vollständig erhalten ist. 1873 gegründet, 1879 als unrentabel vorübergehend stillgelegt, wurde das damals noch kleine Hüttenwerk 1881 von der Familie Röchling erworben. Unter der Leitung von Carl Röchling und später dessen Sohn Hermann wuchs es bald zur größten Produktionsstätte für Eisenträger im Deutschen Reich, zog Menschen aus dem gesamten Saarland und von weiter her an. Das Dorf Völklingen erblühte rasch zur Stadt, dank der vielen tausend Zugezogenen. Nicht allein ihre Größe, mehr noch einige bahnbrechende Neuerungen sicherten der Völklinger Hütte eine technische Spitzenstellung in Europa: so von 1911 an die erste Trockengasreinigung, bei der Gichtgas aus den Hochöfen wieder den Gasgebläsemaschinen zugeführt wurde; oder von 1928 an die Sinterung des Eisenerzes, mit der pulveriges Feinerz und Brennstoffe gleichsam „verbacken" wurden, wodurch der Hochofenprozess gleichmäßiger ablief.

Mit der Stahlkrise 1975 begann jedoch auch der Niedergang in Völklingen. 1986 wurden die Hochöfen stillgelegt. Die hütteneigenen Werkstätten in der Handwerkergasse – unter anderen der Maurer, Schlosser oder Zimmerleute – dienten fortan Studierenden der Kunsthochschule als Ateliers. 1994 wurde die Völklinger Hütte als erstes Denkmal des Industriezeitalters in die Welterbe-Liste aufgenommen. Die Anlagen auf dem Hüttengelände zeigen authentisch alle wichtigen Stationen einer historischen Roheisenproduktion: von den Erzbunkern und -brechanlagen über die Kokerei und die Sinteranlage zu den Hängebahnanlagen hin zur Hochofengruppe nebst Winderhitzern. Hinzu kommen die Trockengasreinigung und Gasgebläsehalle und die Walzenzugmaschine für die Erzeugung von T-Trägern. Die Alte Hütte soll zu einem europäischen Zentrum für Kunst und Industriekultur ausgebaut werden – mit Theatervorführungen, Symposien, Ausstellungen, Lichtinszenierungen, Konzerten und anderem mehr.

## The Old Ironworks at Völklingen

The cultural heritage of the world not only includes churches and monasteries, palaces and gardens, towns and landscapes, but also historical industrial sites. From all the steel and ironworks built in the 19th and early 20th centuries in Western Europe and North America, the one at Völklingen in the Saar curve west of Saarbrücken is the only one which is fully preserved. Established in 1873 and temporarily closed in 1879 due to unprofitability, the then still quite small mill was purchased by the Röchling family. Headed by Carl Röchling and later his son Hermann, it soon developed into the largest production site for iron girders in the German Empire, drawing workers from all over the Saar region and beyond. Owing to the many thousands of newcomers, Völklingen, once a village, quickly blossomed into a town. Not only its size, but also some ground-breaking innovations ensured that the Völklingen ironworks retained their top position throughout Europe: in 1911, e.g., the first dry gas cleaning procedure in which furnace top gas was conducted directly back to the gas blowers; or, from 1928 on, the sintering of iron ore, where powdered fine ore and fuel were "baked", in a sense, resulting in more even blast furnace action.

Nevertheless, the steel crisis beginning in 1975 did not spare Völklingen. In 1986, the blast furnaces were shut down. After that, the factory-owned workshops in the Handwerkergasse – those of the bricklayers, fitters and carpenters among them – were used by art students for studios. In 1994, the ironworks at Völklingen were the first industrial age monument to be accepted into the World Heritage Program. The machinery on the factory grounds mirrors all historically important stations of crude iron production from ore bunkers and grinders to coking and sintering plants to a suspension railway system and assorted blast furnaces with heat blowers and, finally, dry gas cleaners, a gas blower hall and a rolling mill for the manufacturing of T-girders. The Old Ironworks will be built up into a European center for art and industrial culture featuring theater performances, symposia, exhibitions, light installations and concerts among other things.

*Den langen Weg vom Erz zum Eisen, wie er im 19. Jahrhundert in großem Maßstab entwickelt wurde, veranschaulicht das Industriedenkmal Völklinger Hütte. Mit ihren riesigen Schwungrädern lieferten die Gasgebläsemaschinen (links) in erster Linie stündlich bis zu 130 000 Kubikmeter Verbrennungsluft, den „Wind" für den Verhüttungsprozess. Getrieben wurden sie von einem genialen (fast) geschlossenen Kreislauf: Aus den Hochöfen anfallendes Gichtgas – trocken gereinigt – diente als Kraftstoff, Frischluft kam hinzu. Zwei Gasmaschinen erzeugten zudem Strom, der in dem Hüttenwerk für andere Aufgaben gebraucht wurde.
Die zwischen 1882 und 1916 errichtete Hochofen-Gruppe (nächste Doppelseite) ist ein markantes Symbol einer vergangenen industriellen Epoche. Bis zu 17 000 Menschen waren in der Blüte des Unternehmens an seinen 6 Hochöfen und in allen anderen Teilen des 6 Hektar großen Hüttengeländes tätig.*

*The Völklingen ironworks industrial monument illustrates the long way from ore to iron, as it developed in the 19th century on a grand scale. With their gigantic flywheels, the gas blowers (far left) served mainly to supply up to 130,000 cubic meters of combustion air per hour, the "wind" for the smelting process. They were propelled by an ingenious, almost closed cycle. Top gas from the blast furnaces – run through a "dry cleaning" process – was used for fuel together with fresh air. Two gas blowers also generated electricity used elsewhere in the plant.
The blast furnace ensemble built between 1862 and 1916 (overleaf) makes for an arresting symbol of a bygone industrial epoch. At the height of production, up to 17,000 people were at work at six blast furnaces and other areas of the factory grounds of six hectares.*

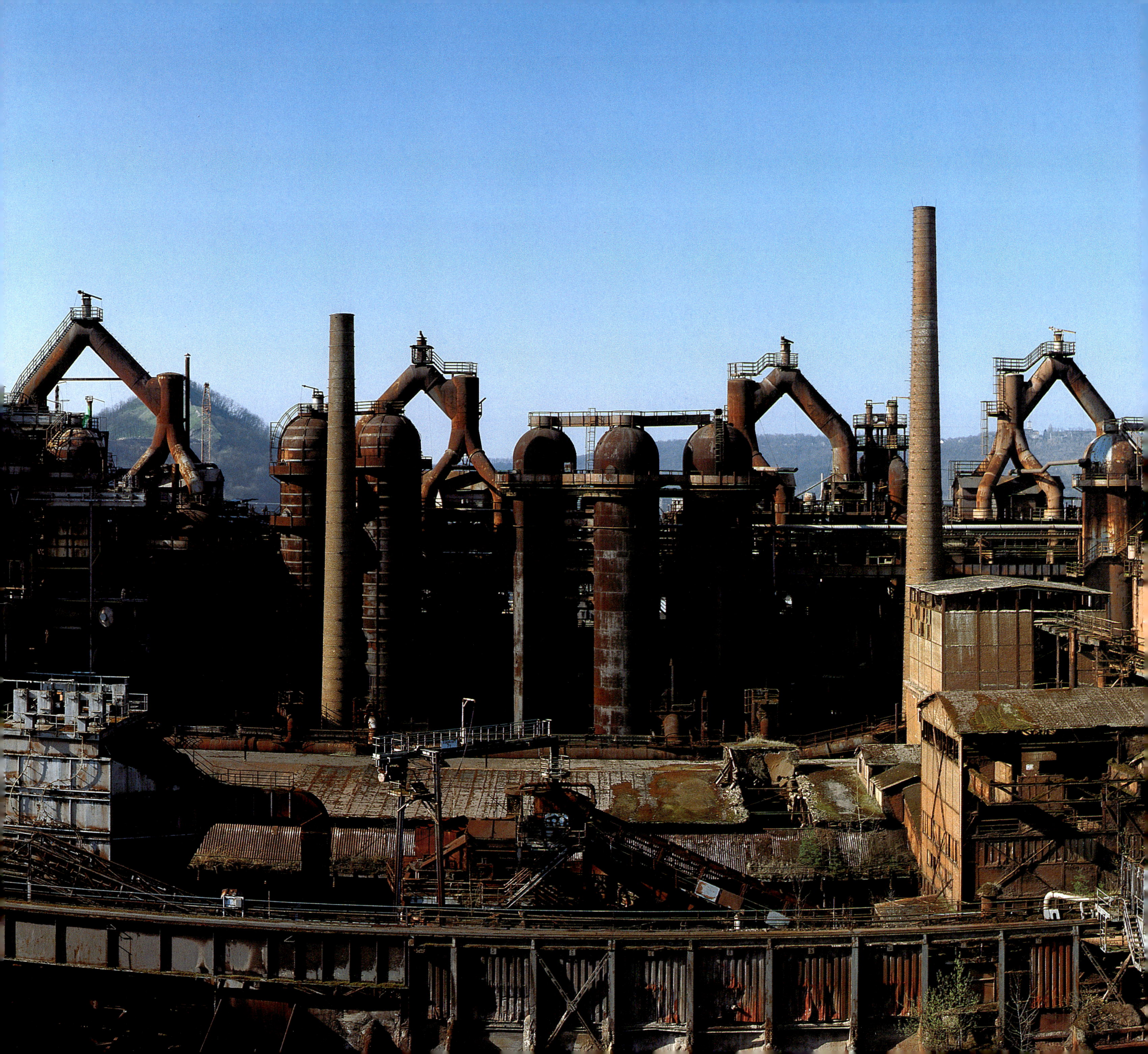

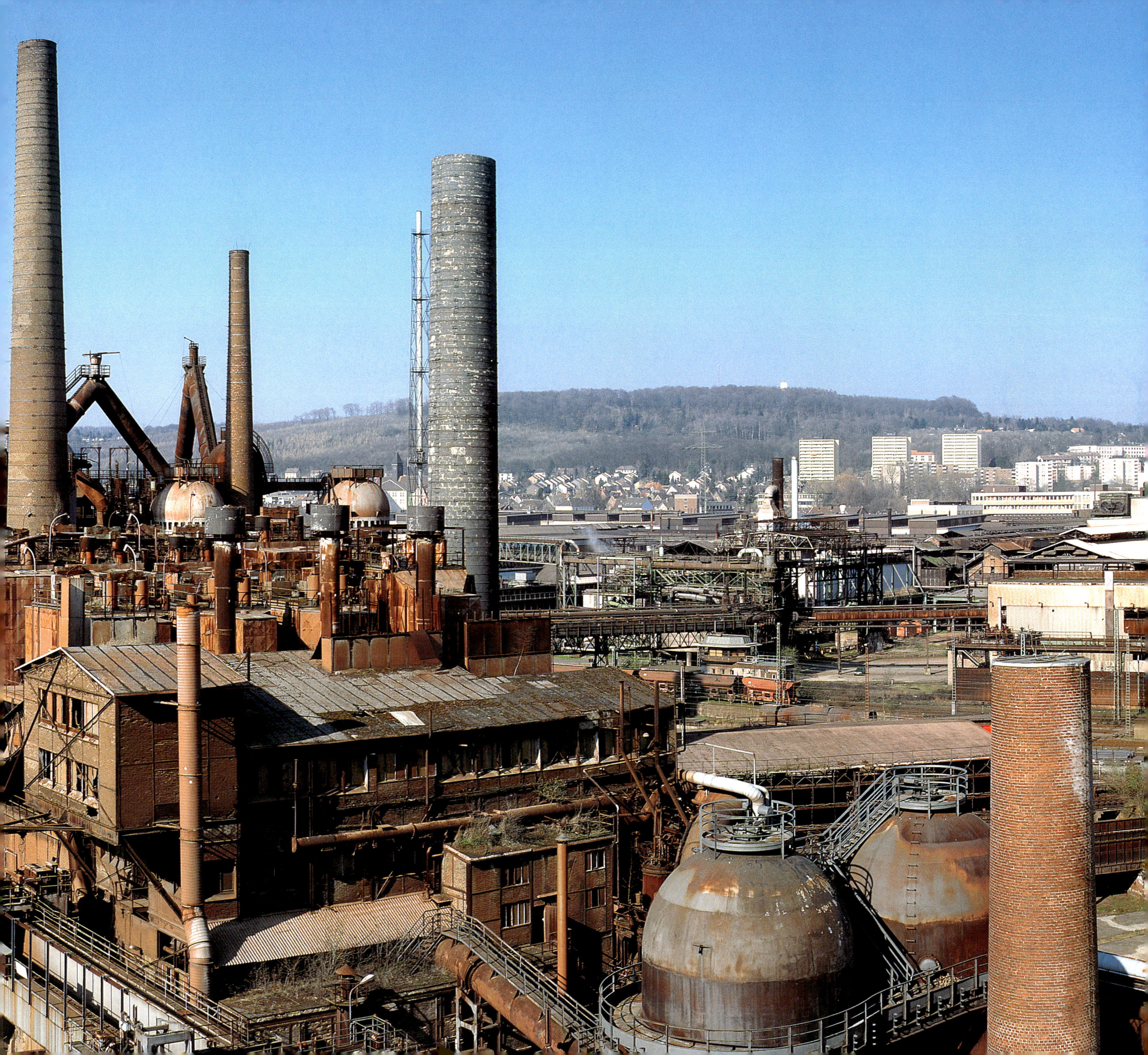

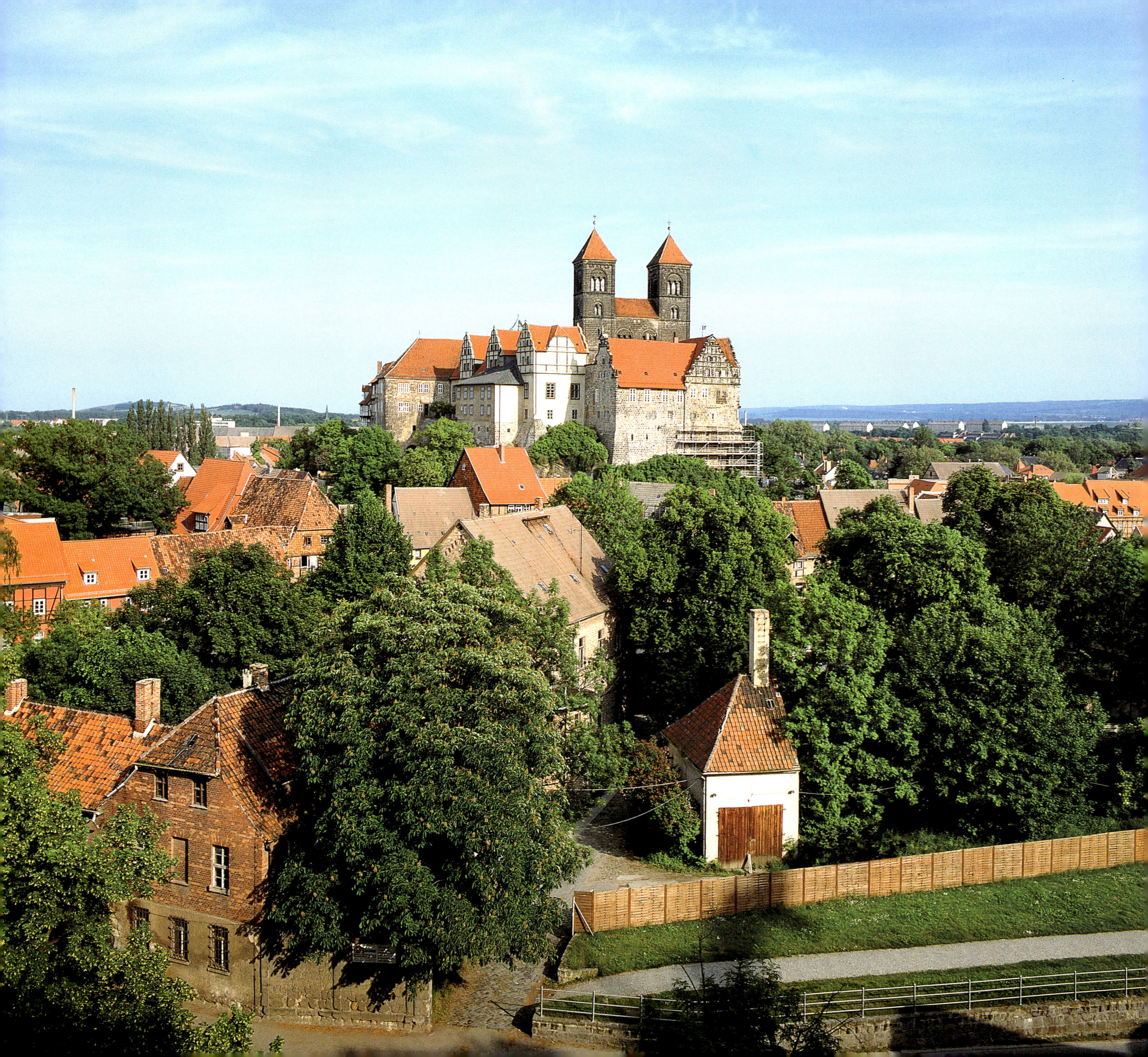

*Aus einem sächsischen Burgdorf, mehreren Ansiedlungen und einem aufblühenden Adelsfrauenstift erwuchs im 10. Jahrhundert das Harzstädtchen Quedlinburg. Von seinem Schlossberg aus, mit der Stiftskirche St. Servatii, schaut man auf das schief verwinkelte Spitzgiebel- und Türmchengewirr seiner Fachwerkhäuser. Einige der schönsten gruppieren sich um den Marktplatz (nächste Doppelseite). Rechts ein Beispiel für die hoch entwickelte oberitalienisch beeinflusste Dekoration an der Außenfassade von St. Servatii.*

## Die Quedlinburger Altstadt

Diese außergewöhnliche mittelalterliche Stadt schart sich um einen bereits von König Heinrich I. nach 929 stark befestigten Sandsteinfelsen. Dieser Burgberg bot auch noch Platz für ein 936 von Otto I., Heinrichs Sohn, und seiner Mutter Mathilde gegründetes Stift, in dem sich bald darauf ein reges Geistesleben entwickelte. Nachdem Otto III. dem Stift Münz- und Zollfreiheit gewährt hatte, verschmolzen Neu- und Altstadt zu einer Doppelgemeinde mit gemeinsamer Stadtmauer. Dieses zusammenhängende städtische Gefüge mit vier alten Pfarreien und mehr als 1 200 Fachwerkhäusern prägt Quedlinburg ebenso wie auf dem weithin sichtbaren Schlossberg Sankt Servatii, die Kirche des ehemaligen Frauenstifts, und das Schlossgebäude aus dem 16. Jahrhundert. Die romanische Basilika – das vierte Gotteshaus am selben Platz – wurde 1129 geweiht, die Krypta aus dem 10. Jahrhundert birgt die Grabstätten von König Heinrich I. und seiner Gattin Mathilde.

Im historischen Stadtkern Quedlinburgs sind rund 800 Häuser als Einzeldenkmäler ausgewiesen, die meisten stammen aus dem 17. und 18. Jahrhundert. Fast alle älteren Fachwerkhäuser stehen am Fuße des Schlossbergs, darunter auch der „Alte Klopstock", ein Erkerbau aus der Mitte des 16. Jahrhunderts. Seinen Namen hat er von einem berühmten Sohn Quedlinburgs, dem Odendichter Friedrich Gottlieb Klopstock. Mit seinem großen Bestand an Fachwerkbauten und einer Reihe von Jugendstilarchitekturen gilt Quedlinburg als eines der größten Flächendenkmäler Deutschlands.

Der historische Kern Quedlinburgs ist allerdings stark sanierungsbedürftig. Die einseitig auf industrielles Bauen ausgerichtete Baupolitik in der DDR hatte die Pflege der Fachwerkhäuser vernachlässigt. Nur durch den Widerstand der Bürger im Herbst 1989 konnten großräumig geplante Abrisse im Nordteil der Altstadt verhindert werden. Schon 1990 erfolgten erste Sanierungsarbeiten. Seitdem werden mit Hilfe von Förderprogrammen und hunderten Millionen Mark zunehmend Fachwerkhäuser repariert und modernisiert. Eines der bisher gelungensten Sanierungsbeispiele ist das Gildehaus der Lohgerber am Markt, das zu einem Hotel ausgebaut wurde.

## Quedlinburg Old Town

This unique medieval town is nestled against a sandstone rock that was strongly fortified as early as 929 by King Heinrich I. The fortified hilltop also held a convent founded in 936 by Otto I, Heinrich's son, and his mother Mathilde, which was soon to be a center of active intellectual life. After Otto III had granted mint and tax privileges to the convent, the new and old town merged into one and joint fortifications were built. This civic structure with its four old parishes and more than 1,200 half-timber houses still characterizes Quedlinburg today, and so does its fortified hill with St. Servatii's, visible from afar, the church of the former women's convent, and the castle dating back to the 15th century. The Romanesque basilica – the fourth church on the site – was consecrated in 1129, the 10th century crypt holds the graves of King Heinrich I and his spouse Mathilde. In the historical old city of Quedlinburg, more than 800 houses are protected monuments. The largest part of these buildings dates back to the 17th and 18th centuries, whereas almost all older half-timber houses are to be found at the foot of the fortified hill, among them the "Alte Klopstock", a structure with bay windows dating to the middle of the 16th century. It derives its name from one of Quedlinburg's great sons, the poet Friedrich Gottlieb Klopstock, famous for his odes. Quedlinburg, with its numerous half-timber structures and a great deal of art nouveau architecture, is said to be one of the largest protected historical sites in Germany.

Quedlinburg's historical core is in dire need of refurbishment, however, as the building policies of the former GDR favored industrial development and neglected the care of the historical half-timber buildings. Large-scale demolitions in the northern part of the old town were prevented only by massive opposition from citizens in fall 1989. First renovation measures followed as early as 1990. Ever since, with the help of support programs and hundreds of billions of DM, more and more half-timber houses have been repaired and modernized. One of the most successful examples is the tanners' guild hall on the market-place, which was converted into a hotel.

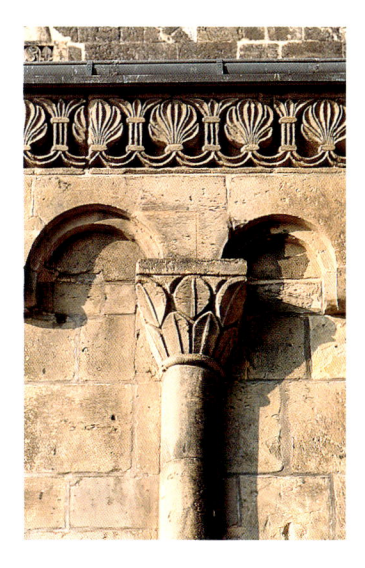

*In the 10th century, the Harz town Quedlinburg developed from a Saxon castle village, a number of surrounding settlements and a blossoming noblewomen's convent. The view from its fortified hill with the convent church St. Servatii shows a maze of odd angles formed by the pointed gables and turrets of its half-timber houses, the most spectacular of which are to be found on the market-place (overleaf). Above, an example of the elaborate Italian-influenced façade decorations on St. Servatii's.*

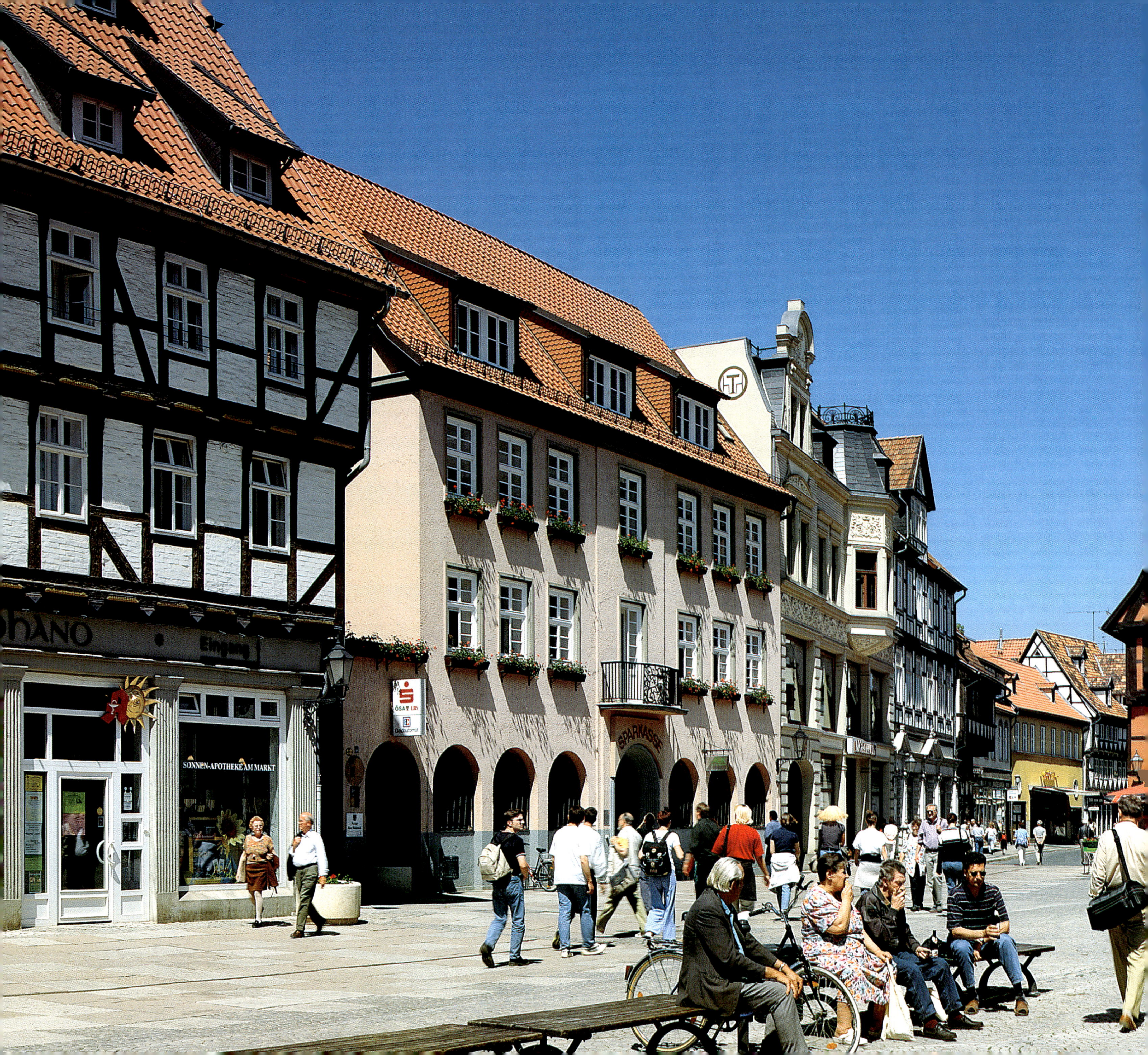
SONNEN-APOTHEKE AM MARKT
SPARKASSE
Eingang

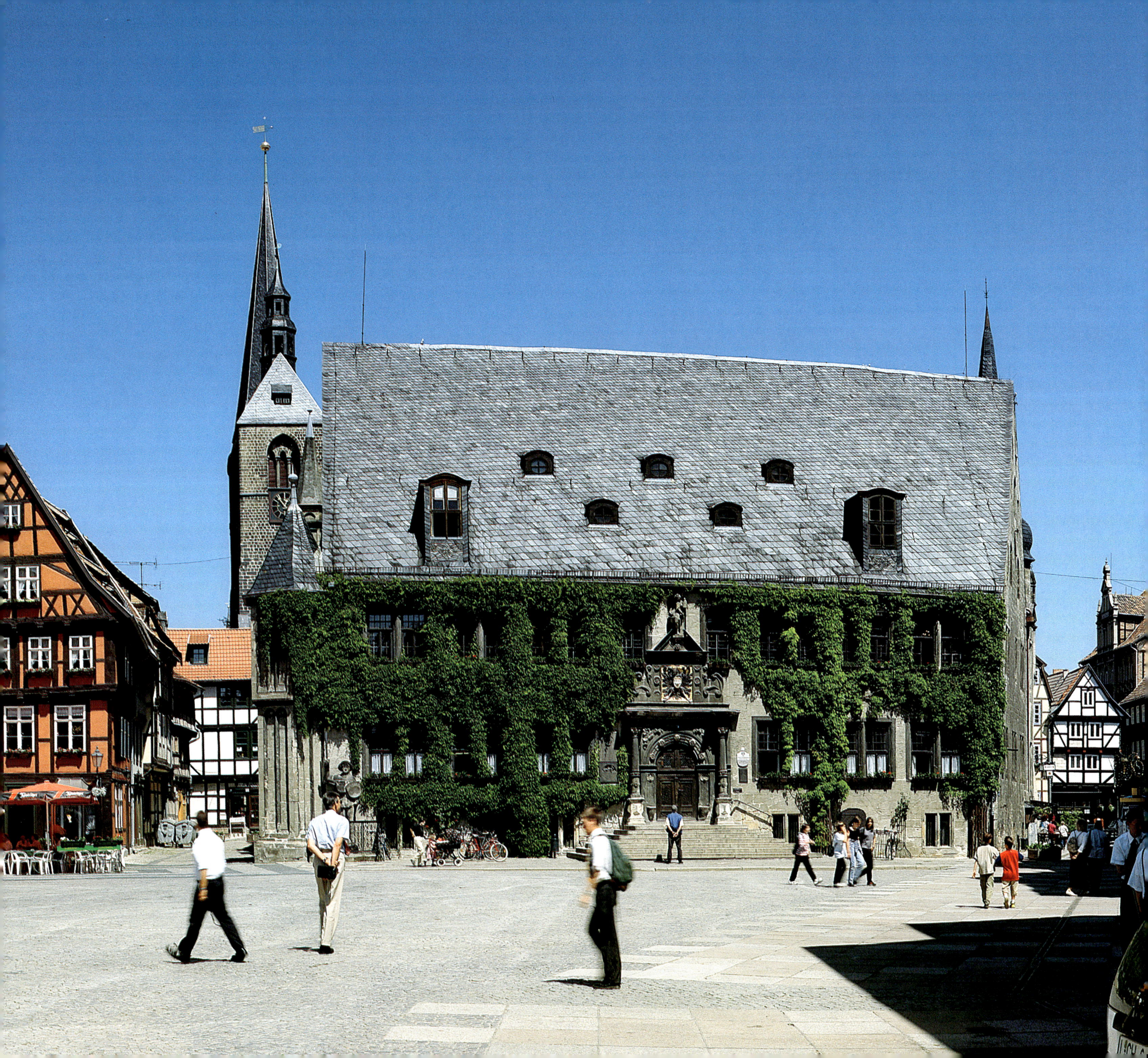

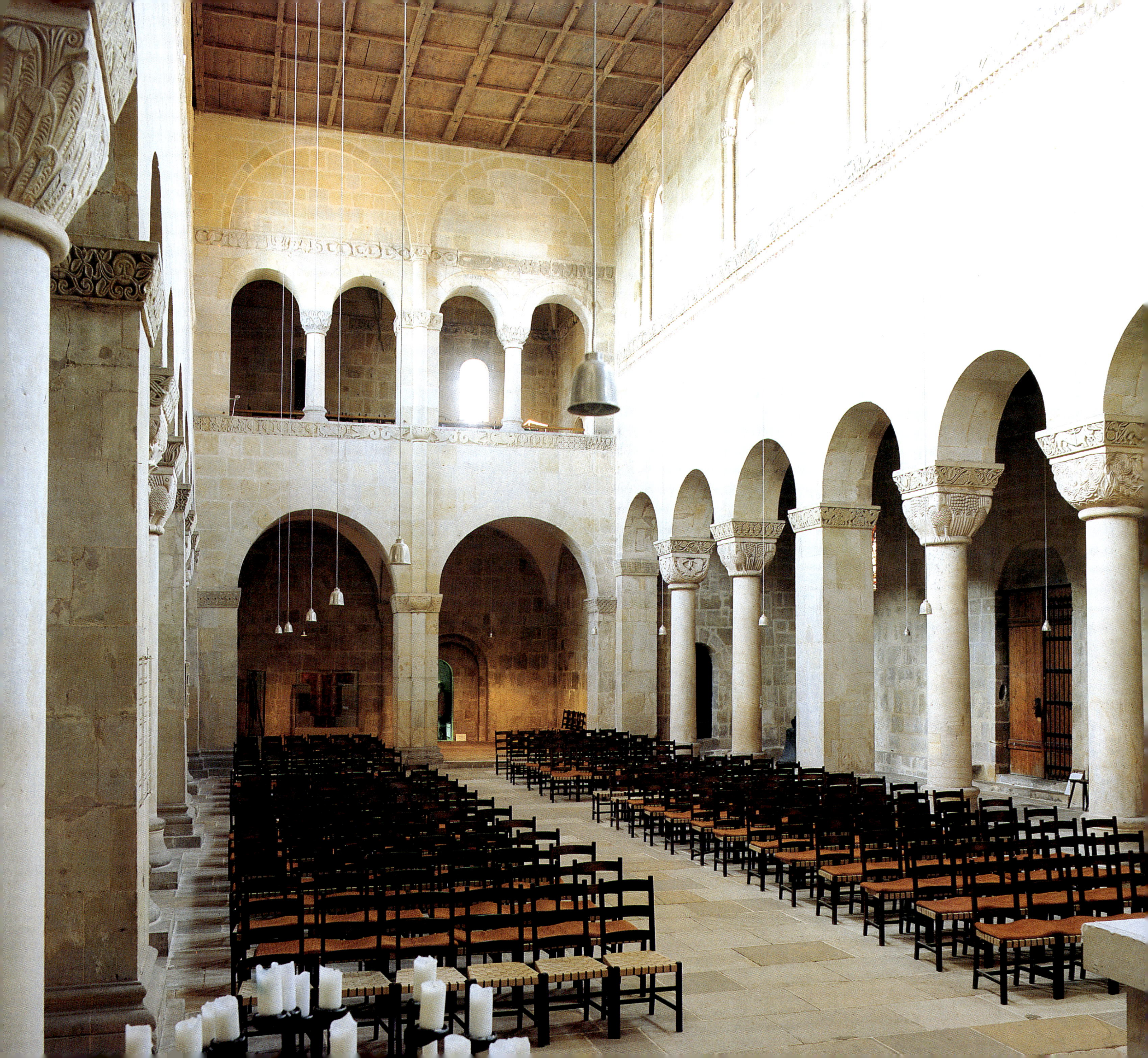

*Quedlinburger Kostbarkeiten: die romanische Stiftskirche, berühmt für ihren Säulenwechsel und die Domschatzkammer mit dem dort ausgestellten Quedlinburger Evangeliar (links); der Nebeneingang des Alten Rathauses (rechts), die Fassaden der Schlossberghäuser (ganz rechts), Deutschlands ältester Ständerbau in der Wordgasse (rechts unten) und schräg gegenüber in der Blasiistraße ein schön restaurierter Innenhof (unten).*

*Quedlinburg's gems: the Romanesque convent church, famous for its alternating columns and the cathedral treasury with the famous Quedlinburg evangeliar (left); the side entrance to the old city hall (right), the façades of the houses on the hill (very right), Germany's oldest wood frame construction in the Wordgasse (bottom right) and opposite, in the Blasiistraße, a nicely redone courtyard (bottom).*

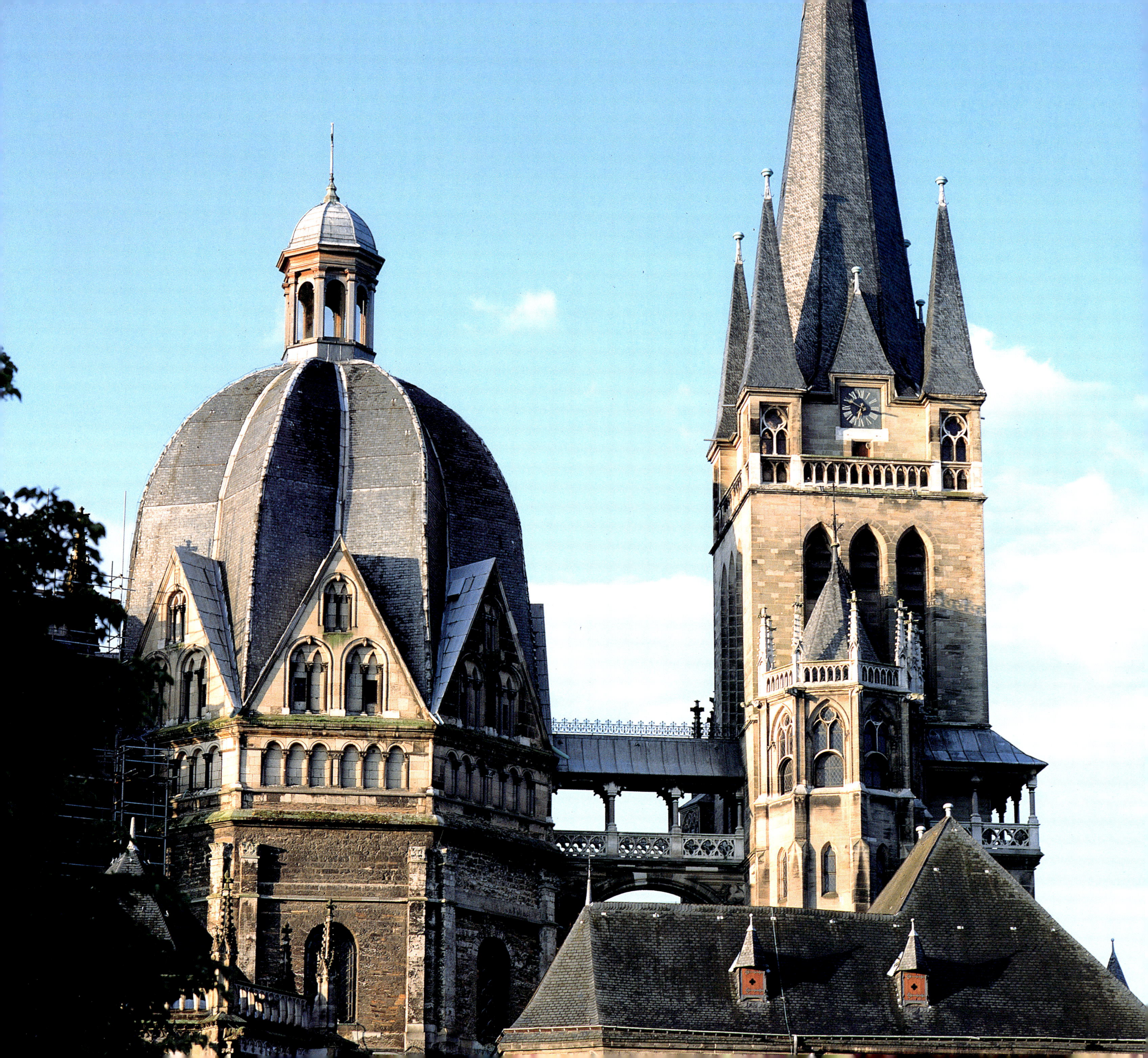

## Der Dom zu Aachen

Als „eine Kirche von wunderbarer Größe" beschreiben schon mittelalterliche Chronisten jene Pfalzkapelle, die Kaiser Karl der Große gegen Ende des 8. Jahrhunderts auf dem eher unbedeutenden Aachener Hofgut seines Vaters Pippin von Odo von Metz hatte erbauen lassen. Die Palastkirche Kaiser Justinians I. in Ravenna, St. Vitale, lieferte die Grundidee für das karolingische Gotteshaus, das erste gewölbte Gebäude nördlich der Alpen seit der Antike. In Aachen erhielten vom 10. bis ins 16. Jahrhundert insgesamt 30 deutsche Könige ihre Herrschaftsweihe. Aus Ravenna und Rom ließ Karl auch einen Großteil der Baumaterialien bringen. Mit der Königshalle, die in ihrem Kern noch heute im Aachener Rathaus erhalten ist, bildete die Pfalzkapelle die beiden Pole des Forums der Pfalz.

Mehr als 30 Meter wölbt sich die stets bewunderte Kuppel der Marien geweihten Kapelle in ihrem höchsten Punkt über den 8 mächtigen Säulen des Mittelbaus, den ein 16-eckiger, 2-geschossiger Umgang konzentrisch säumt. Nach ravennatischem Vorbild sind seine Bögen mit zweifarbigen Quadern gemauert; das Obergeschoss heben Säulen in den Bögen besonders hervor. Waagrechte Tonnengewölbe betonen schließlich die beiden einst wichtigsten Raumpunkte des Baus: im Osten den ehemals vorhandenen oberen Altar, im Westen den Königsstuhl vor der Kaiserloge.

Im Kuppelscheitel hatte Karl der Große, dessen Gebeine bereits einen Tag nach seinem Tod am 28. Januar 814 in der Marienkirche beigesetzt wurden, ein Mosaik-Gemälde anbringen lassen. Es zu verändern, veranlasste jedoch Kaiser Barbarossa, als der von ihm 1165 gestiftete Radleuchter aufgehängt wurde.

Von den später hinzugefügten Bauteilen, die sie wie ein Kranz umgeben, hebt sich die oktogonale karolingische Kapelle auch für heutige Betrachter deutlich ab. Als erstes deutsches Kulturdenkmal wurde der Aachener Dom 1978 in die Liste des UNESCO-Welterbes aufgenommen. Sein Schatz, bereits von Kaiser Karl sorgfältig initiiert, umfasst sakrale Donationen aus spätantiker, karolingischer, ottonischer und staufischer Zeit. Sie sind als Kunstwerke sowie als archäologische und geschichtliche Dokumente von unschätzbarem Wert.

## The Cathedral of Aachen

The palatine chapel, which Emperor Charlemagne had built by Odo von Metz on the rather insignificant Aachen estate of his father Pippin at the end of the 8th century was already called a "church of marvelous dimensions" by medieval chroniclers. The palace church of Emperor Justinian I at Ravenna, St. Vitale, had served as a model for the Carolingian church, the first vaulted structure north of the Alps since Antiquity. Charlemagne had the greatest part of the building materials brought from Ravenna and Rome. The King's Hall, whose core is still preserved in the Aachen city hall, and the palatine chapel formed the two poles of the forum of the imperial residence. Altogether 30 German kings were consecrated at Aachen between the 10th to 16th century.

At its highest point, the dome of the chapel's much admired cupola extends more than 30 meters above the mighty columns of the center aisle, which is surrounded by a two-story concentric ambulatory with 16 corners. Modeled on Ravenna, the arches of the chapel – which is dedicated to Mary – feature ashlars of two alternating colors, with the upper story enhanced by columns dividing the arches. Horizontal barrel vaults characterize the two erstwhile most important structural points: the former upper altar in the east, and the king's seat in front of the imperial balcony in the west.

Charlemagne, whose bones were buried in the Marienkirche on the day after his death on January 28, 814, had the zenith of the cupola embellished with a mosaic painting. Changes were made when Emperor Barbarossa donated a circular chandelier to be installed in the cupola.

Even for today's visitors, the octagonal Carolingian chapel stands out clearly from all later additions encircling it. In 1978, the cathedral at Aachen was the first cultural monument in Germany to be accepted to the list of the UNESCO World Heritage Program. Its cathedral treasure, carefully initiated by Charlemagne himself, contains sacral donations from Late Antiquity and the Carolingian, Ottonian and Staufer periods. Their value both as works of art and as archeological and historical documents is beyond description.

*Als einzigartiges Symbol von Herrschermacht und Innovation strebt der Dom zu Aachen in den Himmel. Seinen Kern bildet die im Auftrag von Karl dem Großen erbaute achteckige Pfalzkapelle (links) mit ihren zweifarbig gemauerten Bögen und dem mächtigen Kuppelraum (nächste Doppelseite). Die Büste Karls des Großen sowie das Lotharkreuz werden neben anderen Kleinodien in der Domschatzkammer bewahrt (oben rechts und links).*
*Kühn in der Architektur und reich ausgestattet, blieb die Aachener Marienkirche bis ins hohe Mittelalter eines der größten Vorbilder religiöser Baukunst im Abendland. Selten ist ein Bauwerk so oft „wiederholt" oder in Details zitiert worden wie sie.*

*A unique symbol of sovereign power and innovation, the Aachen cathedral aspires to the heavens. The octagonal palatine chapel (left) with two-colored brick arches and an impressive domed hall at its core was built under Charlemagne (overleaf). The bust of Charlemagne and the Lotharkreuz cross are only two of many gems kept in the cathedral treasury (top right and left). Boldly conceived and richly endowed, St. Mary's at Aachen remained one of the greatest models of sacral architecture in the occident well into the High Middle Ages. There is hardly another structure which has been "repeated" or whose details have been quoted as often.*

UCTOR PROTEGAT ATQUE
DEUS HOC TUTUM STABILI FUNDA
PLUM QUOD CAROLUS PRIN

CONDIDIT ESSE VELIT
PACIS COMPAGE LIGANTUR
INQUE PARES NUMEROS OMNIA

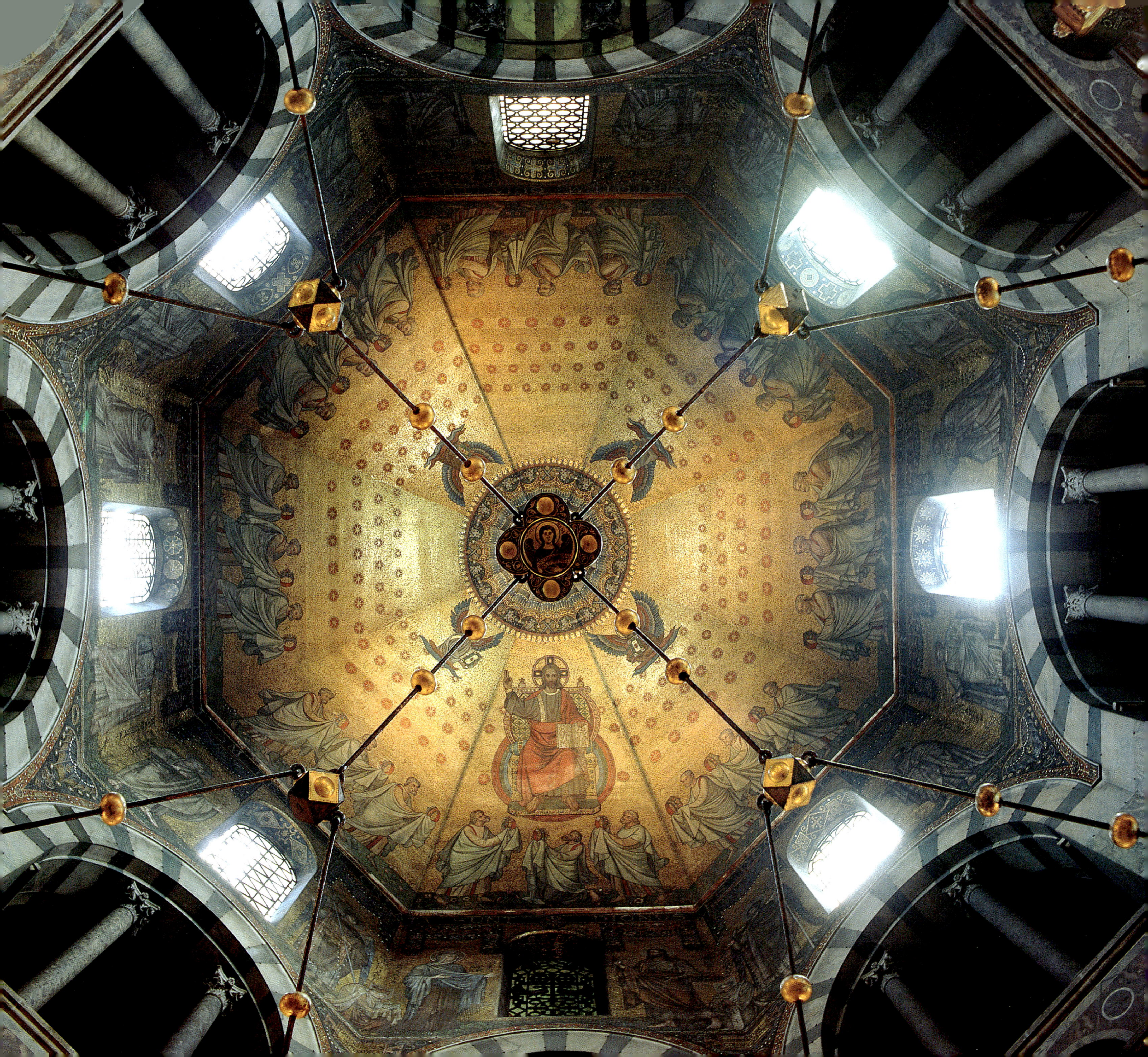

Byzantinisches klingt an bei der kostbaren Ausstattung der Pfalzkapelle, in der auch der Königsstuhl oder -thron Karls des Großen (unten links) steht und der von Kaiser Heinrich II. gestiftete Ambo (Evangelienkanzel) zu bewundern ist (unten rechts). Als Hauptwerk der karolingischen Renaissance vereint der Aachener Dom alle Elemente, die Karl dem Großen zur Legitimation seiner fürstlichen Macht notwendig erschienen. Oben rechts ein Blick aus der gotischen Chorhalle über den Altar hinweg in das Oktogon, dessen Kuppel über 30 Meter hoch ist (linke Seite).

The precious details of the palatine chapel, which also houses Charlemagne's royal seat or throne (bottom left) and the ambo (raised pulpit, bottom right) are reminiscent of Byzantine art. The major work of the Carolingian Renaissance, the Aachen cathedral, includes all elements Charlemagne deemed necessary for the legitimation of his sovereign power. Above left, a view from the Gothic chancel across the altar into the octagon whose domed cupola is more than 30 meters high (left).

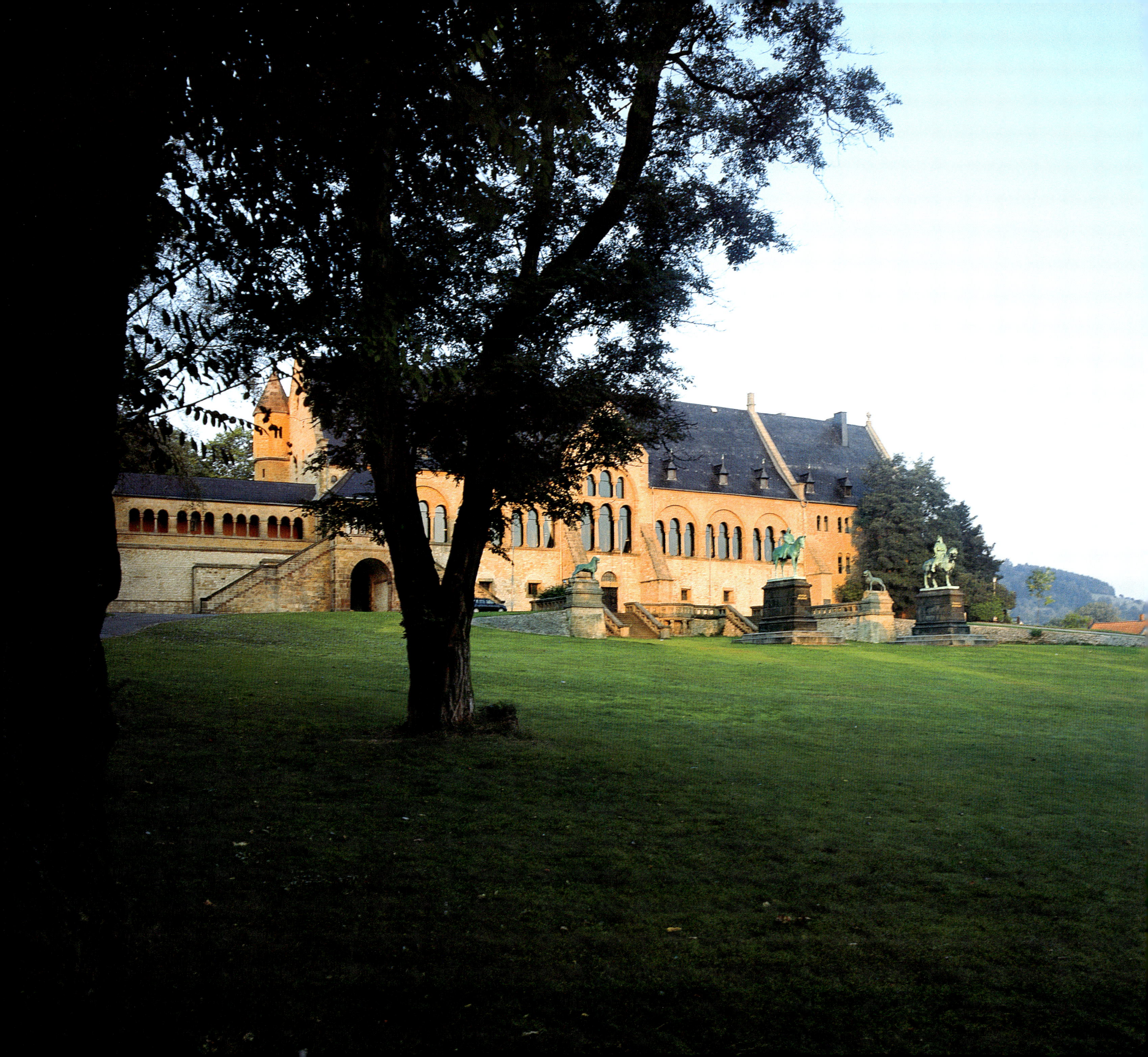

An den Ausmaßen der in großen Teilen im 19. Jahrhundert restaurierten, in einigen Teilen auch frei gestalteten Kaiserpfalz ist noch heute die mittelalterliche Pracht und Macht Goslars abzulesen (links); ebenso an dem Kaiserstuhl in der Vorhalle des 1820 abgebrochenen Domes (rechts).
Nächste Doppelseite: Der Reichtum der Stadt, den ihr das Silber des Rammelsbergs lieferte, zeigt sich auch in den Bauten der Altstadt. Zwei der eindrucksvollsten, das Gildehaus der Gewandschneider „Kaiserworth" (links) und das Rathaus (Mitte) flankieren den Marktplatz. Eines der vielen Kunstwerke, die im Laufe des fast 1000-jährigen Förderbetriebs aus dem Metall des Goslarer Bergwerks hergestellt wurden, ist der aus Bronze gegossene Brunnen auf dem Markt. Seine untere Schale gilt als eines der Hauptwerke mittelalterlicher Großbronzengießerei.

## Goslar und der Rammelsberg

Im späten Mittelalter und in der frühen Neuzeit zählte Goslar am Nordrand des Harz zu den einflussreichsten Städten Europas. Die reichen, seit dem 3. Jahrhundert nachgewiesenen Metallerzvorkommen seines Rammelsberges bescherten ihm eine vielfältige Blüte. Kaiser Heinrich II. machte den Ort bereits Anfang des 11. Jahrhunderts zur Pfalz. Hunderte prächtiger Reichsversammlungen fanden daraufhin in seinen Mauern statt. Das mächtige, im 19. Jahrhundert historisierend restaurierte, so genannte Kaiserhaus – es gilt als der größte Saalbau romanischer Zeit – vermittelt noch immer einen Eindruck davon. Heinrich III., dessen Herz in der Pfalzkapelle bewahrt wird, gab den Auftrag, in Goslar einen mächtigen Dom zu errichten. Berg- und Hüttenbesitzer sowie die verschiedenen Gilden stellten ihren Reichtum mit prachtvollen Bauten wie dem „Brusttuch" oder dem „Kaiserworth" zur Schau; der Rat der Stadt erhielt ebenfalls einen repräsentativen, reich ausgestatteten Sitz. Der Frömmigkeit der Bergleute trug man mit einer Vielzahl von Gotteshäusern Rechnung. Fast 50 Kirchtürme recken sich aus dem mittelalterlichen Stadtkern Goslars in den Himmel. Jenen des Domes indes suchte schon Heinrich Heine vergebens. Nach einem großen Brandschaden blieb von der 1050 geweihten Kathedrale nur die Vorhalle. Der in ihr ausgestellte Kaiserthron ist neben jenem Karls des Großen in Aachen der einzige erhaltene deutsche Herrscherstuhl. Die Bronze für seine Lehnen stammt aus dem Rammelsberg wie für zahlreiche andere Kunstwerke, darunter den Brunnen am Marktplatz.

1988 wurde im Rammelsberg die letzte Schicht gefahren, der Verpackungskünstler Christo ummantelte einen Förderwagen aus ihr samt Erz und machte ihn so zum Kunstwerk. Seit 1990 fungiert der Rammelsberg als Museum, unter anderem mit Abraumhalden aus dem 10. Jahrhundert sowie einem der ältesten und besterhaltenen Stollen des deutschen Bergbaus. Auch Deutschlands ältester gemauerter Grubenraum und das älteste Tagesgebäude des deutschen Bergbaus, der Malermeisterturm aus dem 15. Jahrhundert, zählen zu den Monumenten jenes Berges, der die Geschichte und Entwicklung der Stadt Goslar prägte.

## Goslar and the Rammelsberg Mountain

In the late Middle Ages and early modern times, Goslar, at the northern edge of the Harz mountains, was one of the most influential towns in Europe. Lucrative metal ore deposits on its Rammelsberg mountain, known since the 3rd century, ensured general prosperity. Emperor Heinrich II made the town an imperial residence as early as the beginning of the 11th century. Within its walls, hundreds of splendid imperial assemblies were to take place in the time to come. The so-called Kaiserhaus, a massive structure restored in a historicizing 19th century fashion – it is said to have been the largest hall structure of its time – still testifies to the fact. Heinrich III, whose heart rests in the palatine chapel, commissioned a mighty cathedral to be erected at Goslar. Mountain and smelting works owners as well as the various guilds exhibited their wealth in glorious buildings such as the "Brusttuch" or "Kaiserworth". The city council also received a representative, elaborately embellished seat. The piety of the miners gave rise to a great number of churches. Almost 50 steeples keep watch over Goslar's medieval old town. Yet, already Heinrich Heine was looking in vain for the cathedral tower. A ravaging fire spared only the porch of the building, which was consecrated in 1050. Charlemagne's seat at Aachen and the imperial throne exhibited in the porch are the only two extant German royal seats. The bronze for its backrest comes from the Rammelsberg, and also that for numerous other works of art, including the well on the market-place.

In 1988, the last miner's shift clocked in on the Rammelsberg, and the artist Christo wrapped a mining car full of ore, turning it into a work of art. The Rammelsberg has been a museum since 1990. Among other things, visitors may admire slagheaps from the 10th century as well as one of the oldest and best preserved mining tunnels in Germany. Germany's oldest bricked-in miner's shaft and the German mining industry's oldest day building, the Malermeisterturm from the 15th century, also belong to the numerous sights on the mountain, which determined much of the history and development of the city of Goslar.

*The size of the imperial residence, large parts of which were restored and some even newly conceived in the 19th century, still testifies to Goslar's medieval prosperity and might (left); the imperial seat in the porch of the cathedral, which was dismantled in 1820 (above). Overleaf: The wealth of the town, grounded on silver from the Rammelsberg, is also evident in numerous old town buildings. Two impressive examples, the guild hall of the tailors "Kaiserworth" (left) and the city hall (center), are situated on the market-place. One of the many works of art made of the metal of the Goslar mines in the course of its mining history of almost 1000 years is the cast bronze well on the market-place. Its lower basin is considered to be a major medieval example of large bronze casting.*

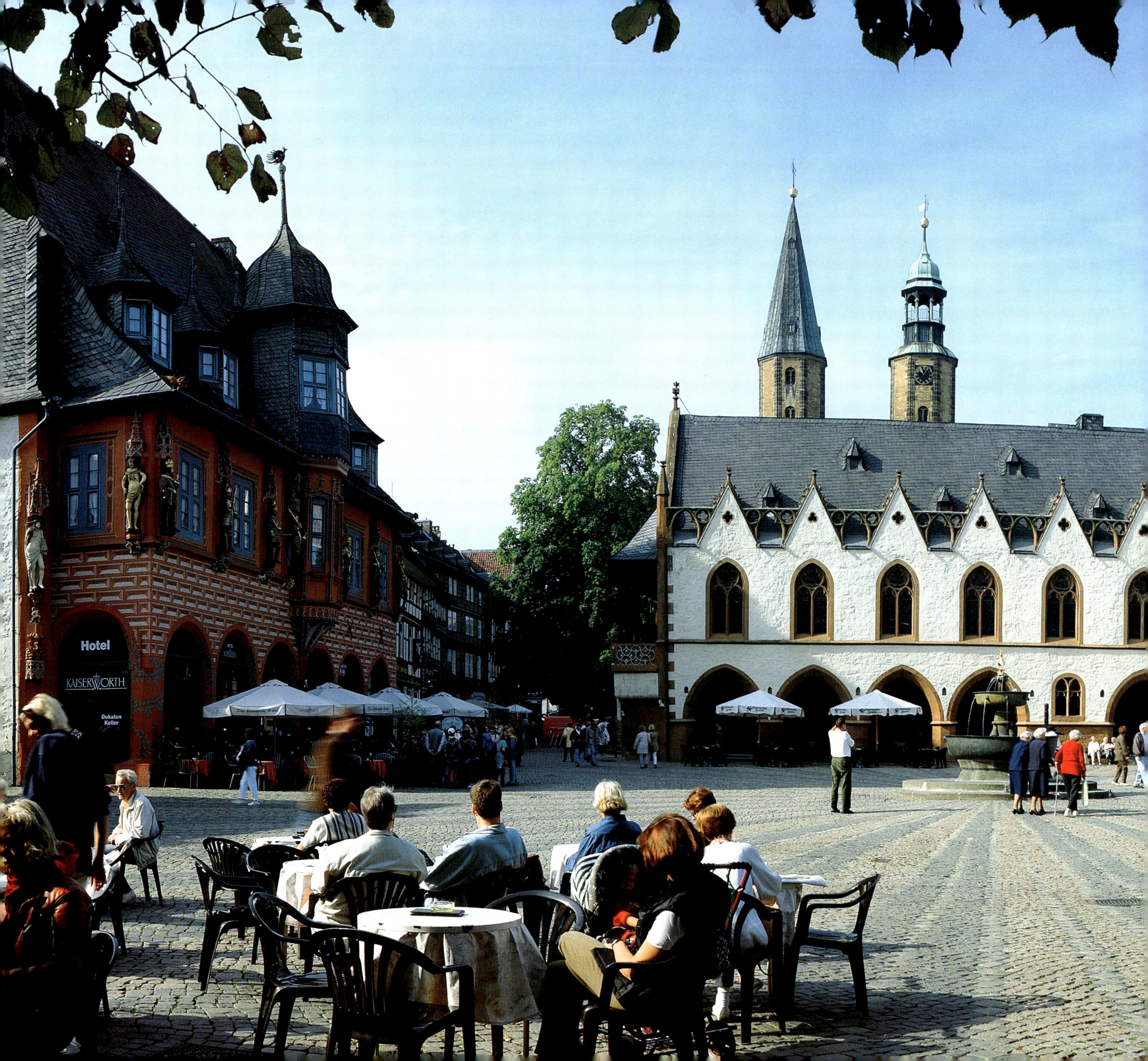
Hotel
KAISERWORTH
Dukaten
Keller

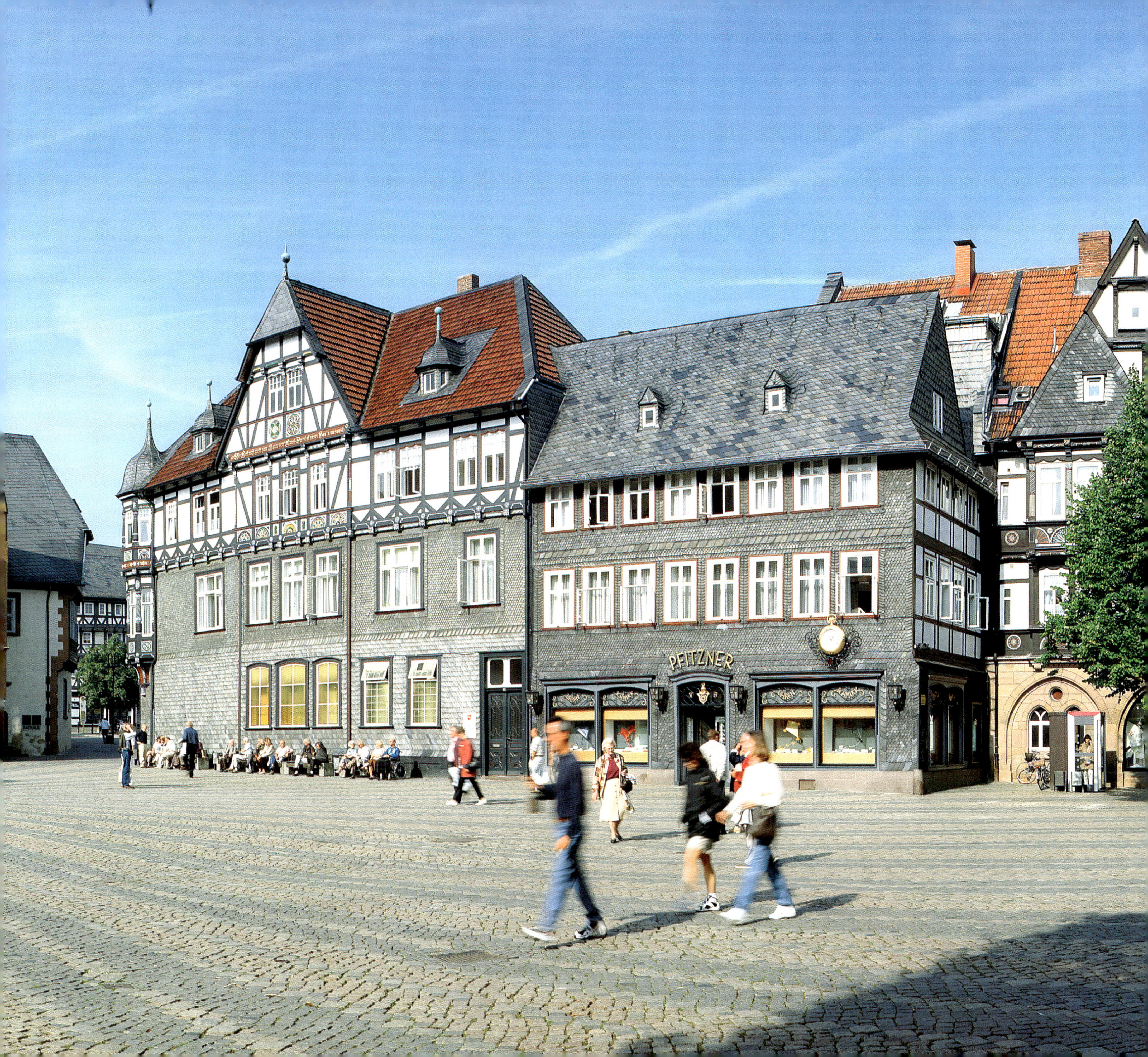
PFITZNER

*Üppiges Schnitz- und Balkenwerk für innen wie außen: im Stift St. Annahaus (links) und in der Halle des im 13. Jahrhundert entstandenen Spitals „Großes Heiliges Kreuz" (ganz rechts oben). Reizvolle mittelalterliche Pflastergassen führen zu immer neuen architektonischen Juwelen – aber auch zurück zum nächtlich beleuchteten Marktplatz mit Brunnen und Haus Kaiserworth (rechts oben).*

*Rich carvings and woodwork both inside and outside: in the hall of the 13th century infirmary "Großes Heiliges Kreuz" (above, very right) and at the St. Annahaus convent (left). Quaint medieval cobblestone alleyways lead to ever new architectural gems and also back to the illuminated market-place with its well and the "Kaiserworth" house at night.*

45

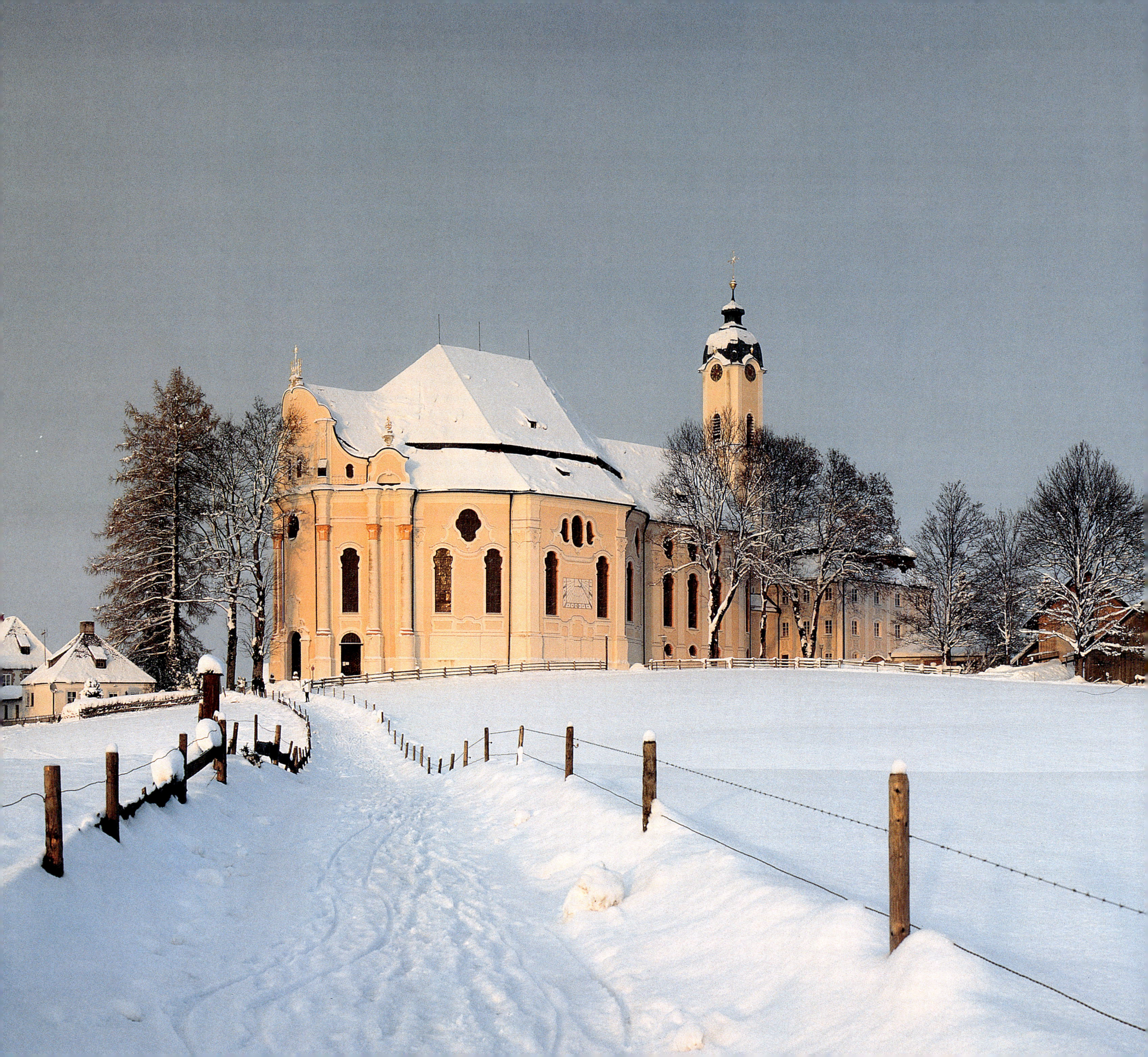

*Im Wiesengelände zu Füßen der Ammergauer Alpen schufen Dominikus Zimmermann, sein Bruder Johann Baptist und ihre Mitarbeiter eines der großartigsten Kunstwerke des bayerischen Rokoko. Viele günstige Umstände lassen „die Wies" gerade hier voll zur Geltung kommen: eine jahrhundertealte Tradition der Wallfahrt, eine enge Verzahnung von Glauben und Lebensgefühl – und nicht zuletzt eine berückend schöne Landschaft. So kann sich auch ein nüchterner Betrachter der Wirkung kaum entziehen, die von diesem Bauwerk bereits von außen ausgeht. Umso mehr gilt dies für innen: ob nun für den großen Überblick zur barocken Orgel hin, die im 20. Jahrhundert restauriert wurde (nächste Doppelseite), oder für die Betrachtung von Details, beispielsweise der Rocailles, die an den architektonischen Nahtstellen allgegenwärtig sind (rechts).*

## Die Wieskirche

Schöne Kirchen und Klöster gibt es zwischen Lech, Ammersee und Staffelsee nicht wenige, der „Pfaffenwinkel" trägt seinen Namen zu Recht. Und dennoch ragt die Wieskirche seit mehr als 250 Jahren heraus. Ein schlichter, von zwei Prämonstratenser-Mönchen des nahen Klosters Steingaden aus Teilen alter Holzfiguren zusammengesetzter Christus gab den Anlass zu ihrem Bau. Das armselige Bildnis des Gottessohnes geriet als Geschenk auf den Hof der Wiesbäuerin Maria Lory. Dort vergoss es, wie die Bäuerin ihrem Beichtvater am 15. Juni 1738 mitteilte, Tränen, während sie und ihr Mann zu ihm beteten.

Das Tränenwunder auf dem Wieshof spricht sich rasch herum, Nachbarn und Fürbittende aus der näheren Umgebung beginnen, zur „Wies" zu pilgern. Bereits 1740 wird für den „Gegeißelten Christus" eine schlichte Wallfahrtskapelle am Fuß des Trauchbergs gebaut. Bald kann sie den Zustrom der Pilger jedoch nicht mehr fassen. Und der Abt von Steingaden kann den Wessobrunner Dominikus Zimmermann als Architekten für ein größeres, glanzvolles Heiligtum gewinnen, einen damals im süddeutschen Raum gerühmten und gefragten Spezialisten. Nach vier Jahren Bauzeit wird 1749 das „gnadenreiche Bildnis" in den Chor der neuen Kirche übertragen. Am 1. September 1754 erfolgt ihre feierliche Weihe.

Gemeinsam mit seinem älteren Bruder, dem Maler und Stuckator Johann Baptist hat Dominikus Zimmermann mit der Wieskirche eines der vollkommensten Kunstwerke des bayerischen Rokoko geschaffen: Er konzipierte ein ovales Kirchenschiff, dessen Höhepunkt der rechteckige Chor mit dem monumentalen doppelgeschossigen Hauptaltar bildet. Marmelierte Holzpfeiler, filigran wirkende Zwillingssäulen, seitliche Galerien und üppiges Muschelwerk – fachsprachlich Rocaille – bezaubern das Auge. 342 Engel schließlich, die allerorten in dem meisterlichen, bis 1991 für gut 10 Millionen Mark restaurierten Gotteshaus schweben, tragen das ihre dazu bei, dass die Wieskirche von vielen auch als „Himmel auf Erden" angesehen wird. Einer der Engel soll übrigens an jedem 22. September um halb sechs Uhr abends auf einem Sonnenstrahl tanzen …

## The Wieskirche Church

There are quite a few beautiful churches and monasteries between the Lech, Ammersee and Staffelsee – the "Pfaffenwinkel" (priest's nook) is called rightfully so. Nevertheless, the Wieskirche church has held a special place for more than 250 years. A simple Christ figure, assembled from parts of old wood carvings by two Premonstratensian monks from the nearby monastery Steingaden was the occasion for its construction. The humble likeness of the son of God ended up as a present on the Wieshof farm of Maria Lory. There, as the lady of the house explained to her confessor on June 15, 1738, it shed tears while she and her husband sat at prayer. The teary miracle of the Wieshof farm quickly became known, neighbors and intercessors from nearby initiated pilgrimages to the "Wies". A modest pilgrimage chapel for the figure of the "scourged Christ" was built at the foot of the Trauchberg mountain as early as 1740, but it was soon too small to accommodate all arriving pilgrims. Subsequently, the abbot of Steingaden succeeded in commissioning the Wessobrunn architect Dominikus Zimmermann, then a well-known and renowned Southern German specialist, for a larger, more representative sanctuary. After four years of construction, the "merciful likeness" was transferred to the chancel of the new church, which was solemnly consecrated on September 1, 1754.

Together with his elder brother, the painter and plasterer Johann Baptist, Dominikus Zimmermann created one of the most finished works of art of the Bavarian rococo: The oval nave culminating in a rectangular chancel with a monumental, two-story altar are his conception. Marmorated wooden pillars, filigree-like twin columns, side galleries and opulent rockwork (rocaille) delight the eye. And finally, 342 angels suspended here and there in the splendid church, which was renovated for about 10 million DM between 1984 and 1991, contribute to the Wieskirche's popular epithet "heaven on earth". Incidentally, one of the angels is said to dance on a sunbeam each September 22nd at five-thirty …

*On the meadows in the foothills of the Ammergau Alps, Dominikus Zimmermann, his brother Johann Baptist and their associates created one of the greatest works of the Bavarian rococo. A number of favorable circumstances work in favor of the "Wies" church on this site: a century-old tradition of pilgrimage, tightly interlocking religious beliefs and lifestyles, and not least a breathtaking landscape. Even sober-minded viewers can hardly resist the effects of its splendid exterior, and even less those of the inside: the grand view onto the Baroque organ, which was restored in the 20th century (overleaf), for instance, or the contemplation of such details as the rocaille work adorning all architectural seams (above).*

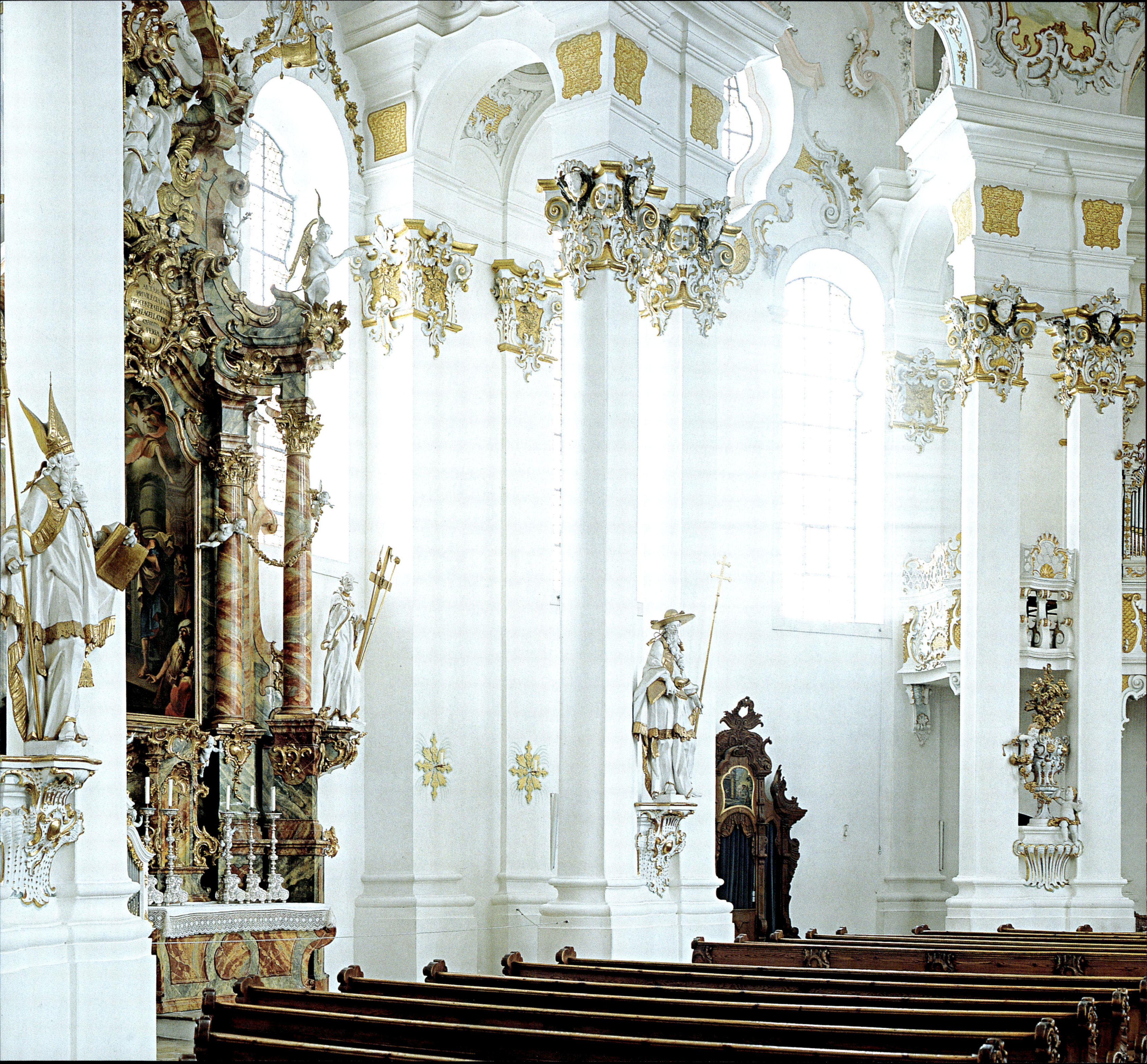

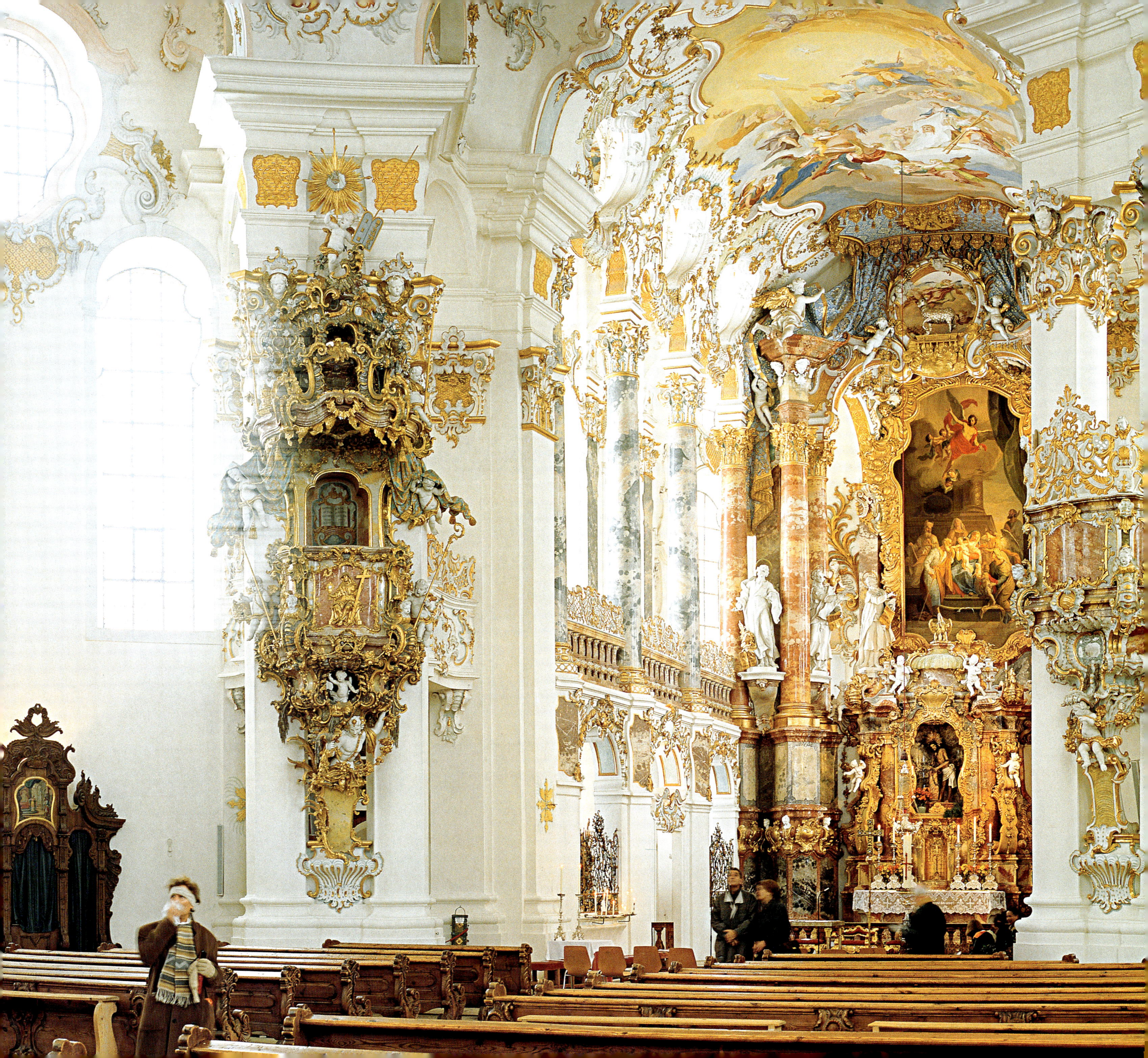

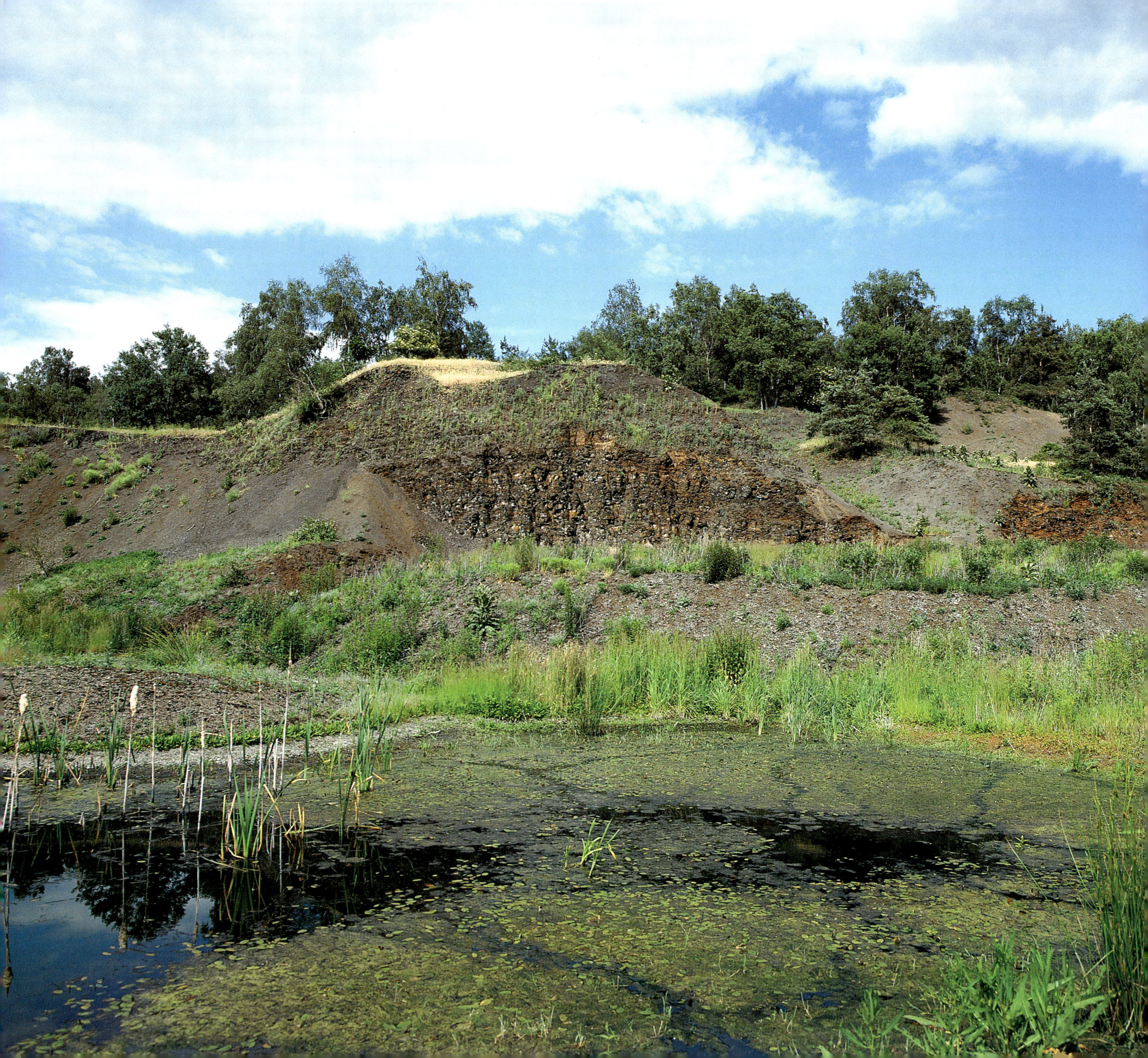

*Aufregende Funde in Natur „aus zweiter Hand": Die tertiäre Grube Messel zwischen Darmstadt und Dieburg mitten in der südhessischen Industrielandschaft ist ein Kleinod aus der erdgeschichtlichen Vergangenheit. Sie gibt in bislang einzigartiger Weise und Fülle Aufschluss über die Tier- und Pflanzenwelt aus der rund 20 Millionen Jahre währenden Zeit des Eozän, als es in unseren Breiten viel wärmer war.*

## Grube Messel

Vom Aschenputtel zur Königin – fast wie ein Märchen klingt die Geschichte der Grube Messel. Denn hätten sich engagierte Bürger nicht über 20 Jahre unermüdlich für das circa 1 Quadratkilometer große eozäne Ölschiefer-Gebiet im Nordosten von Darmstadt eingesetzt, wäre die 1995 als erstes deutsches Naturdenkmal in die Liste des Welterbes aufgenommene Fossilienfundstätte zu einer riesigen Mülldeponie verkommen.

Die Grube Messel dokumentiert, wie sich nach dem Aussterben der Saurier die Tier- und Pflanzenwelt auf der Erde explosionsartig veränderte. Fast 200 Meter mächtig waren die Ölschiefervorkommen der Grube. Sie bergen Fossilien, die das gesamte Spektrum der Lebewesen im Eozän (vor 57 bis 36 Mio. Jahren) umfassen, in einer Artenvielfalt und Qualität, wie sie bislang von keiner anderen Fundstelle belegt ist, und das in großer Zahl: Bisher wurden rund 10 000 Funde gemacht.

Die Fundauswertung der Grube Messel, die der Senckenbergischen Naturforschenden Gesellschaft anvertraut ist, öffnet das Fenster in die Vorgeschichte menschlichen Lebens, gibt Aufschluss über Kontinentaldrift und Sedimentation, über Ozeanbildung und Landbrücken zwischen sich verschiebenden Kontinenten, über Tiefe und Erstreckung der Biosphäre und über Klima- und Lebenszyklen. Möglich ist meist auch ein präzises Bild von Anatomie und Lebensweise der bislang 100 nachgewiesenen Wirbeltierarten, darunter 40 Säugetiere. Zu den spektakulärsten Funden gehören die Überreste von mehr als 70 Urpferden, darunter gut 30 vollständige Skelette. Von Wirbeltieren blieben Skelette mit Weichteilkonturen und sogar Mageninhalten erhalten. Fossilienfunde von Vögeln versprechen neue Erkenntnisse über die Zusammensetzung der artenreichen frühtertiären Vogelwelt. Die Vielfalt der Reptilien- und Amphibienfauna – beispielsweise der Krokodile – erlaubt, Nahrungsketten und das einstige ökologische System zu rekonstruieren. Messel ist auch eine der bedeutendsten Fundstellen fossiler Insekten. Zudem gilt die Flora von Messel unter Paläobotanikern als eine der artenreichsten des Alttertiärs. Die Pflanzenreste von Palmen und Schlinggewächsen lassen Rückschlüsse auf das Klima und besondere Standortbedingungen zu.

## The Messel Pit

From Cinderella to queen – the history of the Messel Pit sounds almost like a fairytale. If involved citizens had not fought for the preservation of the Eocene schist area to the northeast of Darmstadt, the fossil site, which was added to the World Heritage list in 1995 as the first natural site in Germany, would have been turned into a huge dump.

The Messel Pit illustrates how, after the demise of the dinosaurs, flora and fauna on earth underwent dramatic changes. The schist layers in the pit were almost 200 meters thick, holding fossils covering the whole range of life in the Eocene (57 to 36 million years ago), in a biodiversity and quality which has yet to be matched, and also in great quantities: So far, about 10,000 findings have been recorded.

The evaluation of findings from the Messel pit, which rests in the hands of the Senckenbergische Naturforschende Gesellschaft, opens up a window onto the history preceding human life, providing insights into processes such as continental drift and sedimentation, the forming of oceans and land bridges between shifting continents, the depth and extension of our biosphere as well as climatic and life cycles. For the most part, a precise picture of the anatomy and habits of the 100 vertebrae species which have so far been unearthed, among them 40 mammals, has been established. One of the most spectacular finds is the remainder of 70 prehistoric horses including about 30 complete skeletons. Other findings include vertebrae skeletons with abdominal contours and even stomach contents. Bird fossils promise new insights into the diversity of bird life in the Early Tertiary. The wealth of reptile and amphibia fauna – crocodiles, for example – allows the reconstruction of food chains and former ecological systems. Messel is also an important source for fossilized insects. Among paleobotanists, its flora is valued as one of the most diverse of the Early Tertiary. Plant remnants of palms and climbers provide clues to climatic and local conditions.

*Exciting "second hand" findings in nature: the Tertiary Messel Pit between Darmstadt and Dieburg, situated among industrial sites in Southern Hesse, is a historical and geological gem. It allows conclusions about the fauna and flora of the Eocene, a period of about 20 million years, in which the local climate was much warmer.*

Zu den berühmten Fossilienfunden in der Grube Messel zählt neben dem Skelett einer Riesenschlange (Paläopython, oben) auch jenes eines Wolfsbarschs (Paläoperca proxima).

The skeletons of a gigantic snake (paleopython, above) and of a sea perch (paleoperca proxima) belong among the famous fossil findings from the Messel Pit.

*Große Tiere, kleine Tiere: Den versteinerten Abdruck des Knochenbaus eines Urhuftieres (Kopidodon spec., oben) entdeckten Forscher in Messel ebenso wie jenen einer Fledermaus (Paläochiropterix tupaiodon). Im Magen des Nachtfliegers fanden sich sogar noch Nahrungsreste: Schmetterlingsflügel.*

Von 1888 bis 1964 gruben Bergleute bei Messel nach Ölschiefer. An der Stelle der Grube lag einst ein riesiger, von Urwald umgebener Süßwassersee. Dessen Algenreichtum sorgte dafür, dass abgesunkene Tierkadaver und Pflanzen nicht verwesten. Die Grube wurde als erstes Naturdenkmal in Deutschland unter den Schutz der UNESCO gestellt; weitere einmalige – auch von Menschen gestaltete – Landschaften sollen folgen.

From 1888 to 1964, miners were digging schist at Messel. The site of the pit once was a huge fresh water lake surrounded by primeval forest. Large quantities of algae prevented animal carcasses that sank to the bottom from decomposing. The pit was put under the protection of the UNESCO as the first natural site in Germany. More – also man-made – landscapes are to follow.

*Large animals, small animals. Messel scientists discovered the petrified imprints of the bone structure of a prehistoric hooved animal (kopidodon spec., above) as well as those of a bat (paleochiropterix tupaiodon). The stomach of a night flyer still contained food rests: butterfly wings.*

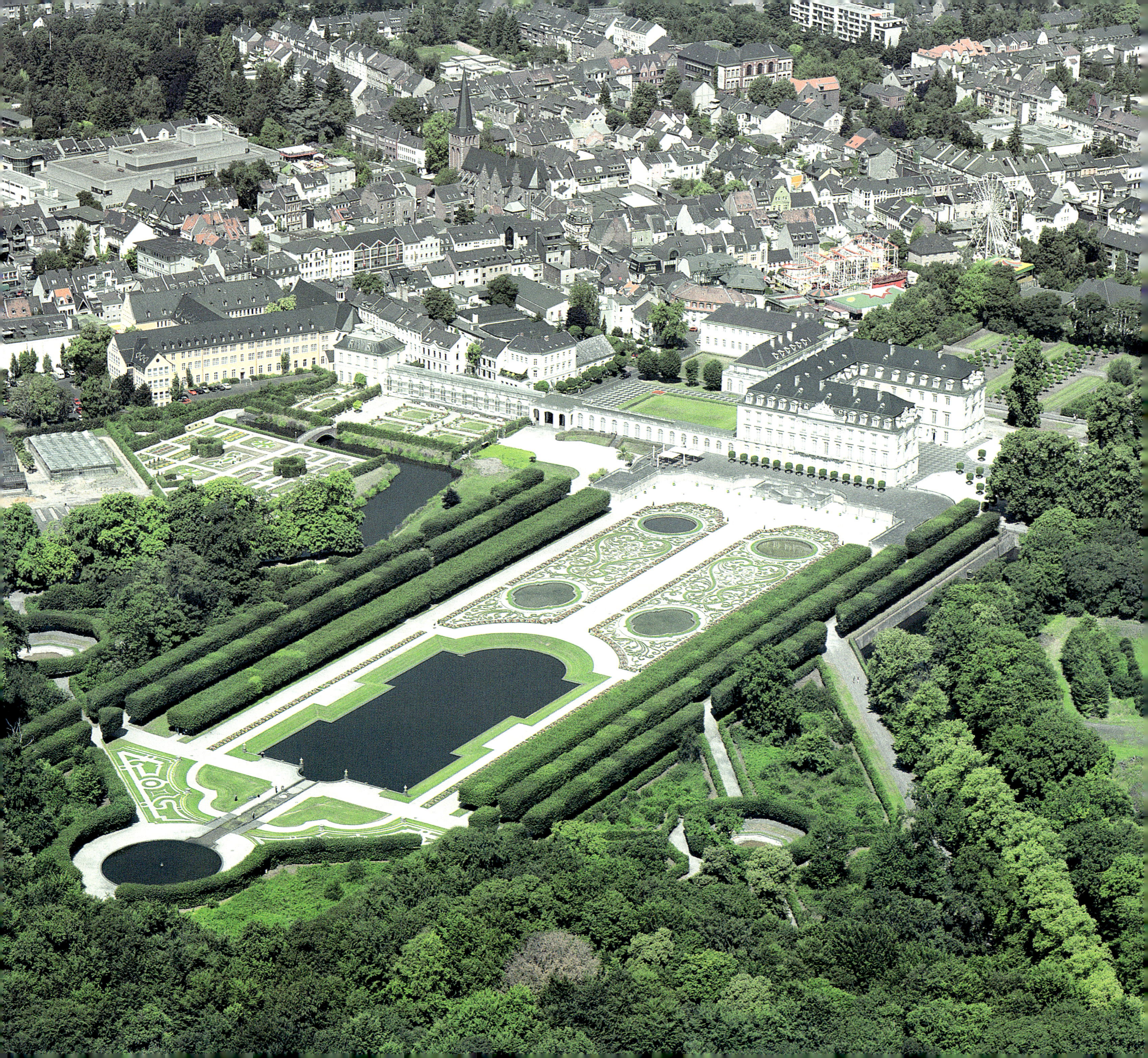

*Mehr als drei Jahrzehnte wurde an Schloss Augustusburg zu Brühl gebaut. Johann Conrad Schlaun und François de Cuvilliés haben hier die Baugeschichte des Rokoko umfassend dargestellt. Kernstück der an ihrer Südflanke von prächtigen Parks akzentuierten Anlage ist die Prunk-Treppe im Mittelflügel (nächste Doppelseite). Sie geht nach allgemeiner Expertenmeinung wohl auf Balthasar Neumann, den kongenialen Erbauer der Würzburger Residenz zurück, wahrscheinlich aber auch zu großen Teilen auf Michel Leveilly, den Kurkölner Hofbaumeister, und wurde in den Jahren 1743 bis 1748 geschaffen.*

## Die Schlösser in Brühl

Ursprünglich sollte Schloss Augustusburg nur ein Jagdschloss werden. Doch dann ließ sich der junge Wittelsbacher Prinz Clemens August zur Änderung seines Planes bewegen. Und François de Cuvilliés, der gebürtige Wallone und Meister des Ornaments, formte den schlichten Rohbau seines westfälischen Kollegen Johann Conrad Schlaun um. Dieser hatte Teile der 1689 zerstörten mittelalterlichen Wasserburg der Kölner Erzbischöfe mit einbezogen, de Cuvilliés schuf nun eine opulente dreiflügelige Residenz mit Lustschlosscharakter. Die Wassergräben wurden zugeschüttet und nach den Plänen von Dominique Girard entstand vor der Südfront des Bauwerks ein prächtiges Gartenareal im französischen Stil. Balthasar Neumann wird die Krönung des Brühler Rokoko-Glanzes zugeschrieben: der prachtvolle Treppensaal. Doppelsäulen und Gewölbebrücken gliedern plastisch den hohen Raum, farbiger Stuckmarmor und das Deckenfresko von Carlo Carlone – dem seinerzeit bestbezahlten Maler – in der Flachkuppel vereinigen sich zu grandioser Farbharmonie.

Nach seinem Niedergang in der Französischen Revolution ließ erst Preußenkönig Friedrich Wilhelm IV. das rheinische Kleinod Augustusburg restaurieren und kaufte Teile seiner ursprünglichen Innenausstattung zurück. Der Zweite Weltkrieg brachte dann erneut schwere Schäden für das einstige Wittelsbacher Traumschloss. Doch auch diese Wunden konnten geschlossen werden. Seit den 70er Jahren diente das Schloss der Bundesrepublik als Kulisse für Staatsempfänge.

Mit Augustusburg durch eine – inzwischen wiederhergestellte – Allee verbunden war Falkenlust, das intime Jagdschlösschen des „durchleuchtigsten Churfürsten und hochwürdigen Erzbischofs von Köln", Clemens August. Ebenso nach Plänen von Cuvilliés erbaut, ist es ein bezauberndes Beispiel für künstlerische Freiheiten und Überraschungen: mit einem polygonalen Mittelteil, der im Erdgeschoss einen ovalen Salon aufweist. Clemens August hielt hier illustre Jagdgesellschaften ab und lud gelegentlich zu Diners à deux. Augustusburg und Falkenlust sind die ersten bedeutenden Schöpfungen des Rokoko in Deutschland und wurden daher 1984 in die Welterbe-Liste aufgenommen.

## The Palaces at Brühl

Originally, Augustusburg Palace was intended only as a hunting lodge. But as the young Wittelsbach prince Clemens August changed his mind, François de Cuvilliés, the Walloon master of ornament, was entrusted to reconceive the rather plainly designed shell his Westphalian colleague Johann Conrad Schlaun had left. Schlaun had incorporated the medieval moat-encircled castle of the Cologne archbishops destroyed in 1689, and Cuvilliés created an opulent summer residence with three wings. The moats were filled in, and Dominique Girard devised a huge French-style garden area extending on the southern front of the palace. The showpiece of the Brühl rococo splendour, however, is attributed to Balthasar Neumann: the palace's marvelous staircase. The lofty space is structured with sculptural elements such as twin columns and vaulted arches, while colorful stucco marble and the ceiling fresco by Carlo Carlone – the best-paid painter of his time – extending over the flat dome all blend into a grandiose color harmony.

After its demise in the course of the French Revolution, it was the Prussian King Friedrich Wilhelm IV who had the gem on the Rhine restored, repurchasing some of its original fittings. World War II once more spelled heavy damages for the wonderful former Wittelsbach residence. Yet, these wounds, too, could be healed. Since the seventies, the palace has been used as a backdrop for official state receptions of the Federal Republic of Germany.

Augustusburg was connected to Falkenlust via a tree-lined avenue which since has been restored. The cozy hunting-lodge of "His Grace the Elector and the Most Reverend Archbishop of Cologne" was also built according to plans from Cuvilliés and is a charming example for artistic inventiveness and surprise details, e.g. a polygonal middle with an oval salon on the ground floor. Here, Clemens August entertained hunting parties of rank and fame and occasionally indulged in diners à deux. Augustusburg and Falkenlust are the first important rococo creations in Germany and were accepted into the World Heritage Program in 1984.

*The construction of Augustusburg Palace at Brühl took more than three decades. Johann Conrad Schlaun and François de Cuvilliés created a prime example of rococo architecture between them. The heart of the structure, whose southern side is accentuated by a gorgeous park, is the representative staircase in the center wing (overleaf). It was built between 1743 and 1748 and has been attributed to Balthasar Neumann, the ingenious master builder of the Würzburg Residence, with some parts by Michel Leveilly, the Cologne court master builder.*

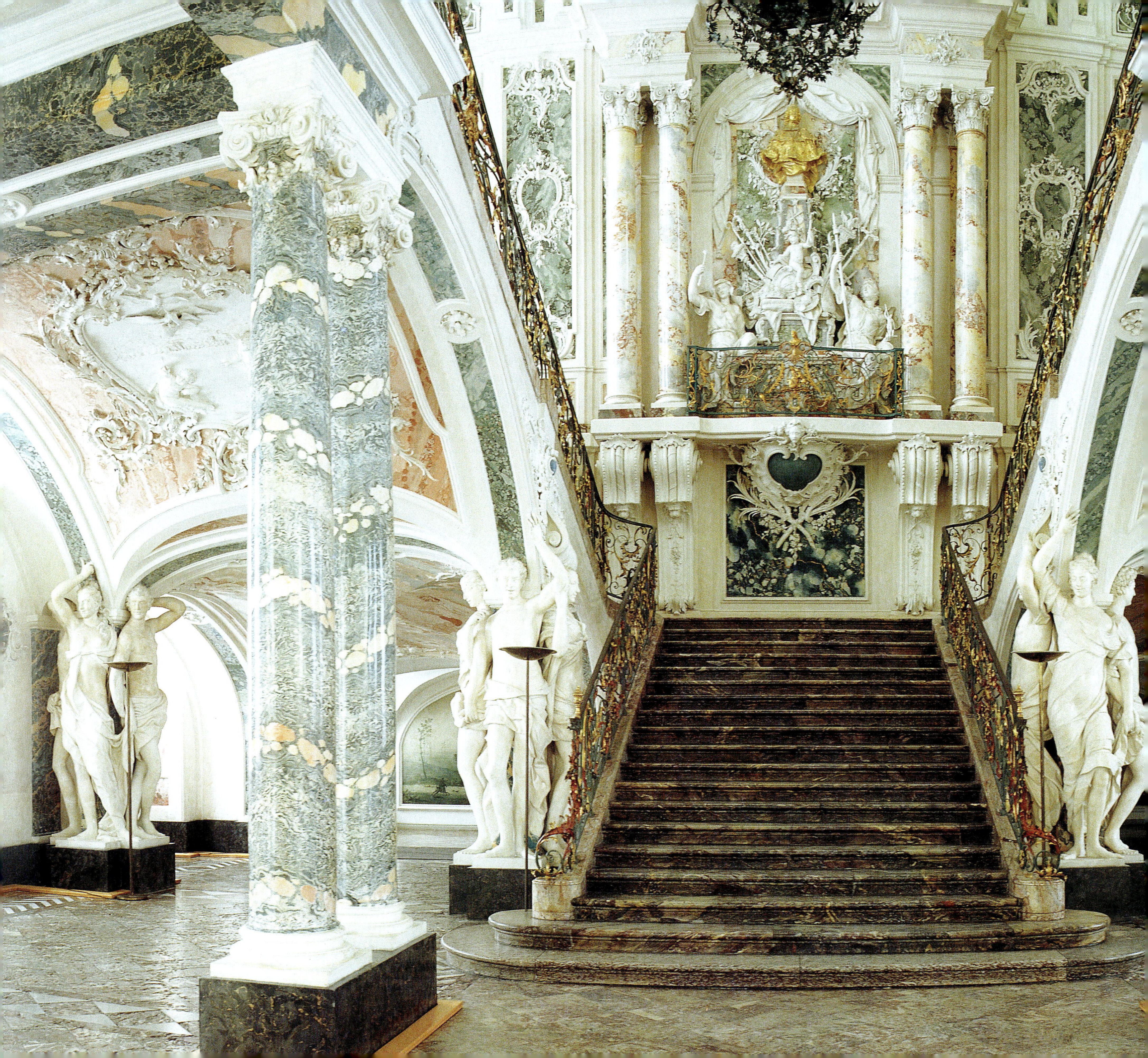

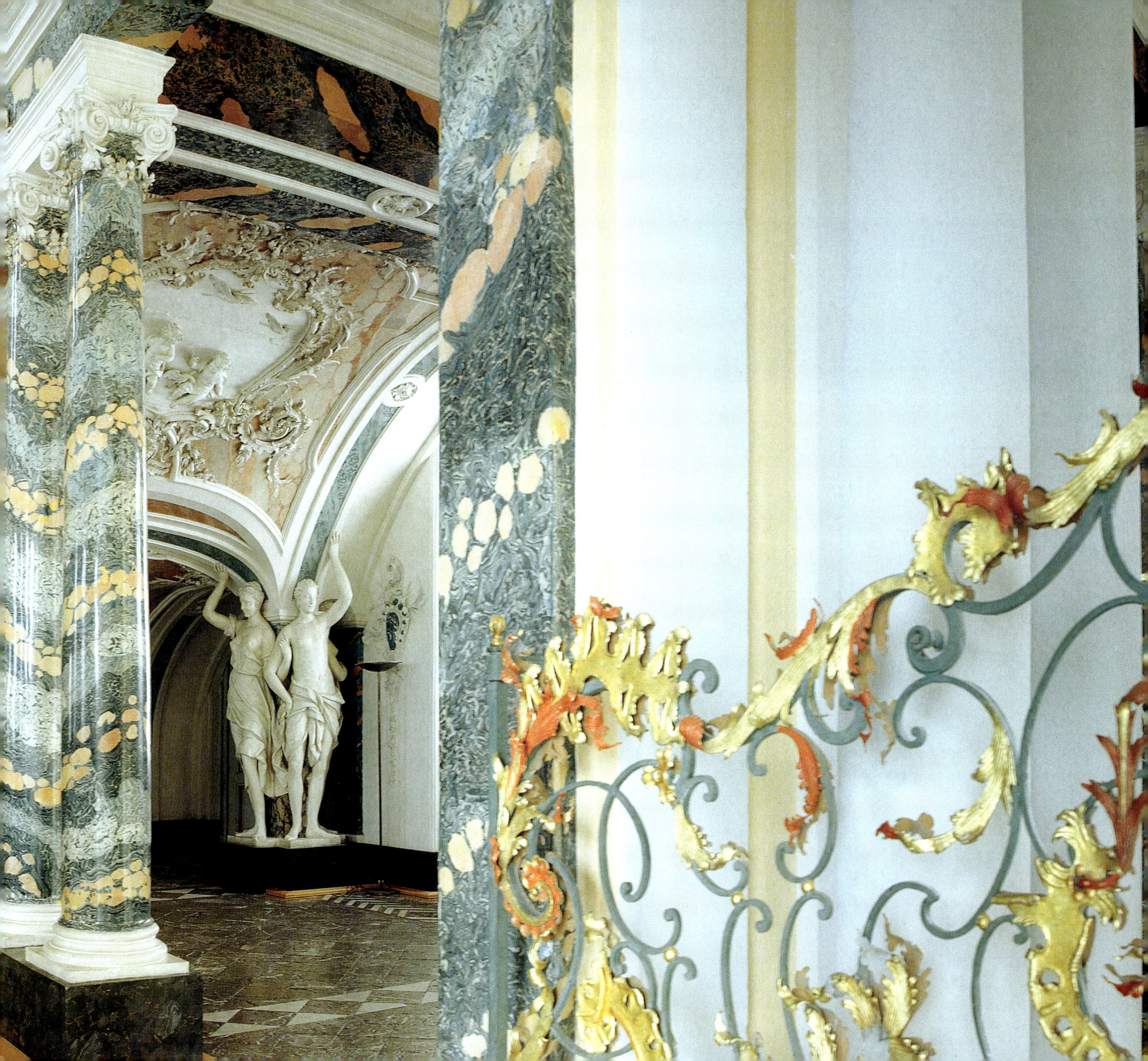

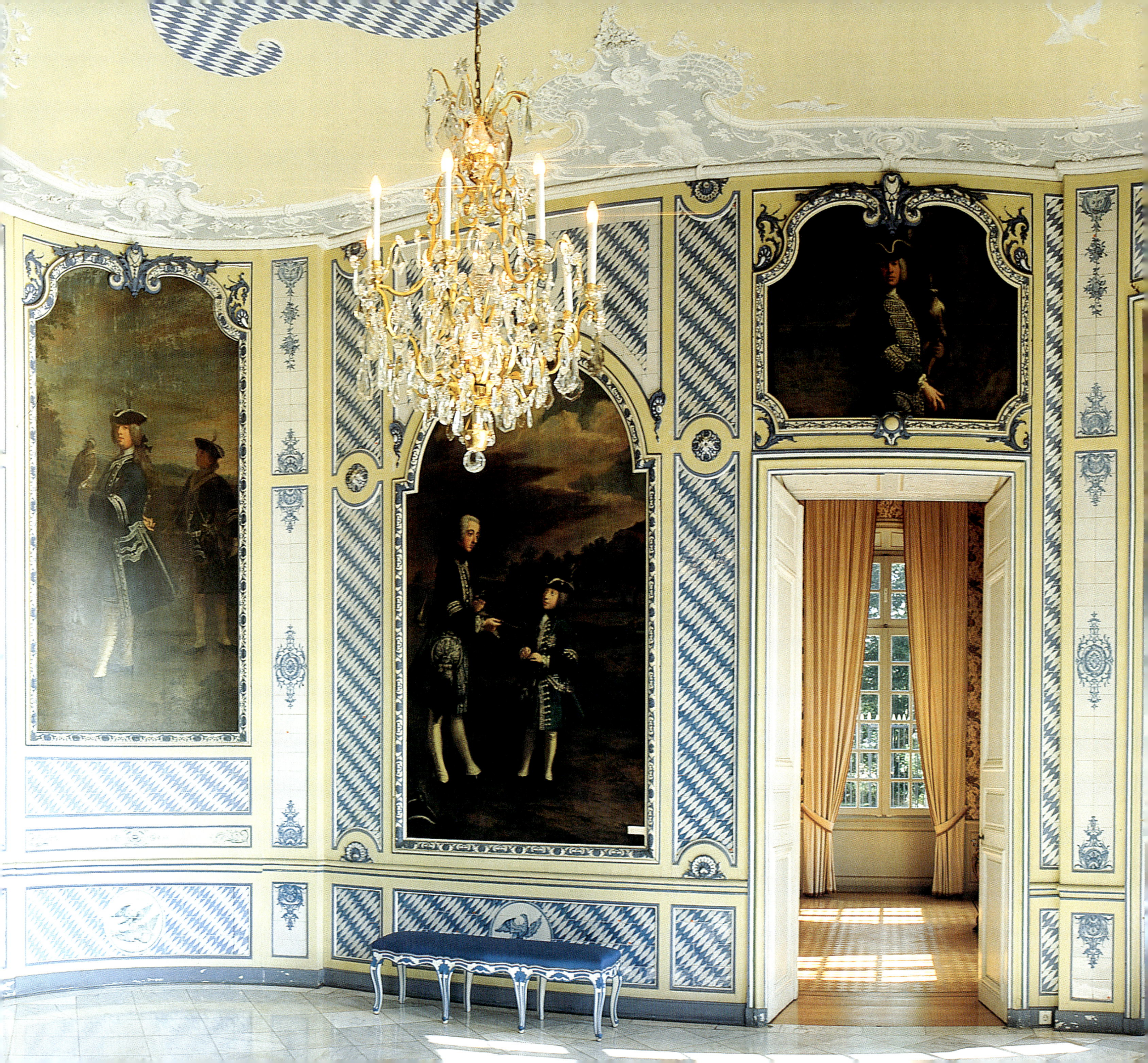

*In einem kleinen Wald im Anschluss an den weitläufigen Park von Augustusburg liegt südöstlich von Brühl das Jagdschlösschen Falkenlust. In seiner Innenausstattung dominieren die Farben des Hauses Wittelsbach sowie der kurkölnischen Falkenjagd: weiß und blau.*

*The Falkenlust hunting lodge is situated in a small wooded lot bordering the spacious park of Augustusburg Palace southeast of Brühl. Its interior decorations show the Wittelsbach colors, white and blue, as well as motifs of falconry.*

*1729 wurde Falkenlust von Clemens August in Auftrag gegeben; François de Cuvilliés entwarf die Pläne für eines der intimsten Bauwerke des frühen Rokoko in Deutschland, und Michel Leveilly hatte bis zur Fertigstellung im Jahre 1740 die Bauleitung. Die Kapelle von Falkenlust wurde in der Form einer Eremitengrotte errichtet.*

*Clemens August commissioned Falkenlust to be built in 1729. François de Cuvilliés designed the plans for one of the coziest early rococo structures in Germany, while Michel Leveilly was in charge of the building supervision until its completion in 1740. The Falkenlust chapel was built as a hermit's grotto.*

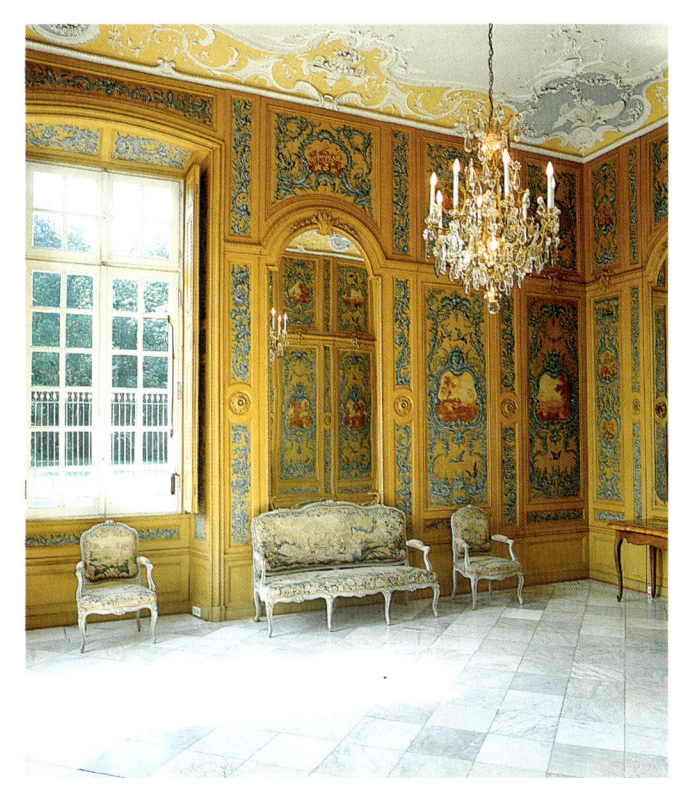

Die Farben des Hauses Wittelsbach und der Falken- oder Beizjagd findet man in Falkenlust in den niederländischen Wandfliesen, in den Boiserien des Spiegelkabinetts und in der exquisiten Sammlung von Chinaporzellan. Nebenbei bemerkt: Die Beizjagd mit eigens dafür abgerichteten, pfeilschnellen Raubvögeln – meist aus der Familie der Falken – genoss bis zum Ende des Mittelalters allerhöchstes Ansehen in Deutschland. Heute wird sie noch in ihrem vermutlichen Ursprungsgebiet – in Arabien – mit Leidenschaft betrieben.

The Dutch wall tiles, the paneling in the mirror cabinet and in the exquisite china collection feature the Wittelsbach family colors and motifs of falconry and hawking. Incidentally, hawking with specially trained, swiftly moving predatory birds – mostly of the falcon family – was a highly respected sport in Germany well into the late Middle Ages. Today, it is still very popular in its supposed area of origin – various Arabian countries.

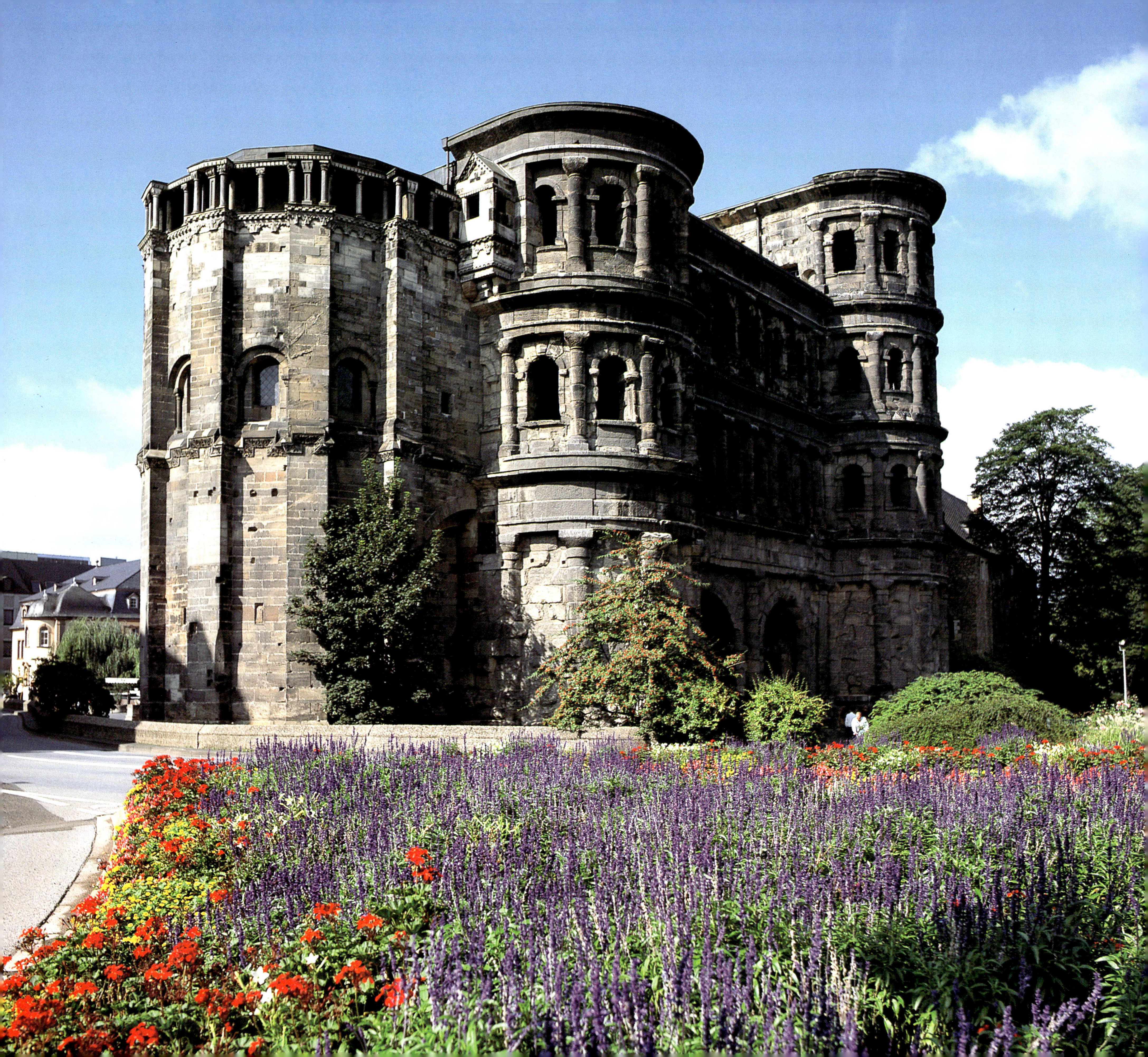

*Lebendige Antike in der Moselstadt Trier: Ein Symbol für den Glanz der einstigen Kaiserresidenz und Metropole des Weströmischen Reiches ist die eindrucksvolle Porta Nigra, das unvollendet gebliebene nördliche Stadttor mit zwei halbkreisförmig vorspringenden, viergeschossigen Türmen (links). Den Namen „Schwarzes Tor" bekam es erst im Mittelalter, der nachdunkelnde helle Sandstein gab den Anlass. Seine zeitweise Nutzung als Kirche schützte es vor der Zerstörung durch Feindeshand. Ein anderes römisches Monument war die Doppelkirchenanlage am selben Platz, an dem sich heute Dom und Liebfrauenkirche erheben (nächste Doppelseite). Das Bauwerk des 4. Jahrhunderts war das größte seiner Art. Im Ostteil des heutigen Doms sind Teile des römischen Baus erhalten.*

# Trier

Bereits im Jahre 16 v. Chr. von Kaiser Augustus als Augusta Treverorum gegründet, rühmt sich die Moselstadt nicht nur, die älteste Stadt Deutschlands, sondern auch weitaus früher als Rom erbaut worden zu sein. Im 3. und 4. Jahrhundert erlebte Trier seine Blüte als „caput mundi": Residenz der Herrscher des Römischen Reiches mit mindestens 70 000 Einwohnern.

Die im 12. Jahrhundert errichtete Stadtmauer indes musste nur noch knapp 10 000 Menschen schützen. Die Trierer Erzbischöfe, seit dieser Zeit auch gleichzeitig Kurfürsten, trachteten jedoch an den Glanz der Römerzeit anzuknüpfen und fügten Triers Stadtbild immer wieder neue, prunkvolle Bauten hinzu. Das kurfürstliche Schloss, von Johann Seitz im barocken Stil umgestaltet, ist eines von ihnen.

Zu den berühmtesten architektonischen Erinnerungen an die römische Epoche Triers gehört die Porta Nigra, das mächtige nördliche Stadttor aus dem 2. Jahrhundert. Es ist hier aber nicht das älteste Bauwerk der Römerzeit. Diese Ehre gebührt dem Amphitheater. In seiner Arena fanden einst Gladiatorenkämpfe statt.

Römische Baukunst und Macht spiegeln außerdem die Reste der riesigen – anders als die intimeren Barbarathermen allerdings niemals genutzten – Kaiserthermen. Und natürlich die Basilika, ein trotz seiner imposanten Ausmaße – rund 70 Meter lang, 28 Meter breit, 33 Meter hoch – ohne Stützpfeiler errichteter Bau mit wechselvoller Geschichte und Nutzung: Nach seiner Errichtung um das Jahr 310 unter Kaiser Konstantin diente er als Palastaula, wies verschwenderische Ausstattung und Technik auf. Die Frankenkönige nutzten die alte Aula, später die Trierer Erzbischöfe, die sie aber im 17. Jahrhundert stark veränderten und in ihren Palast eingliederten. Zu preußischen Zeiten stilrein wiederhergestellt, dient die Basilika heute als evangelische Pfarrkirche und Konzertsaal.

Eine technische Meisterleistung ist Triers Römerbrücke. Fünf ihrer sieben Pfeiler stammen noch aus dem 2. Jahrhundert. Die ursprüngliche hölzerne Fahrbahn, die sie trugen, wurde im 18. Jahrhundert erneuert. Die gesamte Konstruktion zeigte sich bislang als uneingeschränkt belastbar für den modernen Autoverkehr.

# Trier

Founded as Augusta Trevorum by the Roman Emperor Augustus as early 16 B.C., the Moselle town cannot only boast of being the oldest town in Germany, but also of having been built quite a bit earlier than Rome. Trier, then "caput mundi" with more than 70,000 inhabitants, flourished in the 3rd and 4th centuries, when it was the residence of the rulers of the Roman Empire.

The city wall built later in the Middle Ages only needed to protect 10,000 people, however, even if the archbishops of Trier, at the time also electors and intent on picking up where the splendor of the Roman period had left off, added ever more magnificent buildings to the town. The electoral palace, redesigned in the Baroque style by Johann Seitz, is among them.

One of the most famous architectural remainders of the Roman epoch at Trier is the Porta Nigra, the massive northern city gate dating back to the 2nd century. Yet, the honor of being the oldest Roman building goes to the amphitheater whose arena was used for gladiator fights.

Roman architecture and might are also reflected in the huge Imperial Thermal Baths, which – unlike the more intimate Barbara Springs – were never in use, however, and also in the basilica, a structure built without supporting pillars despite of its imposing dimensions – it is about 70 meters long, 28 meters wide and 33 meters high and has a rather eventful history of use. Constructed around the year 310 under Emperor Constantin with lavish decorations and some technical sophistication, it first served as the palace auditorium. It was also used by the Frankish kings and later the Trier archbishops, who in the 17th century redesigned and integrated it into their palace. In the Prussian era, the basilica was restored true to style, and today it is a Protestant parish church and concert hall.

Trier's Roman bridge is a technological masterpiece. Five of its seven pillars still date back to the 2nd century. The surface, originally wood, was renewed in the 18th century. So far, the entire construction has invariably held up to modern traffic.

*Antiquity lives on in the Moselle town Trier: The impressive Porta Nigra, the never finished northern city gate with its two projecting semi-circular four-story towers (left) is a symbol for the splendor of the former imperial residence and metropolis of the Western Roman Empire. The name "black gate", coined in the Middle Ages, is due to its darkening, originally light sandstone. It was temporarily used as a church and thus spared from enemy destruction. The twin church structure on the same site also dates back to the Roman period. The 4th century building was the largest of its kind. Today, its place is taken by the Liebfrauenkirche church and the cathedral (overleaf), whose eastern part includes pieces of the old Roman building.*

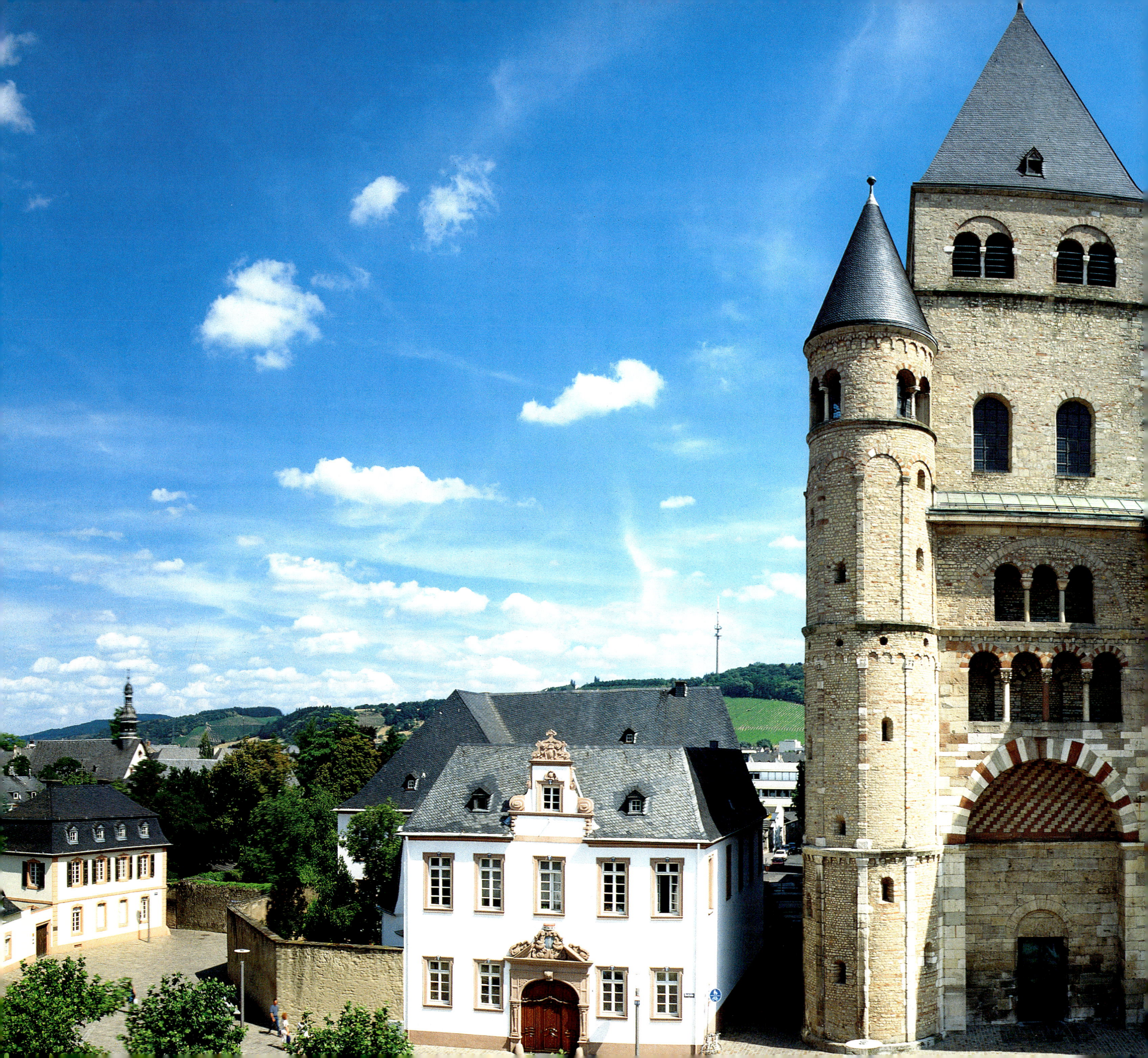

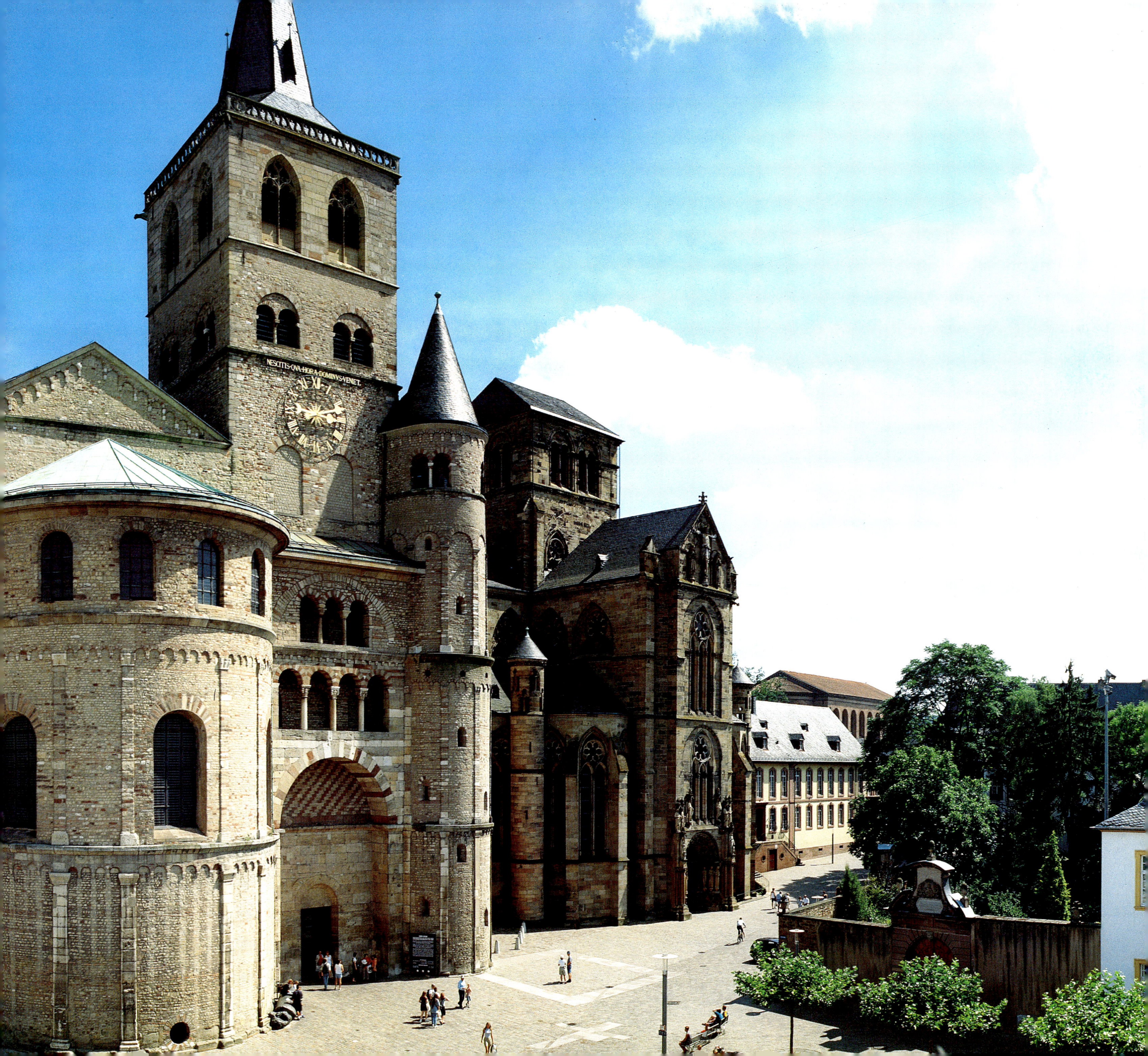
NESCITIS·QVA·HORA·DOMINVS·VENIET.

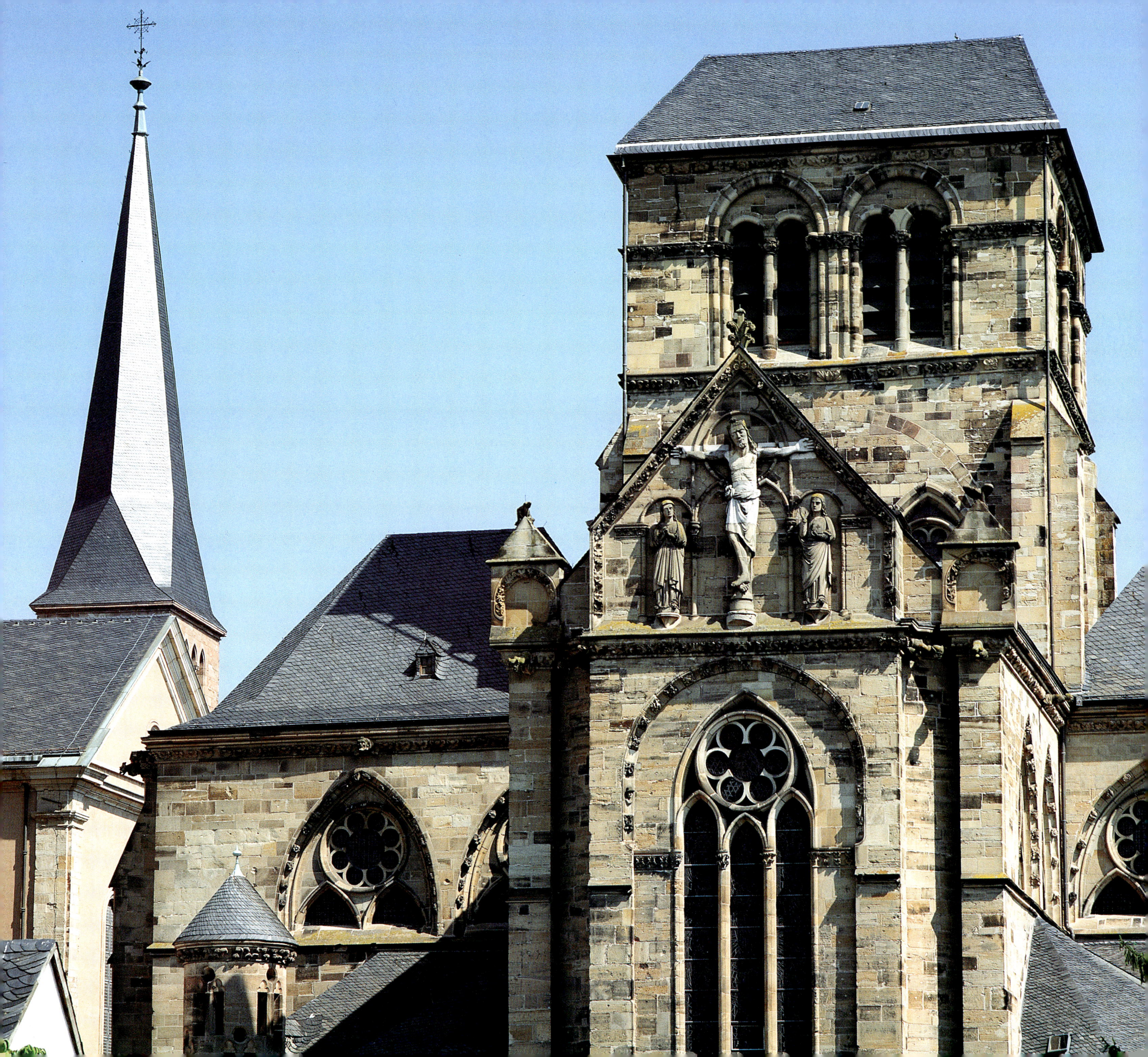

Während sich in der Doppelkirche von Dom und Liebfrauen (linke Seite) Romanik, Gotik und Barock ergänzen, bezaubert das Kurfürstliche Palais (oben) mit seiner restaurierten Farbigkeit aus dem Rokoko. Die ehemals als Westflügel der Schlossanlage dienende römische Basilika oder Palastaula, hier halb verdeckt, dient heute als evangelische Pfarrkirche. Sie wurde einst auf einem großen römischen Gräberfeld errichtet und die unter ihrer Nordhälfte gefundenen Fragmente einer gemalten Decke, auf der man zwei Damen – Helena und Fausta vielleicht – der kaiserlichen Familie zu erkennen glaubt, bezeugen den höfischen Charakter der Architektur.
An den Kaiserthermen (unten links und rechts) wurde lange Zeit gebaut und umgebaut: vom 3. bis ins späte 4. Jahrhundert. Gewaltig sind die Ausmaße ihrer Überreste und kunstvoll die gemauerten Bögen.

The twin structure of the cathedral and the Liebfrauenkirche church (far left) features elements of the Romanesque, Gothic and Baroque periods, and the Kurfürstliches Palais (above) sparkles in its restored rococo colors. The Roman basilica or palace auditorium (partially hidden), formerly the western wing of the palace, today houses a Protestant parish church. It was built on a large Roman graveyard, and the fragments of a painted ceiling found below its northern half and perhaps showing two ladies of imperial descent – possibly Helena and Fausta – testify to the courtly character of the architecture.
Construction, including various changes, of the Imperial Thermal Baths (below left and right) took a long time: from the 3rd to the late 4th century. Of enormous dimensions, the remainders of the brick-laid arches are quite ornate.

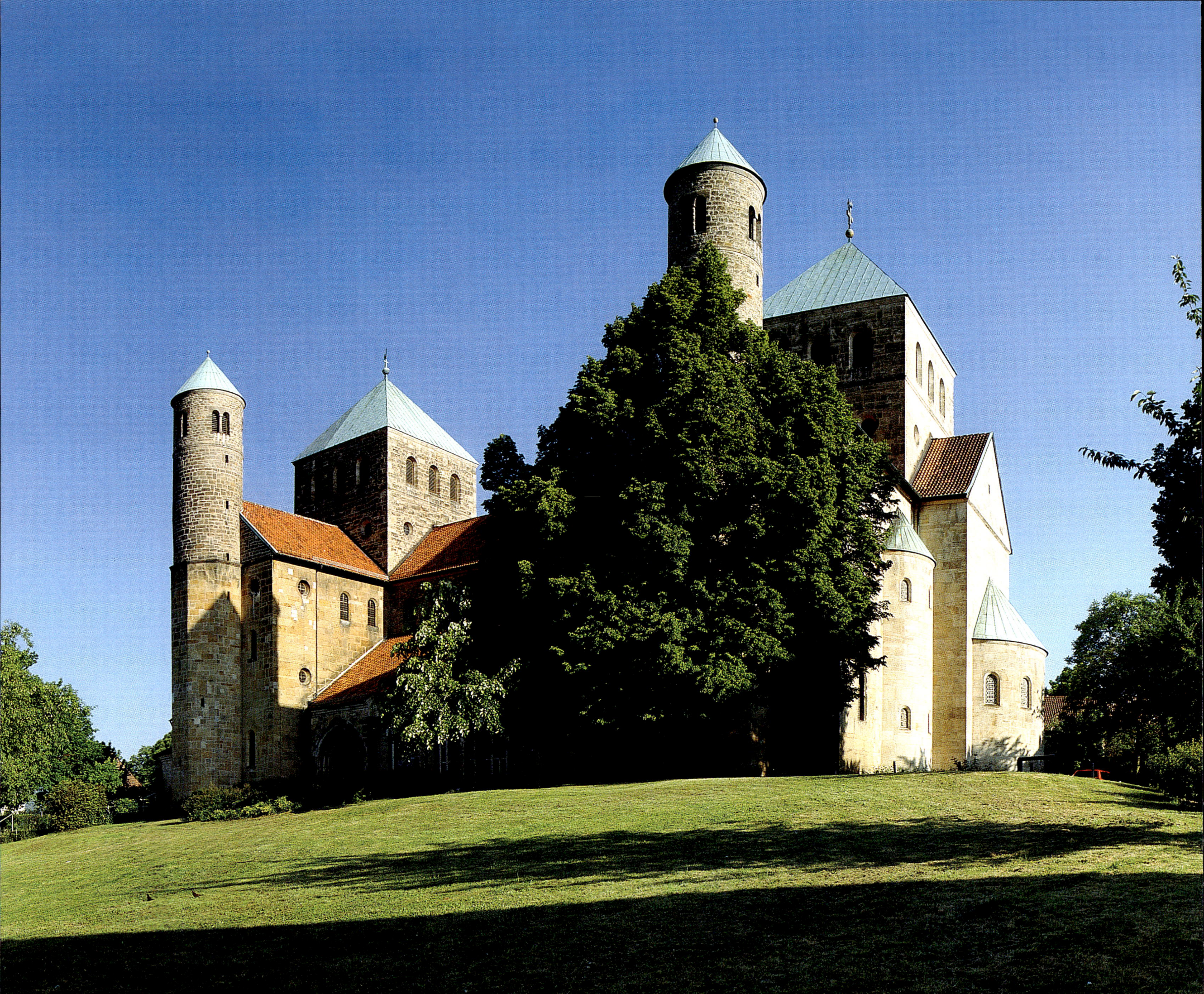

*Von Süden gesehen wird die geradezu mathematische Architektur der Michaeliskirche zu Hildesheim (links) besonders gut offenbar. Das unter dem kunstsinnigen Bischof Bernward von 1010 an erbaute und nach dem Zweiten Weltkrieg rekonstruierte Gotteshaus präsentiert sich wunderbar geschlossen nach außen und innen (nächste Doppelseite). Säulen, Bögen und Ornamente sind klar strukturiert und fügen sich zu einer geometrischen Sinfonie schlichter Schönheit. Dazu passt das auf 1 300 Eichenbretter gemalte Deckengemälde, das im 13. Jahrhundert entstand und das unbeschädigt blieb, da man es 1943 vorsorglich ausgebaut hatte. Wer Hildesheim kennt, denkt auch in der Regel an den so genannten Tausendjährigen Rosenstock (rechts). Seit dem 13. Jahrhundert nachweisbar, grünt und blüht er im Kreuzgang an der Chorapsis des Doms St. Mariae.*

# Hildesheim

Ganz auferstanden aus seinen Ruinen ist Hildesheim zwar nicht mehr; das einst geschlossene mittelalterliche Stadtbild ging in einem verheerenden Brandbombensturm kurz vor Ende des Zweiten Weltkriegs unwiederbringlich verloren. Zwei der architektonischen Glanzstücke des 11. Jahrhunderts gereichen der kleinen niedersächsischen Großstadt inzwischen wieder zur Ehre: St. Michael und der Dom, beide rekonstruiert.

Die Michaeliskirche wurde zwischen 1010 bis 1022 im Auftrag des damaligen Bischofs von Hildesheim erbaut, des kunstsinnigen und selbst künstlerisch tätigen, aus vornehmer einheimischer Familie stammenden Bernward. Die doppelchörige, in ihrem Grundriss durch strenge Symmetrie gekennzeichnete Basilika gilt als einer der bedeutendsten romanischen Kirchenbauten und als Schlüsselwerk mittelalterlicher Architektur. Ohne baulichen Prunk und Zierrat beeindruckt sie durch ihre allein in der Zuordnung der Raumteile begründete Ästhetik. Den beiden Chören im Osten und Westen ist je ein weit über die Seitenschiffe hinaus vorspringendes Querhaus vorgeschaltet; an den Giebelseiten erheben sich beiderseits schlanke Rundtürme, die mit den gedrungenen Vierungstürmen kontrastieren.

Eine von Bernward in Auftrag gegebene Bronzesäule mit Szenen aus dem öffentlichen Leben Jesu bildete einst das bauliche und liturgische Zentrum von St. Michael, und über dem Altar ließ der Bischof eine ähnliche Lichterkrone aufhängen, wie er sie für den Hildesheimer Dom gestiftet hatte, der nach einem Brand anno 1046 neu errichtet wurde. Das prächtige Deckengemälde, das sich über das gesamte Mittelschiff der Michaeliskirche erstreckt und den Stammbaum Christi in Form der Wurzel Jesse darstellt, stammt jedoch nicht mehr aus der Amtschaft von Bernward; es wurde um 1230 angefertigt.

Die Christussäule aus St. Michael kann heute im Dom bewundert werden; thematisch ergänzt sie den rechten Flügel des dortigen bernwardinischen Doppelportals aus Bronze. Beide Türflügel sind übrigens je aus einem einzigen Stück gegossen und waren, wie die Inschrift auf der Mittelleiste verrät, ursprünglich „an der Schauseite des Engelstempels" aufgehängt.

# Hildesheim

Unfortunately, Hildesheim did not quite rise from its ashes – the formerly unified medieval townscape vanished in a devastating air raid shortly before the end of World War II. Yet, two architectural gems from the 11th century once more have become a credit to the small city in Lower Saxony: St. Michael's and the cathedral. Both buildings were reconstructed.

The Michaeliskirche church was built between 1010 and 1022 under the auspices of the then ruling bishop of Hildesheim, the art-loving and artistically inclined Bernward of local descent. The double-ended basilica, whose floor plan is characterized by strict symmetry, is one of the most important Romanesque church buildings and a key to medieval architecture. No architectural frills and ornaments detract from an effect that rests solely on an aesthetics based on the assignment of space. The twin chancels in the east and west are preceded by transepts projecting far beyond the side aisles, the fronts feature slender circular towers that contrast with thickly set crossing towers.

The structural and liturgical center of St. Michael's was once formed by a bronze column with scenes from Christ's public life commissioned by Bernward. Bernward also had the altar illuminated with a crown of lights similar to the one he had donated to the cathedral, which was being rebuilt after a devastating fire in 1046. The splendid ceiling fresco extending across the entire nave of St. Michael's and depicting the lineage of Christ in the shape of the Tree of Jesse was not completed until 1230, after Bernward's rule.

Today, the column of Christ from St. Michael's may be admired in the cathedral; thematically, it is related to the right panel of St. Michael's Bernwardian bronze twin portals. Both panels of the portal are cast from a single piece of bronze and were originally mounted on the "state side of the temple of the angels" as indicated in an inscription in the center molding.

*Seen from the south side, St. Michael's at Hildesheim (left) with its almost mathematical architecture that set the standards for the Romanesque style appears in all its splendor. The church, built after 1010 under the art-loving bishop Bernward and reconstructed after World War II, presents itself as a unified architectural feat, inside and outside (overleaf). Pillars, columns, arches and ornaments are clearly structured, blending into a harmonic work of unpretentious beauty. The ceiling fresco, painted onto 1,300 oak panels, dates back to the 13th century and survived the war undamaged; it had been taken down as a precautionary measure in 1943.*
*Hildesheim connoisseurs usually also point out the Thousand-Year-Old Rose Tree (above): It apparently has been flourishing and blooming in the cloister of the chancel apse of the St. Mariae cathedral since the 13th century.*

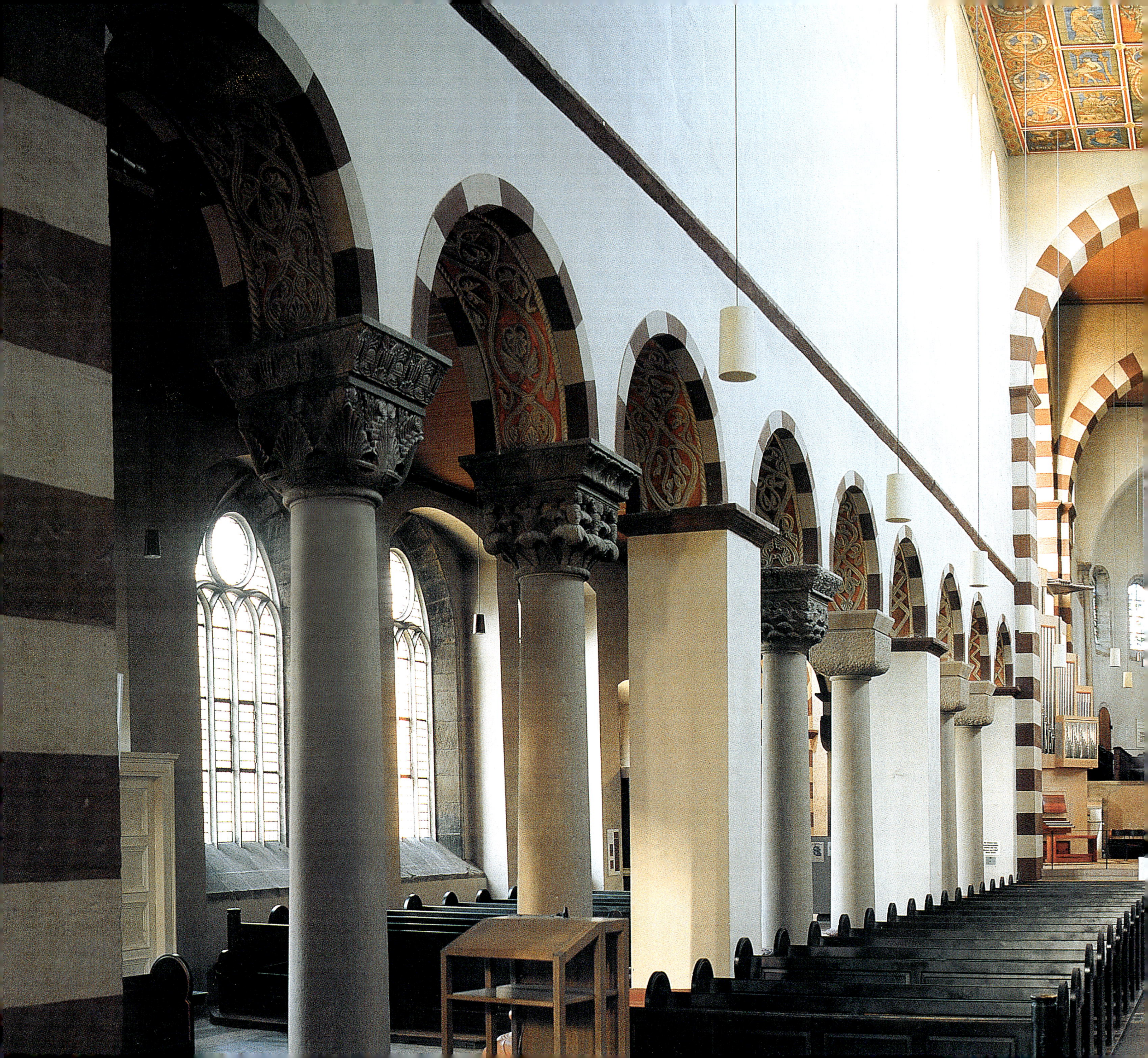

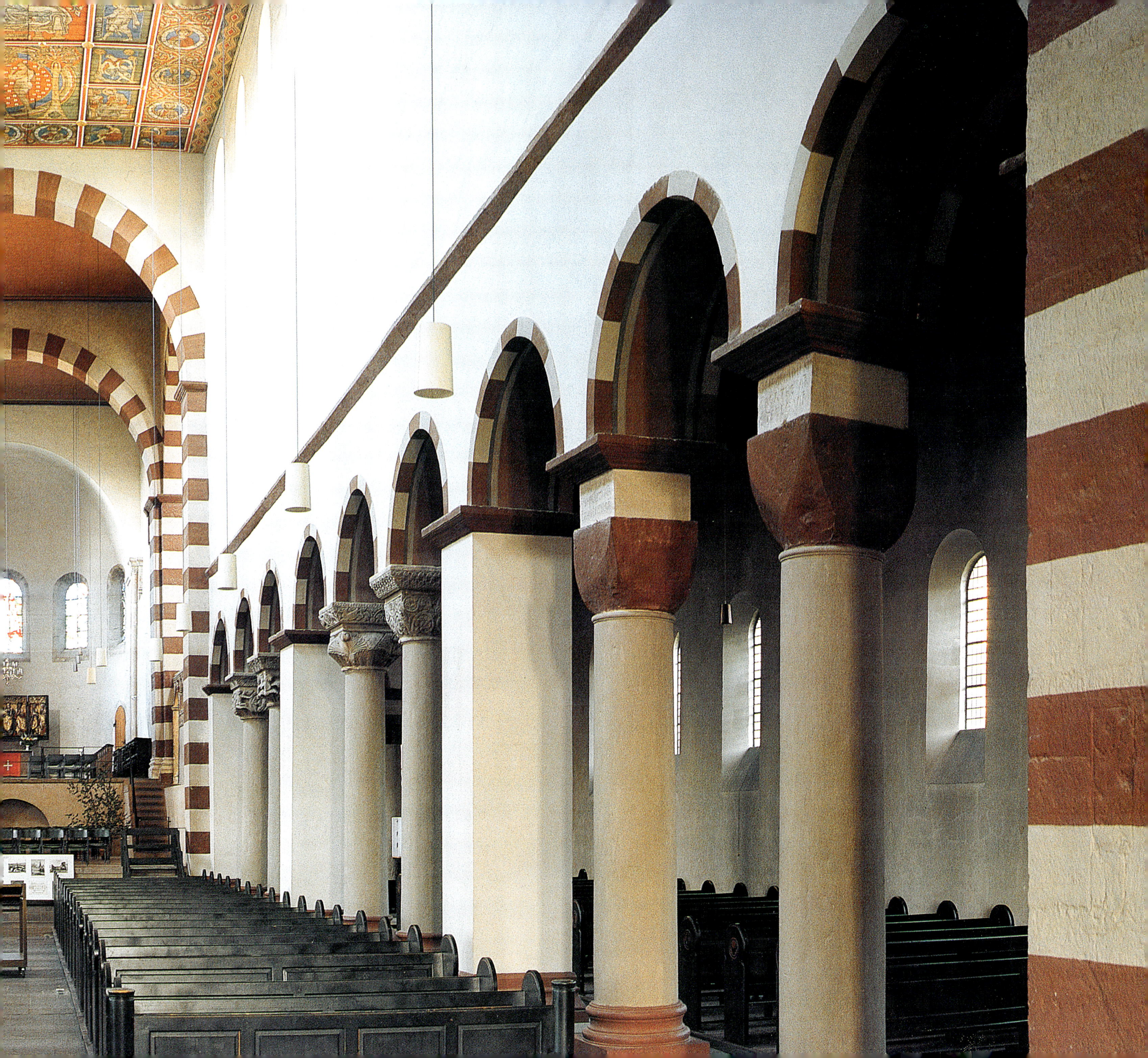

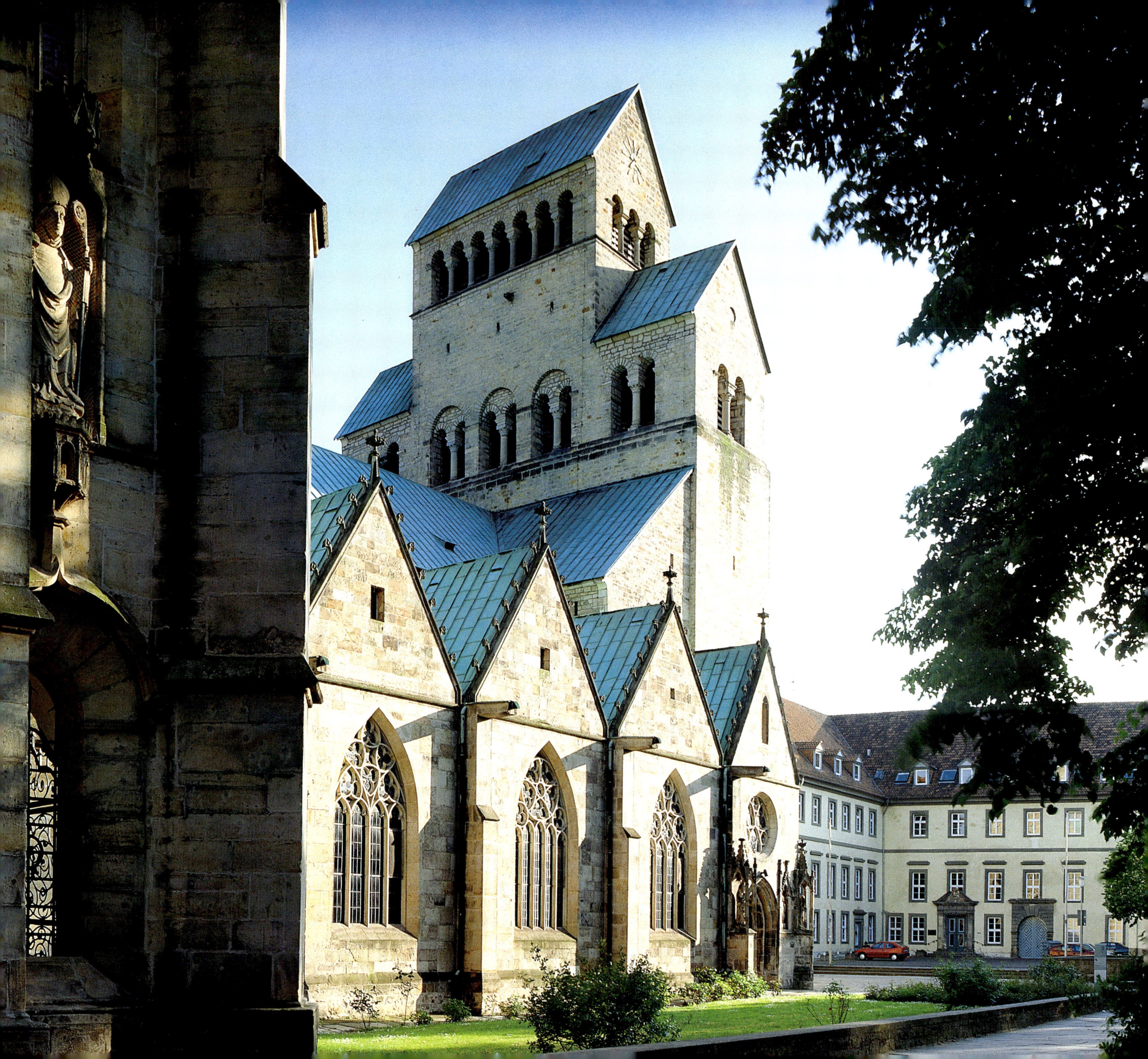

Bernwards künstlerischer Einfluss spiegelt auch der Hildesheimer Dom wider. Vor allem zwei mächtige Bronze-Werke zeugen in ihm von den einzigartigen Leistungen des engagierten Kirchenmannes: die Christussäule und das doppelflügelige Portal. Der kostbare Radleuchter von etwa 1060, der die Stadtbefestigung von Jerusalem symbolisiert, ist als Nachfolgewerk der großen Lichterkrone zu sehen, die Bernward einst gestiftet hatte.

Bernward's artistic influence also characterizes the Hildesheim cathedral. Two impressive bronze pieces testify to the rarified taste of this clergyman: the column of Christ and the twin portals. The precious circular chandelier dating to about 1060 and symbolizing the fortifications of Jerusalem, is the successor to the immense crown of lights once donated by Bernward.

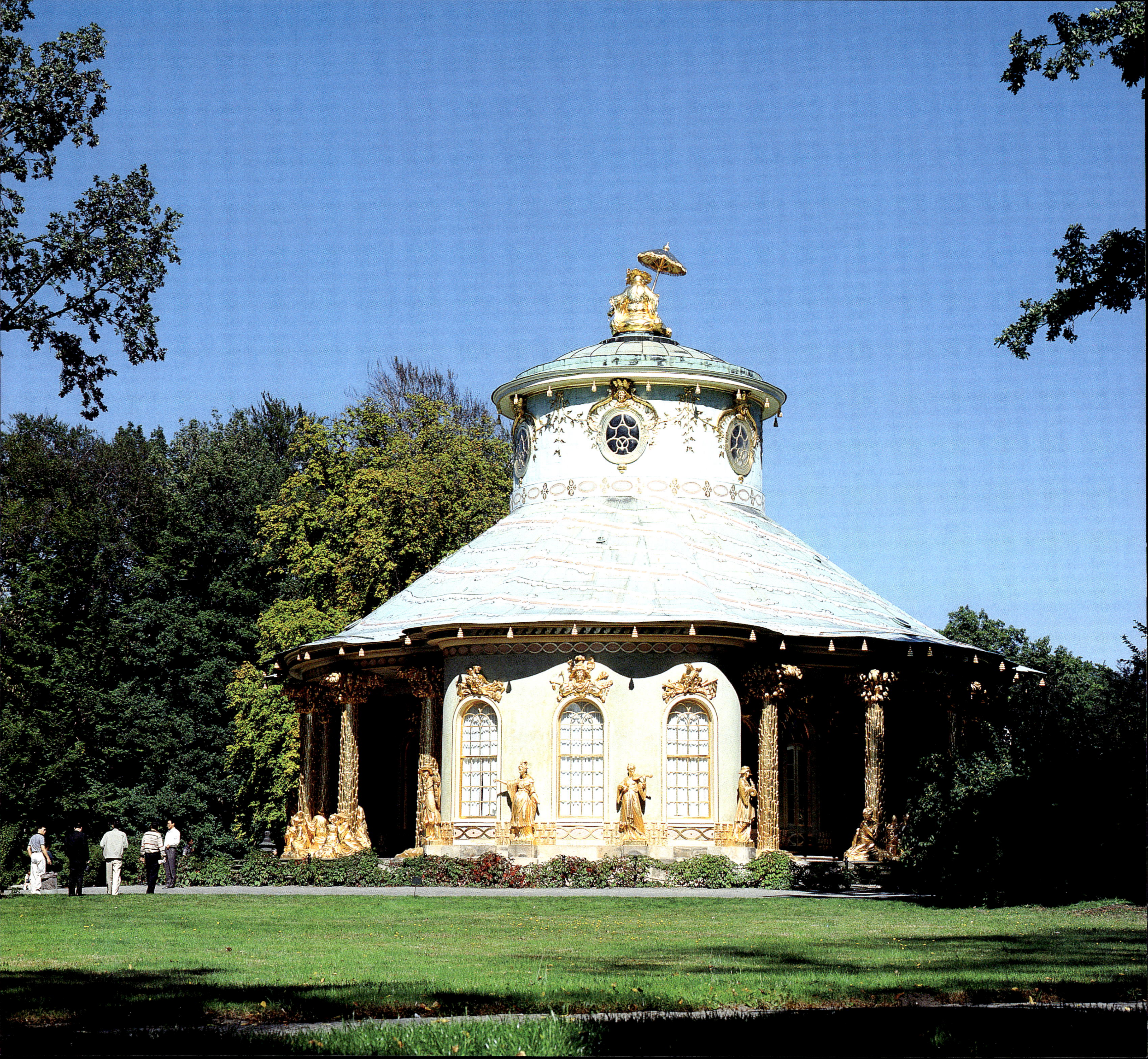

*Schloss Sanssouci (nächste Doppelseite) mit seiner sechsstufigen Wein- und Feigenterrasse, die als Nutzgarten diente, und der umgebende Park mit all den anderen Bauwerken werden gerne als „preußisches oder märkisches Versailles" bezeichnet. Das weitläufige Areal im Westen Potsdams birgt eine Vielzahl von Architektur- und Landschaftsschöpfungen aus dem 18. bis ins frühe 20. Jahrhundert. Sie bilden eine einzigartige Synthese der damaligen europäischen Kunstrichtungen. Das nach Entwürfen von Johann Gottfried Büring erbaute Chinesische Teehaus (links und rechts) zählt zu den intimsten Gebäuden des Ensembles.*

## Schlösser und Parks von Potsdam

Friedrich II., landläufig der Große genannt, begann in der sandig-sumpfigen Mark Brandenburg ein „preußisches Paradies" zu schaffen. Er ließ seine heiter-klare Sommerresidenz Schloss Sanssouci zwischen 1745 und 1747 nach den Plänen von Georg Wenzeslaus von Knobelsdorff über einem terrassierten Nutzgarten errichten. Fast 40 Sommer verbrachte er danach in seinem „Maison de Plaisance" vor den Toren Potsdams und beschloss auch dort im Schlaf- und Arbeitszimmer im August 1786 sein Leben. Um das anmutige Sanssouci wuchs über viele Jahre ein einzigartiges Ensemble: auf etwa 500 Hektar sechs miteinander verwobene Gartenanlagen und 150 Gebäude, darunter zahlreiche Schlösser und Schlösschen. So ließ Friedrich II. um seine Sommerresidenz nicht nur einen riesigen Park mit Bildergalerie, Grotte und Chinesischem Teehaus anlegen. Nach dem Siebenjährigen Krieg befahl er am äußersten Westende des Areals zudem den Bau des Neuen Palais.

Nach dem Tod Friedrichs des Großen wurde auf Geheiß von Friedrich Wilhelm IV. im frühen 19. Jahrhundert der Park im Süden von Sanssouci erweitert. Karl Friedrich Schinkel errichtete dort das klassizistisch-elegante Schloss Charlottenhof; der königliche Gartendirektor Peter Joseph Lenné legte einen romantischen Landschaftsgarten nach englischem Vorbild an. Schinkel und Persius bauten bis 1860 zudem die Römischen Bäder sowie die ebenfalls mediterran inspirierte Orangerie und die Friedenskirche.

Friedrich Wilhelm II., Friedrichs II. Neffe und Nachfolger auf dem Thron, zeigte an Sanssouci hingegen wenig Interesse. Er ließ sich im Osten des Areals, am Heiligen See und am Jungfernsee, einen eigenen Park anlegen, den Neuen Garten. Gontard entwarf für ihn darin das Marmorpalais. Später wurde als Residenz des preußischen Kronprinzen im Neuen Garten Schloss Cecilienhof errichtet, wo im August 1945 das Potsdamer Abkommen unterzeichnet wurde.

1990 erklärte die UNESCO das oft als „preußisches Versailles" gerühmte Potsdamer Ensemble zum Weltkulturerbe: Sanssouci, den Neuen Garten, Schloss und Park von Babelsberg, Schloss Glienicke und die Pfaueninsel mit dem Kavaliershaus und dem Palmenhaus.

## The Palaces and Parks of Potsdam

Frederick II, commonly called the Great, set out to create a "Prussian Paradise" in the wet sands of the Mark Brandenburg as he had his bright, clear summer residence Sanssouci and its terraced garden plot built between 1745 and 1747 according to plans by Georg Wenzeslaus von Knobelsdorff. He spent almost 40 summers in his "Maison de Plaisance" outside the Potsdam town limits and finally passed away there in his bedroom and office in August 1786. It took many years to transform the surroundings of the charming Sanssouci palace into the unique ensemble it is today: Six interconnected gardens and 150 buildings, among them numerous small and big palaces, are spread over an area of about 500 hectares. Frederick II first had an immense park with a picture gallery, grotto and Chinese teahouse laid out, and, after the Seven-Years-War, he ordered the building of the "Neues Palais" on the very western edge of the area.

After the death of Frederick the Great, it was Friedrich Wilhelm IV who at the beginning of the 19th century had the park extended towards the south of Sanssouci. Karl-Friedrich Schinkel conceived the elegant Classicist Charlottenhof Palace and the royal garden designer Peter Joseph Lenné drew the plans for a romantic landscape garden according to English models. By 1860, Schinkel and Persius had also built the Roman baths, the orangery, which was inspired by Mediterranean styles, and the Friedenskirche church.

In contrast, Frederick's nephew and immediate successor to the throne showed little interest in Sanssouci. He had his own park, the Neuer Garten, laid out in the eastern parts of the complex at the Heiliger See and Jungfernsee lakes, and the Marmorpalais Palace in it was conceived by Gontard. Cecilienhof Palace in the Neuer Garten was built later as the residence of the Prussian crown prince, and in 1945, the Potsdam Agreement was signed there. The Potsdam Ensemble – often called "Versailles of Prussia" – consisting of Sanssouci, the Neuer Garten, Babelsberg Palace and Park, Glienicke Palace and the Pfaueninsel island with its Kavaliershaus and Palmenhaus buildings was accepted into the UNESCO World Heritage Program in 1990.

*Sanssouci Palace (overleaf) with its sequence of six terraces where grapes and figs were cultivated for actual use, and its surrounding park with numerous other buildings, is often called the "Versailles of Prussia (or the Mark)". The extensive area to the west of Potsdam includes a wealth of architectural and landscape creations from the 18th to the early 20th century, a unique synthesis of European styles in vogue at the time. The Chinese teahouse (left and above), built according to plans by Johann Gottfried Büring, is one of the coziest buildings in the ensemble.*

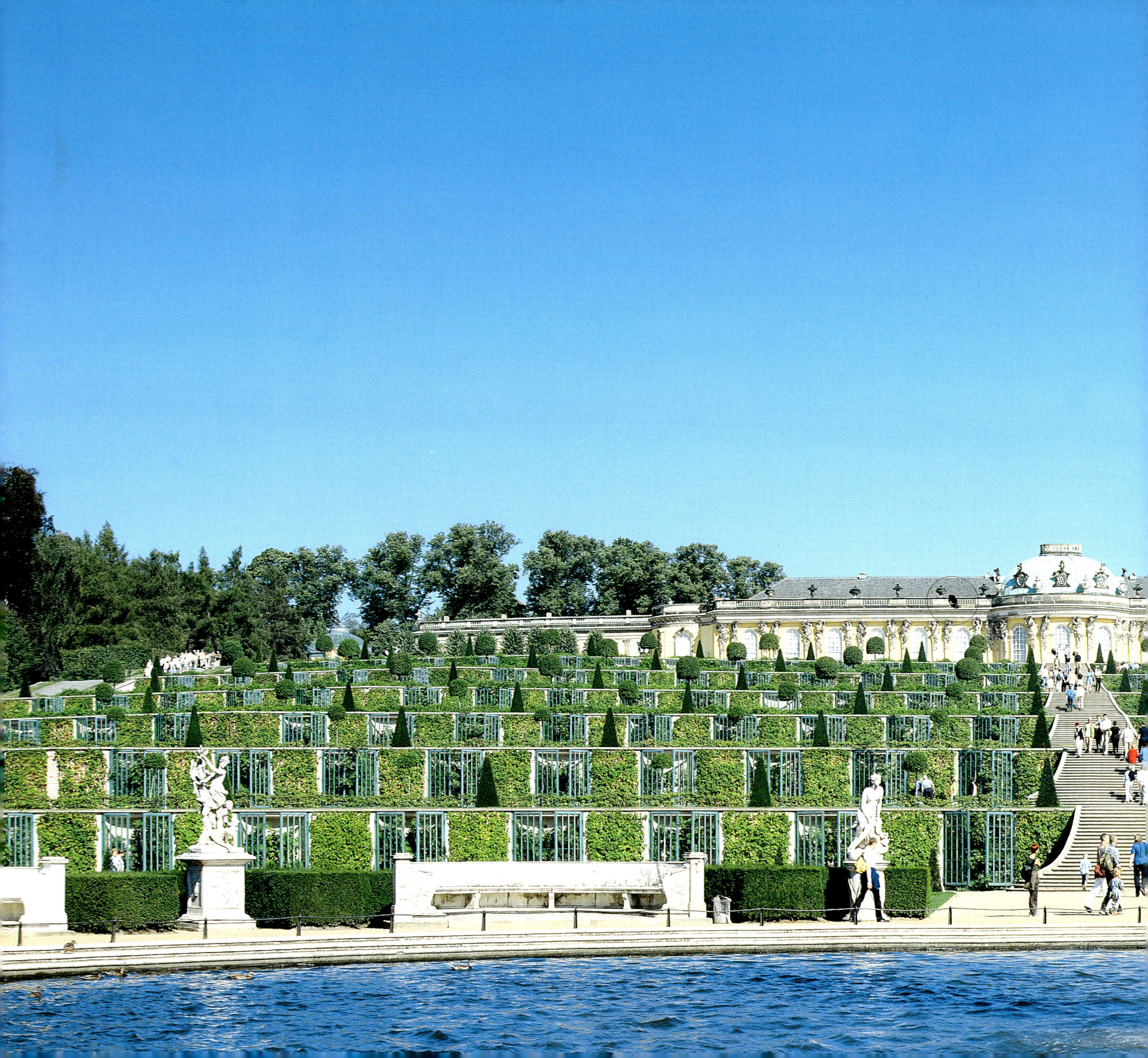

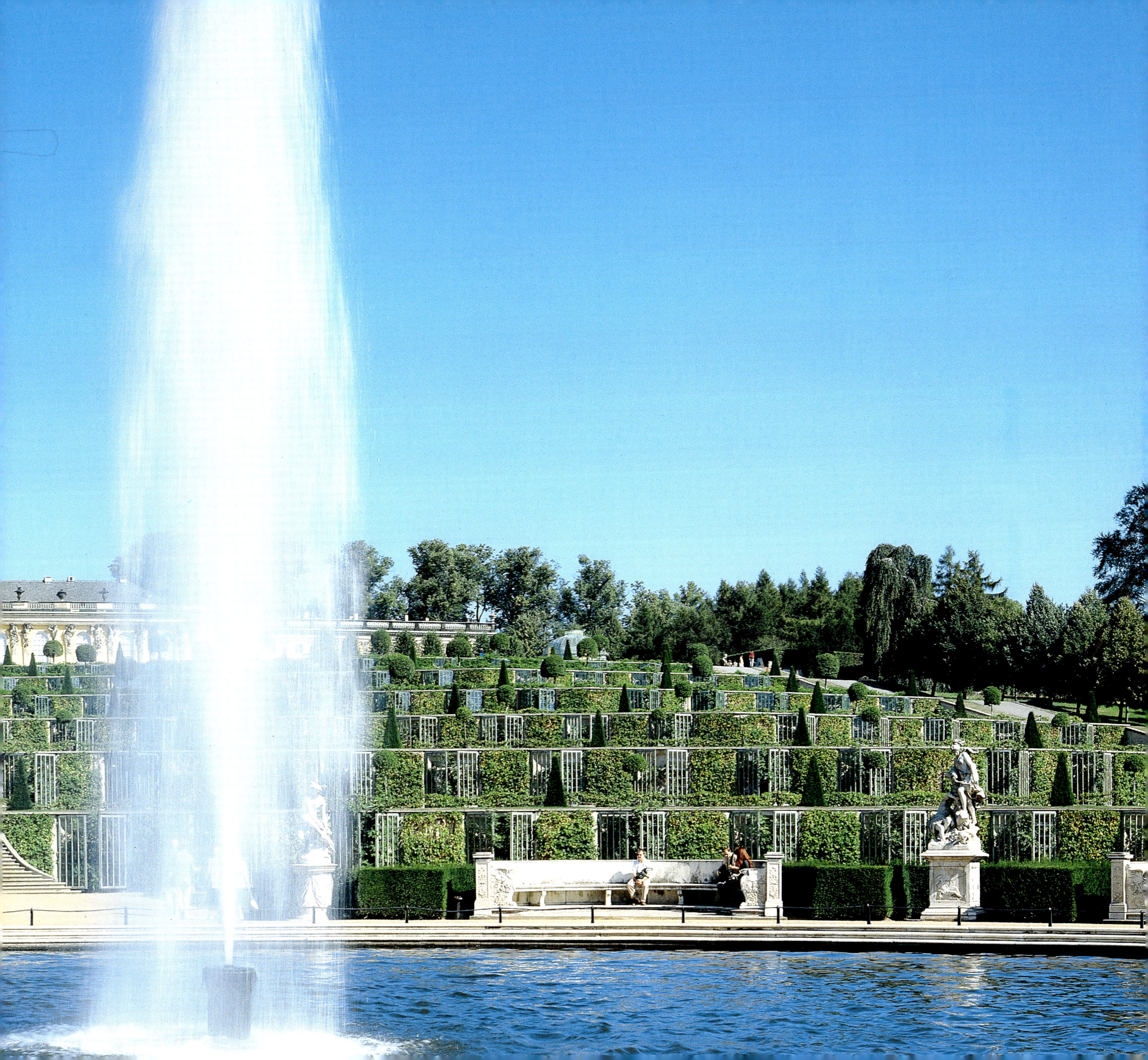

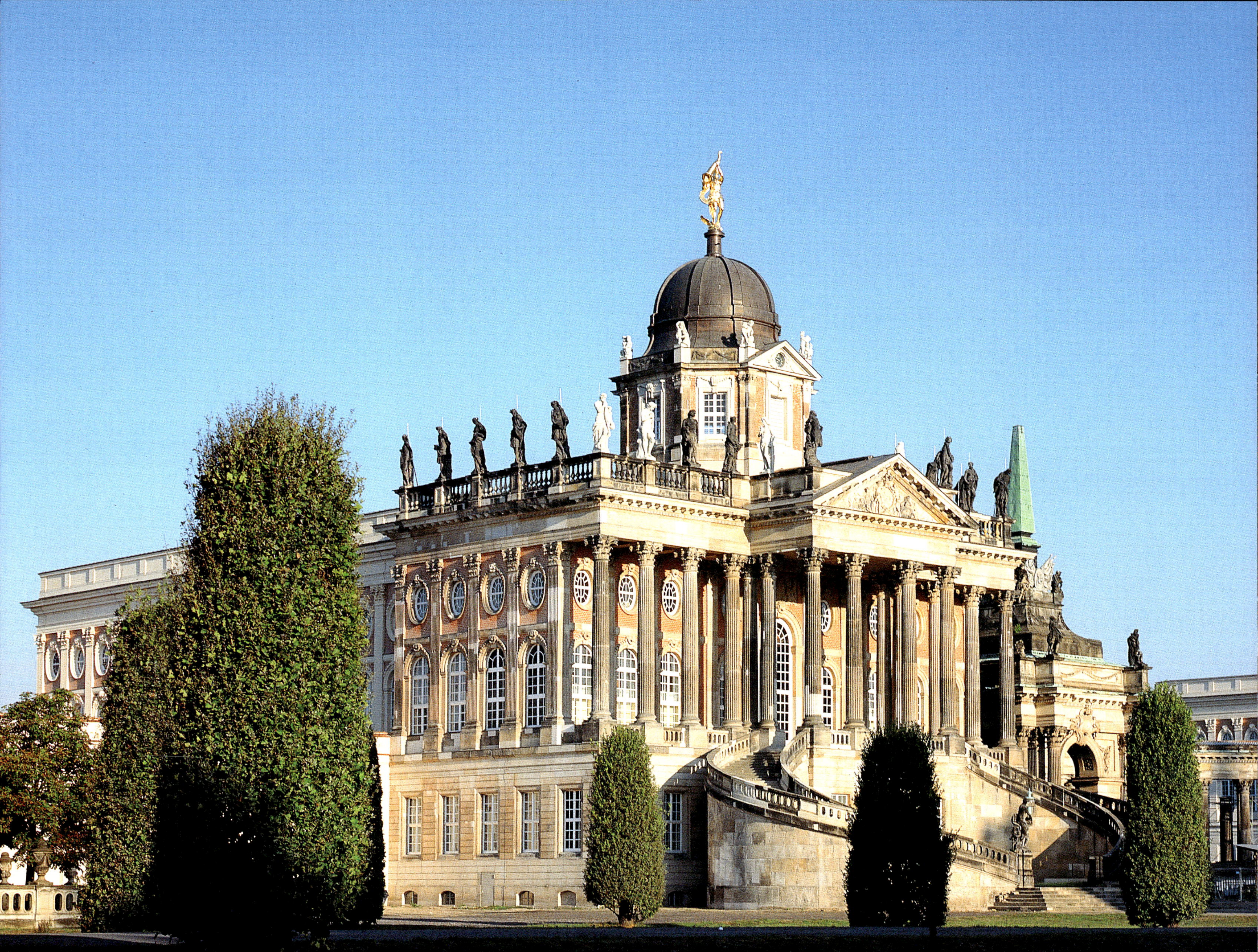

*Zu Sanssouci gruppieren sich in den Parks und an ihren Rändern die Communs (links), das ist gleichsam die „Verkleidung" der Wirtschaftsgebäude des Neuen Palais (nächste Doppelseite). Der ausladende Rokokobau sollte Besuchern des „Alten Fritz" standesgemäße Unterkunft bieten. Hinzu kommen die Friedenskirche (rechts), die Orangerie (unten links) und eine Figur aus den Römischen Bädern, die von einem Bodenmosaik nach pompejanischem Vorbild geschmückt werden.*

*The commons, i.e. the "masked" service buildings (far left) of the Neues Palais (overleaf) are hidden around Sanssouci in the parks and on their outskirts. The Neues Palais is an imposing rococo structure which was to house visitors to the "Old Fritz" in grand style. Above, the Friedenskirche church, the orangery (bottom left) and a sculpture from the Roman baths, which feature floor mosaics fashioned after Pompeian models.*

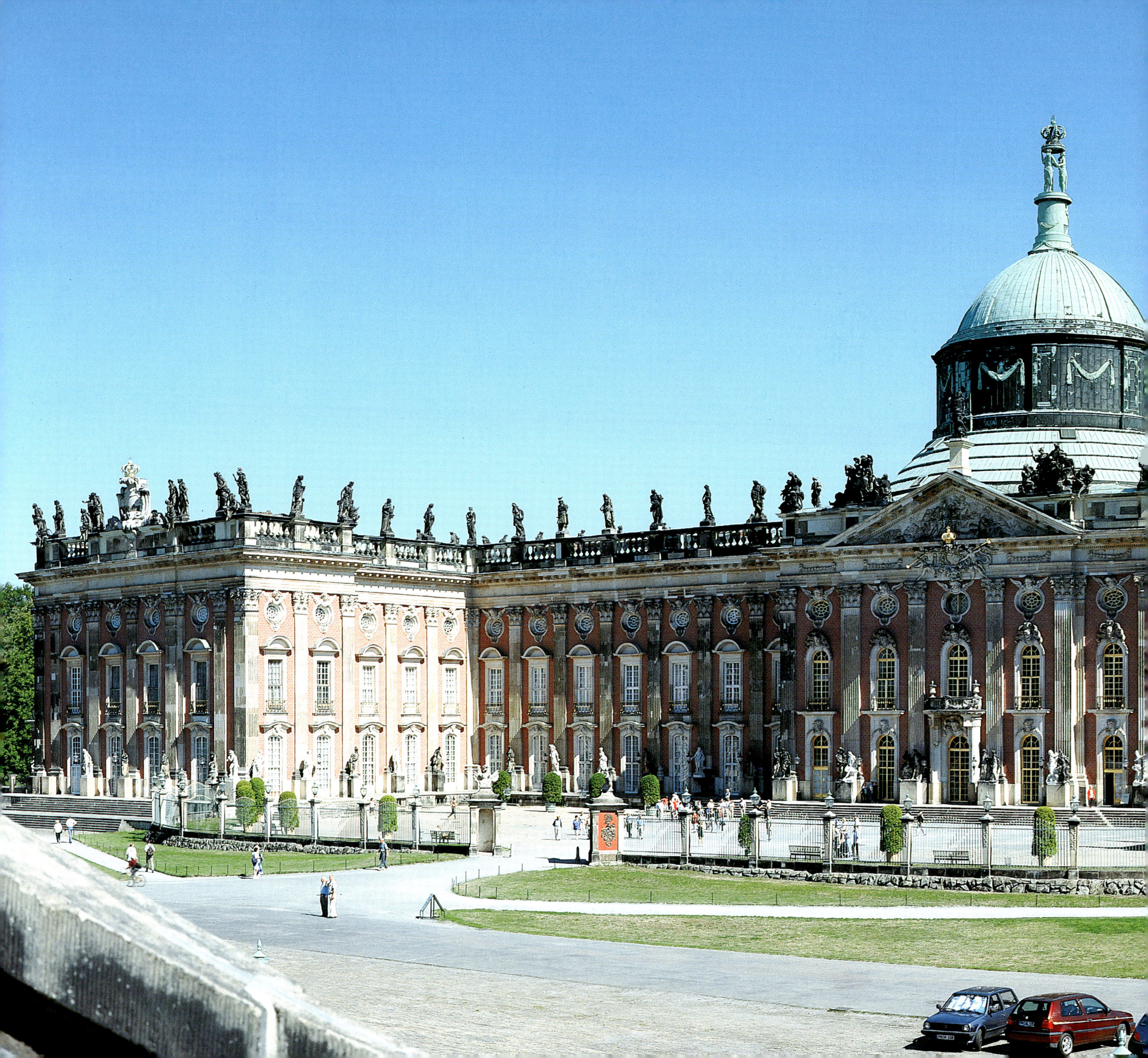

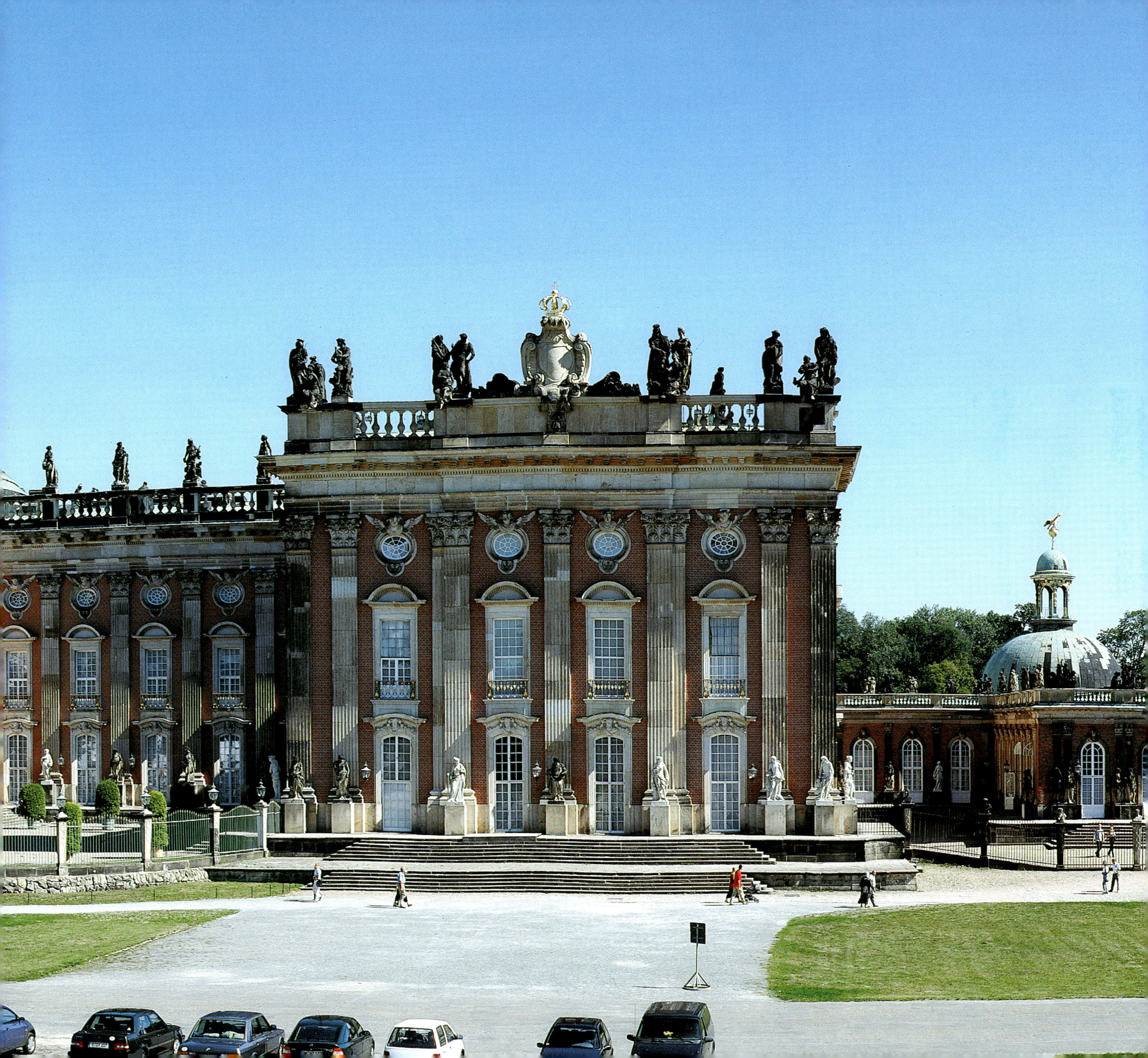

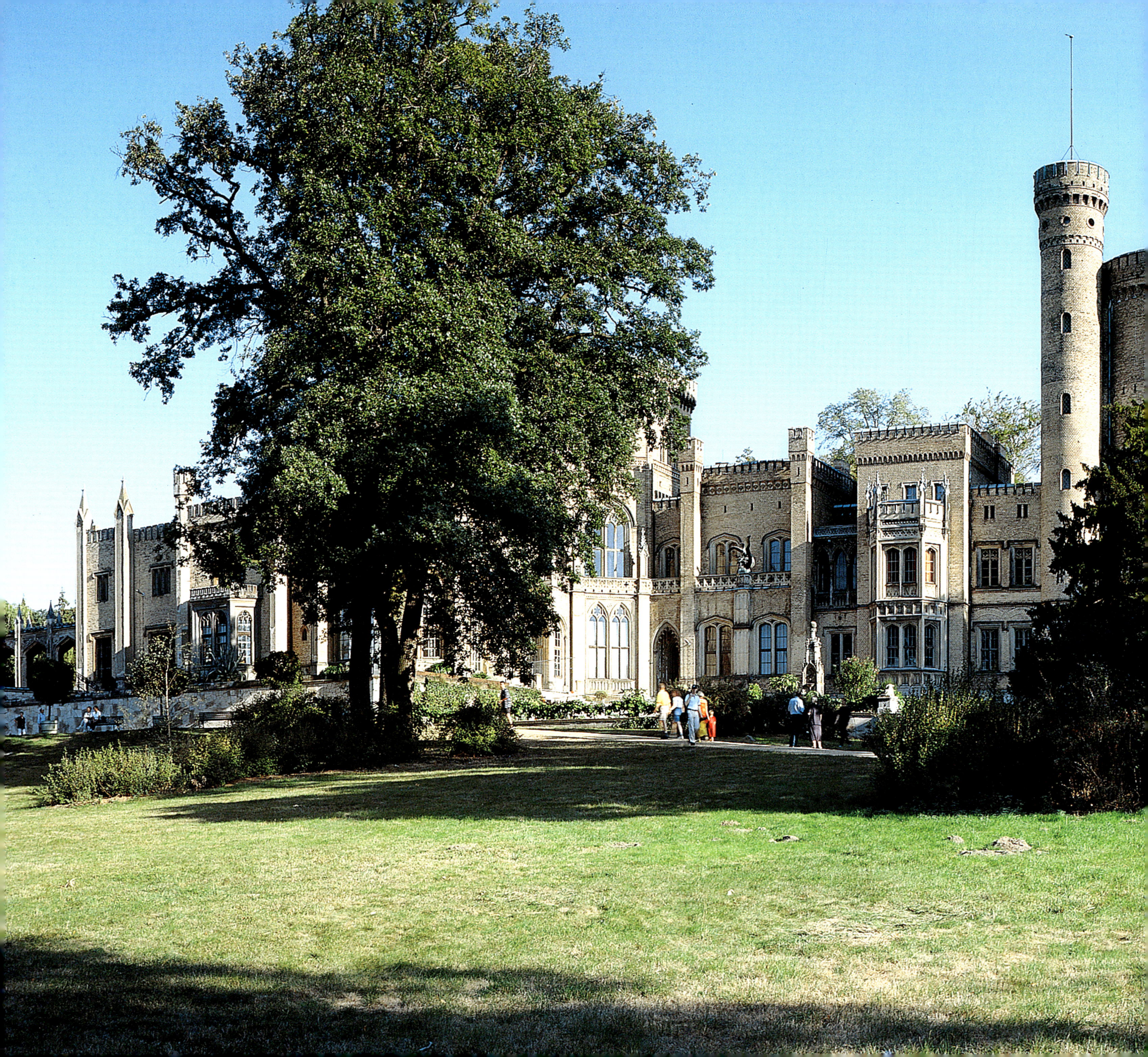

Friedrich Wilhelm II., der Neffe Friedrichs des Großen und sein Nachfolger, bescherte Potsdam nach Sanssouci den Neuen Garten. Karl von Gontard errichtete darin das Marmorpalais (oben) als Sommersitz. Peter Joseph Lenné schuf dann nach 1816 auf dem Gelände neue, große Landschaftsräume, von denen der Blick bis nach Glienicke, Sacrow und zur Pfaueninsel mit dem Schlösschen, einer „gebauten Ruine" (unten rechts) reicht.
Babelsberg ist die dritte große Parkanlage Potsdams. Die ersten Entwürfe für Schloss Babelsberg (linke Seite) stammen von Karl Friedrich Schinkel, der bis 1835 entstandene romantisch-neugotische Landsitz englischer Prägung wurde in den Jahrzehnten danach durch weitere Bauten und Kunstwerke von anderen Künstlern verändert und ergänzt.
Das letzte Schloss der Hohenzollern in Potsdam überhaupt ist Cecilienhof (unten links), 1913 bis 1917 wiederum im Neuen Garten im Stil eines englischen Landsitzes gebaut.

Friedrich Wilhelm II, nephew and successor of Frederick the Great, gave Potsdam and Sanssouci the Neuer Garten park area and its Marmorpalais (above), built by Karl von Gontard as a summer residence. After 1816, Peter Joseph Lenné generously landscaped the entire area, with views as far as Glienicke, Sacrow and the Pfaueninsel island with its small palace that was built as a ruin (below right)
After Sanssouci and the Neuer Garten, Babelsberg is the third large park at Potsdam. The first drafts to Babelsberg palace (left) were drawn by Karl Friedrich Schinkel. The Romantic-Neogothic manor in the English style was completed in 1835, but additional structural parts and works of art by different artists were added in the decades to follow. The last Hohenzollern place to be erected at Potsdam was Cecilienhof Palace (below left), which was built from 1913 to 1917, again in the Neuer Garten park area and in the style of an English manor.

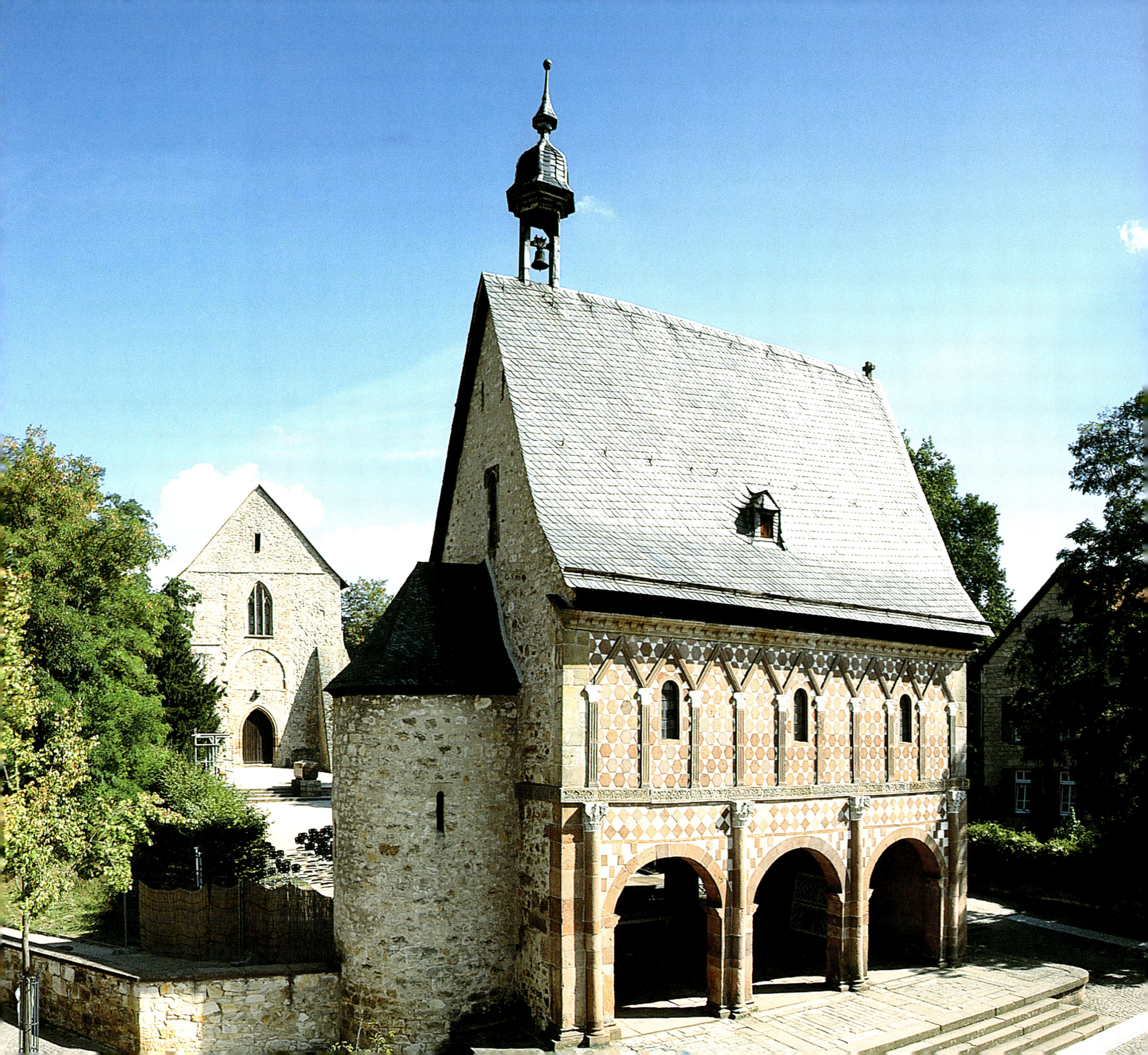

*In dem Städtchen Lorsch zwischen Mannheim und Darmstadt erinnert die berühmte Torhalle (links und rechts) an die vergangene Größe einer einst mächtigen Klosteranlage (nächste Doppelseite). Das Gebäude ist eines der bedeutendsten Baudenkmäler aus der Zeit der Karolinger, der Vorromanik. Es konnte über die vielen Jahrhunderte sein ursprüngliches Aussehen bewahren. Wie ein kostbarer Schrein mutet es an mit seiner mosaikartigen Fassade, die an maurisch-arabische und byzantinische Ornamentik erinnert.*

## Kloster Lorsch

Ein halbes Jahrtausend eines der wichtigsten religiösen, kulturellen und machtpolitischen Zentren des Abendlandes – diese Vergangenheit sieht man dem südhessischen Städtchen Lorsch heute kaum mehr an. 16 Benediktinermönche gründeten anno 764 auf Geheiß von Chrodegang, Erzbischof von Metz und Kanzler des Fränkischen Reiches, zwischen den feuchten Niederungen alter Rheinarme ein Kloster. Karl der Große erhob die imposante Anlage schon 6 Jahre später in den Rang einer Reichsabtei. Davon stehen heute nur noch die Vorkirche und die prächtige Königshalle. Die Vorkirche ergänzte einst die Dimension der 774 geweihten Klosterkirche zusammen mit der Grabkapelle auf eine Länge von 100 Metern. Sie war neben St. Denis in Paris die zweite große Kirche jener Zeit. Manchmal an die 100 Mönche verrichteten in ihr die Gebete. Und bis ins 11. Jahrhundert diente sie als Grablege der ostfränkischen Karolinger. Inzwischen beherbergt sie Grabsteine und einen Sarkophag, unter dessen Steinplatte angeblich die Gebeine von Ludwig (II.) dem Deutschen ruhen.

Die karolingische Torhalle überstand alle Zeiten unbeschadet. Sie ist in Deutschland das älteste vollständig erhaltene Bauwerk aus nachrömischer Zeit und wurde zum Inbegriff der Architektur jener Epoche hierzulande. Das zweigeschossige Gebäude mit zwei Treppentürmen stand ursprünglich frei hinter dem Tor auf dem Vorplatz vor dem Atrium der Klosterkirche. Das Untergeschoss ist mit kräftigen, antikisierenden Pfeilern römischer Provenienz geöffnet, über denen die zart gliedrigen, dicht gestellten Pilaster mit Spitzgiebeln im Obergeschoss wie ein zierliches, der braunroten Fassadenwand vorgeblendetes Gitter wirken. Im Obergeschoss liegt ein Saal, der möglicherweise schon in den Anfängen des Klosters als Kapelle diente.

Bereits während ihrer ersten Jahre in Lorsch erhielten die Benediktiner eine Fülle von Schenkungen. Fast 4000 Gütergaben verzeichnet ihr Urkundenbuch, der Codex Laureshamensis. Ein anderes berühmtes Schriftstück aus den mehr als 300, inzwischen weltweit verstreuten, Manuskripten der Klosterbrüder ist das von 810 datierte Lorscher Evangeliar. Es ist heute im Besitz des Vatikans.

## Lorsch Monastery

For half a millennium it was one of the most important religious, cultural and political centers of the western world – a history that is hard to be believed when looking at Lorsch, a small town in Southern Hesse, today. In 764, sixteen monks of the Benedictine order did the bidding of Chrodegang, archbishop of Metz and chancellor of the Frankish Empire, when they founded a monastery in the wetlands of the Rhine's old side arms. Only six years later, the imposing complex was raised to the ranks of an imperial abbey by Charlemagne. Today, the only fragments left are the antechurch and the splendid king's hall. With the antechurch and the grave chapel, the length of the monastery church, consecrated in 774, came up to 100 meters; it was the second largest church of its time after St. Denis in Paris. At times, up to 100 monks prayed there, and it remained the burial-place for East Frankish Carolingian royalty well up into the 11th century. Today, it houses gravestones and a sarcophagus under whose stone plate the bones of Ludwig (II) the German are presumed to rest.

The Carolingian gate hall withstood the changes of time unharmed. It is the oldest fully preserved structure from the post-Roman period in Germany and has become the epitome of the architecture of its time. The two-story building with two stair towers originally stood unencumbered behind the gate in the forecourt of the monastery church's atrium. The lower story is opened up with powerful, classically inspired pillars of Roman provenance, and on the upper floor, the rapid succession of graceful pilasters with pointed gables appears like a delicate screen covering the red-and-brown façade. The upper story encloses a hall which may have served as a chapel at the monastery's beginnings.

In the first years, the Benedictine monks received quite a number of endowments: The register, the codex Laureshamensis, names almost 4,000 gifts of goods. The famous Lorsch evangeliar dated to 810, now owned by the Vatican, is just one of the monks' altogether more than 300 manuscripts, which today are scattered all around the world.

*In the small town of Lorsch between Mannheim and Darmstadt, the famous gate hall (left and above) testifies to the bygone splendor of a once powerful monastery complex (overleaf). The building is one of the most important works of architecture from the pre-Romanesque Carolingian period and has outlasted many centuries in its original form. With its mosaic-like façade reminiscent of Moorish-Arabic and Byzantine ornamentation, it looks like a precious shrine.*

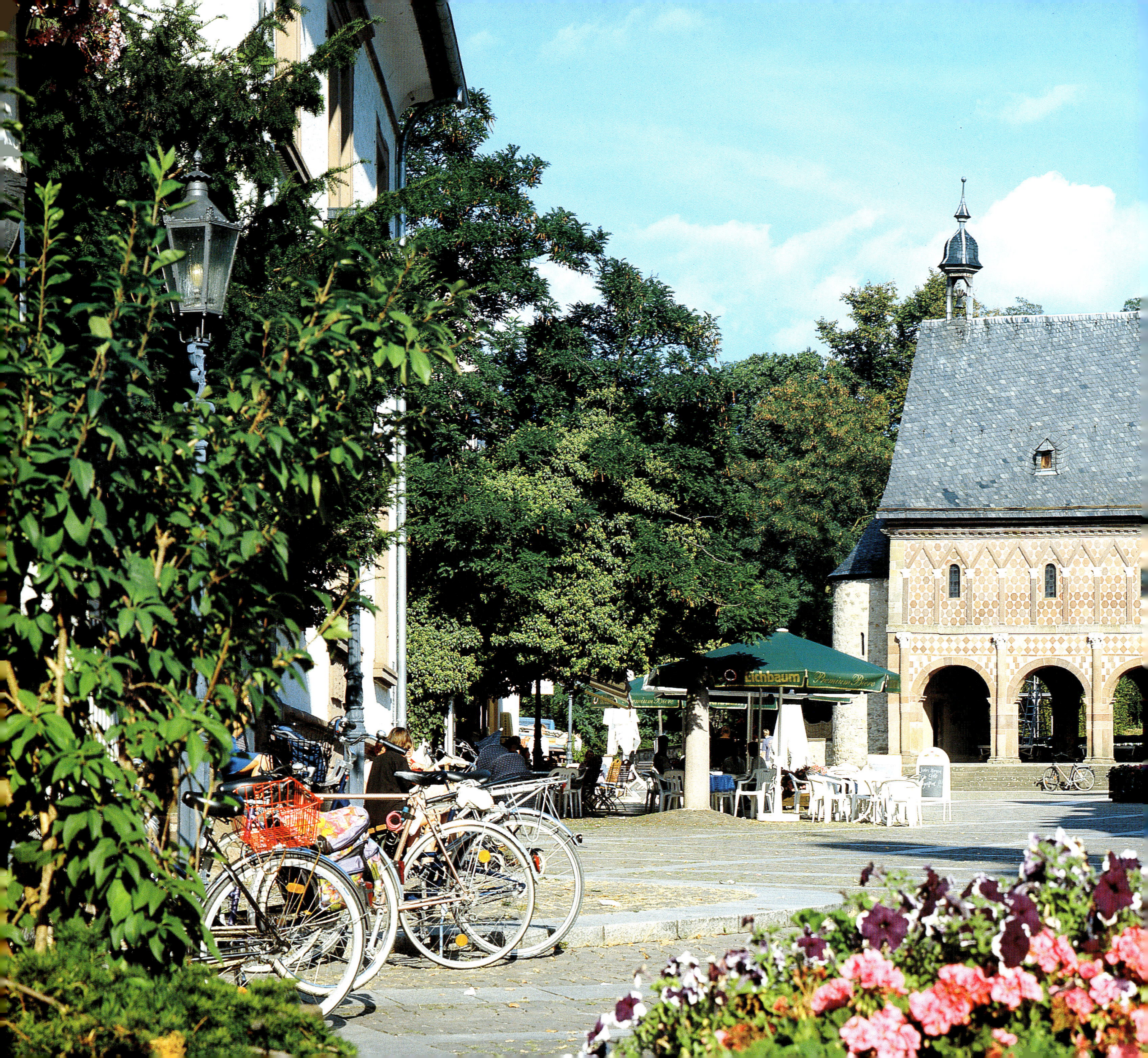
Eichbaum
Premium Biere

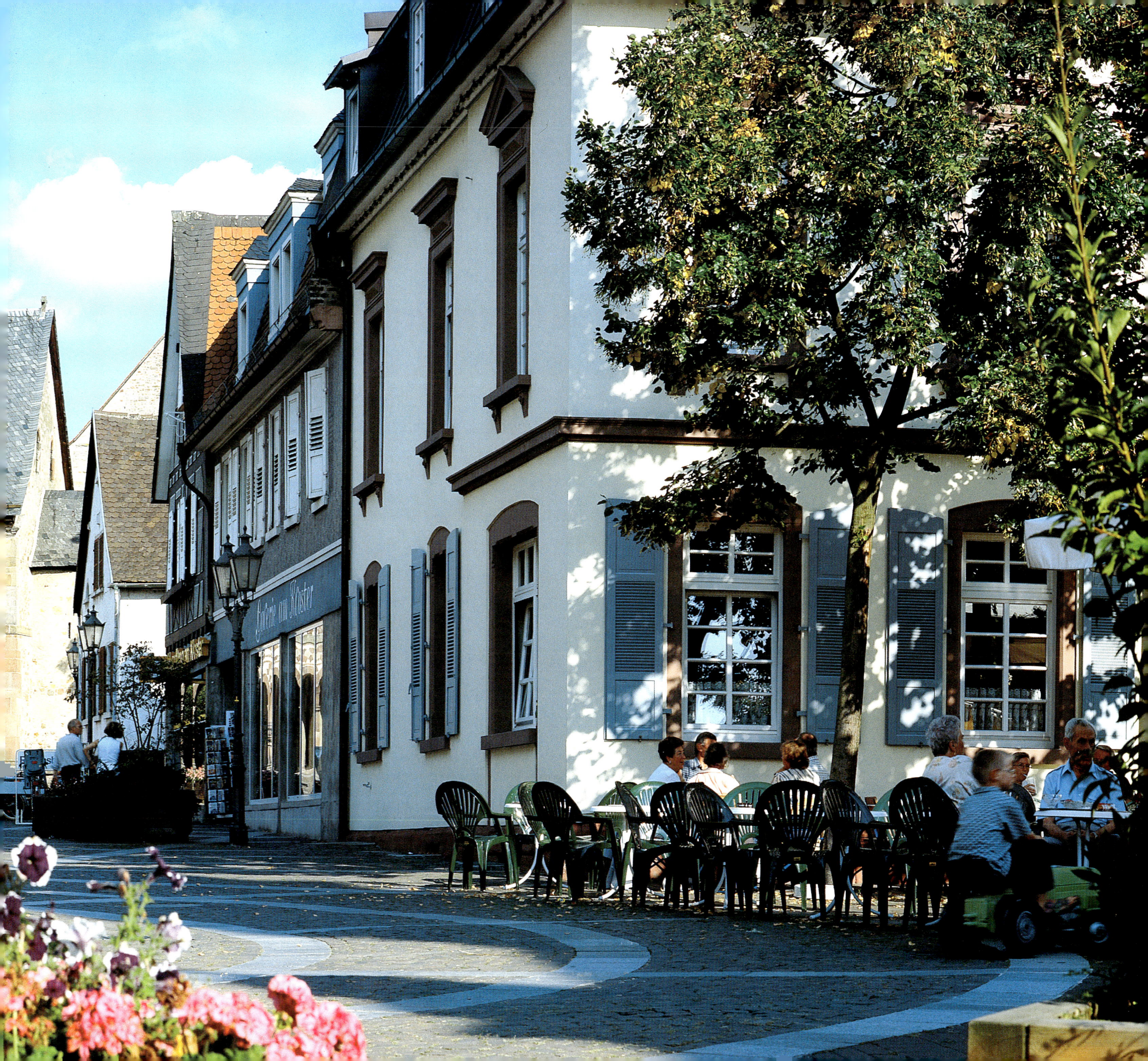
Galerie am Kloster

Karolingische und gotische Fresken (rechte Seite und links oben) zieren die Wände im Obergeschoss der Torhalle – auch Lorscher Königshalle genannt.
Im Inneren der einstigen Vorkirche erinnern verschiedene Werke der Steinmetze an die Lorscher Glanzzeit: wie das Säulenkapitell (links unten), das Mauerdetail (rechts oben) und der Sarkophag von angeblich Ludwig (II.) dem Deutschen (rechts unten).

Carolingian and Gothic frescoes (right and above left) embellish the walls of the upper story of the gate hall, also known as the Lorsch king's hall.
In the former antechurch, numerous works by various stone masons remind of Lorsch's past glory, among them the column capital (bottom left), the wall detail (top right) and the presumed sarcophagus of Ludwig (II) the German (bottom right).

*Erhabene Höhe, strukturiert durch schlanke Säulenbündel und elegante Kreuzrippengewölbe – im „Dom des Lichts" ist genügend Raum für tiefe Empfindungen, für Ehrfurcht und Glauben.*

*Lofty heights, structured by slender groups of columns and elegant rib vaults – in the "Cathedral of Light" there is enough room for deep emotions, awe and piety.*

Die Kölner Dombauer, so heißt es, haben die Kathedrale als Bautyp vollendet. Zugute kam ihnen dabei, dass 1814 in Darmstadt durch puren Zufall Teile des Originalrisses der Westfassade entdeckt wurden und zwei Jahre später in Paris die Reste der mittelalterlichen Pläne. Nach 282 Jahren Unterbrechung – 1560 bis 1842 – entstanden einige Bauabschnitte im neogotischen Stil. Wegen des Umfangs und der Qualität der Arbeiten wurde der Kölner Dom von der UNESCO als Meisterwerk der Gotik 1996 in die Liste des Welterbes aufgenommen.

The builders of the Cologne cathedral, it is said, brought the cathedral as an architectural type to perfection. They benefitted from the fact that in 1814 parts of the original drafts of the western façade were discovered at Darmstadt by a mere accident, and, two years later, the remainders of the medieval plans in Paris. After an interruption of 282 years – 1560 to 1842 – some parts were then built in the neo-Gothic style. Due to the quality and extent of the work, the Cologne Cathedral was accepted into the UNESCO World Heritage Program in 1996 as a masterpiece of Gothic architecture.

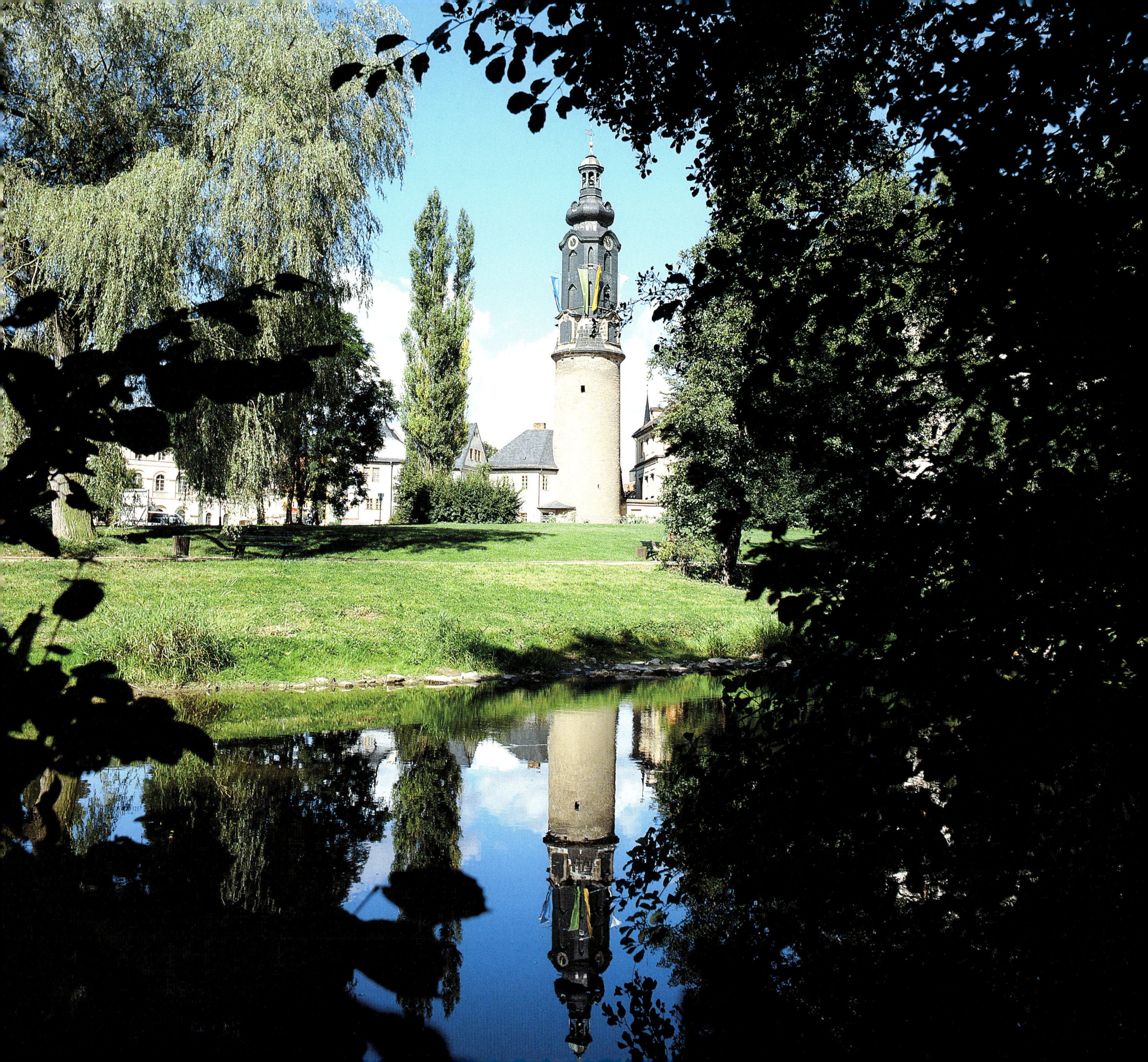

*Johann Wolfgang von Goethe (links) und Friedrich von Schiller (rechts) stehen auf dem Platz vor dem Weimarer Deutschen Nationaltheater seit 1857 im Dioskuren-Denkmal unverrücklich Seite an Seite (Bild rechts). Wie es das Denkmal darstellt, haben die beiden berühmten Weimarer Klassiker von 1794 an eng zusammengearbeitet und wurden Freunde, sorgten gemeinsam für die Glanzzeit des Theaters von 1799 bis 1805.*
*1919 tagte die deutsche Nationalversammlung hier, nach Zerstörung und Wiederaufbau im Zweiten Weltkrieg gab es zu Goethes 199. Geburtstag eine „Faust"-Aufführung zur Eröffnung.*
*Links ein Blick durch den Ilmpark über die Ilm auf den Turm des Schlosses, in dem Karl August, dessen Einladung nach Weimar Goethe Ende 1775 folgte, und vor ihm des jungen Herzogs Mutter Anna Amalia residierten.*
*Nächste Doppelseite: Das barocke Belvedere südlich der Stadt war eine Sommerresidenz der herzoglichen Familie, umgeben von einem herrlichen Park, dessen Gestaltung auf Fürst von Pückler-Muskau zurückgeht.*

## Klassisches Weimar

Ursprünglich ein beschauliches Ackerbürgerstädtchen fern der Handels- und Wirtschaftszentren, erblühte Weimar im späten 18. und frühen 19. Jahrhundert zu einem Mittelpunkt europäischer Geistesströmungen. Den Anstoß dazu gab 1772 die junge, früh verwitwete Herzogin Anna Amalia, als sie den Dichter Christoph Martin Wieland als Erzieher ihres Sohnes Karl August berief. Unter dessen Regentschaft kamen dann 1775 Johann Wolfgang Goethe, ein Jahr später Johann Gottfried Herder und 1799 Friedrich Schiller in die Residenzstadt an der Ilm. Sie verfassten in ihren Mauern literarische Werke von außergewöhnlicher Bedeutung. Ihr Schaffen prägte den Begriff der „Weimarer Klassik". Zahlreiche Spuren künden noch heute von der Welt der Dichter und ihrer Mäzene und von den vorbildhaften künstlerischen, architektonischen, städtebaulichen und landschaftsgestalterischen Leistungen in jener Zeit.

Elf für die Epoche wichtige Monumente nahm die UNESCO 1998 in die Liste des Weltkulturerbes auf. Dazu zählen Goethes barockes, klassizistisch umgestaltetes Domizil am Frauenplan und der Park an der Ilm; in ihm liegt jenes Gartenhaus, das Karl August dem Dichterfürsten geschenkt hatte. Ebenso das Wohnhaus von Schiller an der Esplanade, in dem er unter anderem seinen „Wilhelm Tell" und „Die Braut von Messina" verfasste. Und die Herderstätten, das heißt die spätgotische Stadtkirche St. Peter und Paul, in der er begraben liegt und in der Lucas Cranach d. Ä. das Altarbild gestaltete, Herders Wohnhaus und das Alte Gymnasium. Die Reihe wird ergänzt durch das Stadtschloss und das Wittumspalais der Herzogin Anna Amalia, die dort ihre „Freitagsgesellschaften" mit den „Klassikern" versammelte; durch die prachtvolle, nach ihr benannte Bibliothek mit den kostbaren Handschriften und Drucken des Goethe- und Schillerarchivs, das Schloss Belvedere mit dem herrlichen Barockgarten, das Schloss Tiefurt mit seinem Landschaftspark, das Schloss und den Schlosspark Ettersburg sowie den Historischen Friedhof mit der Fürstengruft, in der Goethe, Schiller und ihr Gönner Karl August bestattet sind, unter dem Weimar sein klassizistisches Aussehen erhielt.

## Classical Weimar

Originally a peaceful agricultural town away from economic centers and trade routes, Weimar blossomed into a center of European intellectual life in the late 18th and early 19th centuries. Duchess Anna Amalia, widowed at an early age, initiated this development when she appointed the poet Christoph Martin Wieland to teach her son Karl August. Under Karl August's regency, in 1775 first Johann Wolfgang Goethe, one year later Johann Gottfried Herder, and in 1799 Friedrich Schiller came to the small residence on the Ilm. Within its walls, literary works of extraordinary importance were written, and the term "Weimar Classics" was coined. The world of the poets, their patrons and the exemplary achievements in the arts, architecture, urban planning and landscaping of that period can still be traced today.

In 1998, eleven sites characteristic for the epoch were accepted to the list of the UNESCO World Heritage Program. Among those are Goethe's Baroque domicile at the Frauenplan, later refurbished in the Classicist style, and the park on the Ilm with the garden house Karl August had given to him; furthermore, Schiller's house on Esplanade street, in which he wrote his "William Tell" and "The Bride of Messina", among other works, as well as the "Herder sites", i.e. the Late Gothic town church St. Peter and Paul where he is buried, with an altarpiece from Lucas Cranach the Older, Herder's residence as well as the "Altes Gymnasium". Other sites are the city palace and the widow's seat of Duchess Anna Amalia, where she held her "Friday Meetings" with the classical poets, the splendid library with precious manuscripts and prints from the Goethe and Schiller archives named after her, the Belvedere Palace with its splendid Baroque gardens, Tiefurt Palace with its landscaped park, Ettersburg Park and Palace as well as the historical graveyard with the royal crypt holding the remnants of Goethe, Schiller and Karl August, who gave Weimar its Classicist appearance.

*Since 1857, Johann Wolfgang von Goethe (left) and Friedrich Schiller (right), unseparably side by side, have been overlooking the square in front of the Deutsches Nationaltheater in the Dioscuri monument (above). As the monument has it, the two famous Weimar classical poets worked together closely after 1794 and became friends, resulting in the theater's golden years from 1799 to 1805. In 1919, it was the site of the national assembly, and after its destruction in and reconstruction after World War II, "Faust" was played at the opening night of Goethe's 199th birthday.*
*Left, a view into the park on the Ilm and onto the tower of the palace, the residence of Karl August and before him his mother, Anna Amalia. It was Karl August who invited Goethe to Weimar in 1775.*
*Overleaf: The Baroque Belvedere Palace south of town was used by the ducal family as a summer residence. It is surrounded by an impressive park designed by Fürst von Pückler-Muskau.*

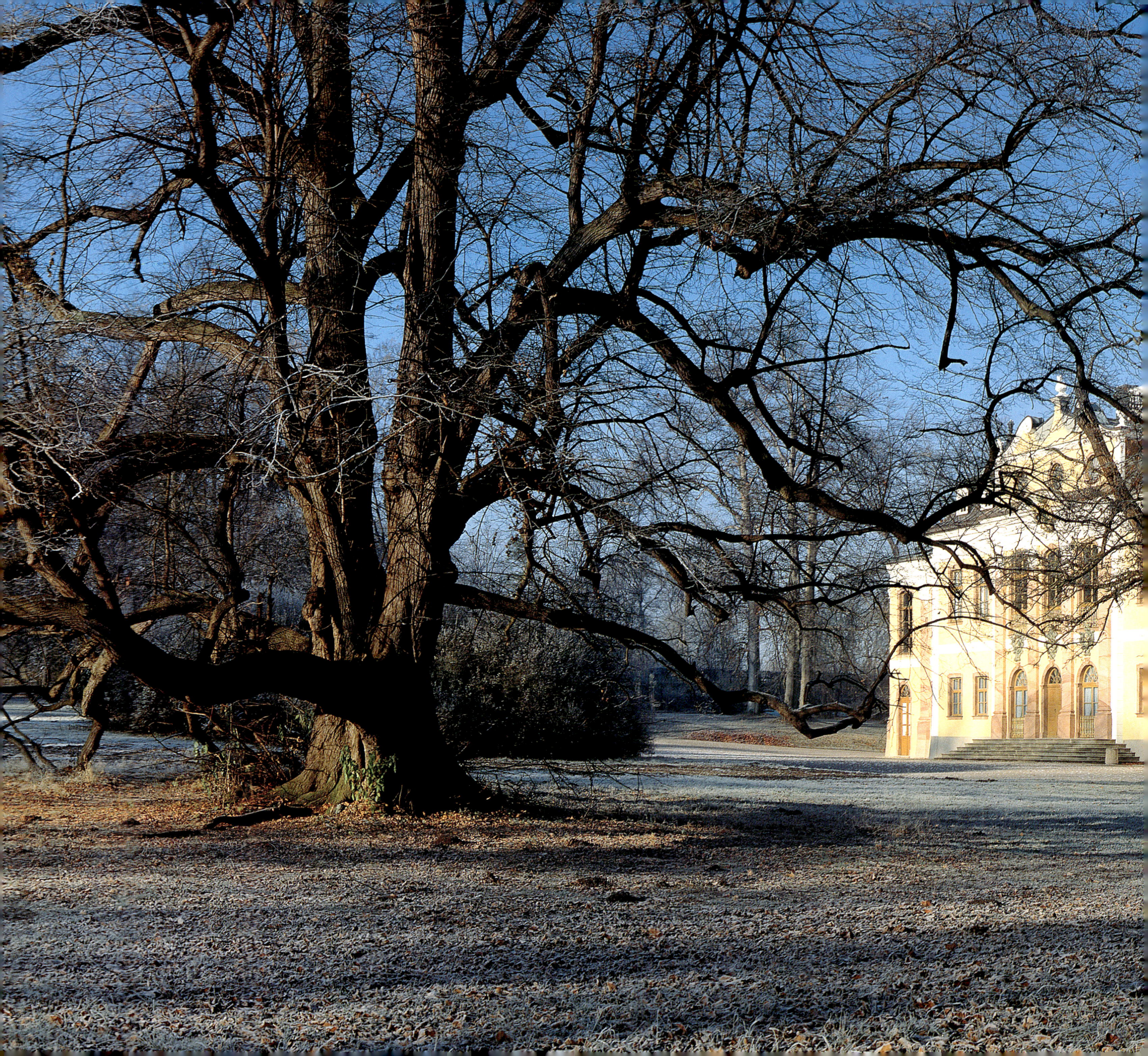

*Mitten im Ilmpark steht Goethes Gartenhaus (oben), in dessen Wänden die Entwürfe zu „Egmont", die Prosafassung von „Iphigenie" und „Wilhelm Meisters theatralische Sendung" entstanden. Das Kaleidoskop der Welterbe-Stätten ergänzen das Schillerhaus (links unten) und das Römische Haus im Park an der Ilm (rechts unten), das erste klassizistische Gebäude in Weimar.*

*Goethe's garden house (above), whose walls witnessed the creation of "Egmont" and the prose versions of "Iphigenie" and "Wilhelm Meister's Theatrical Mission" lies hidden in the park on the Ilm. The Schiller house (bottom left) and the Roman house in the park on the Ilm (bottom right), the first Classicist building at Weimar, round off the caleidoscope of World Heritage sites.*

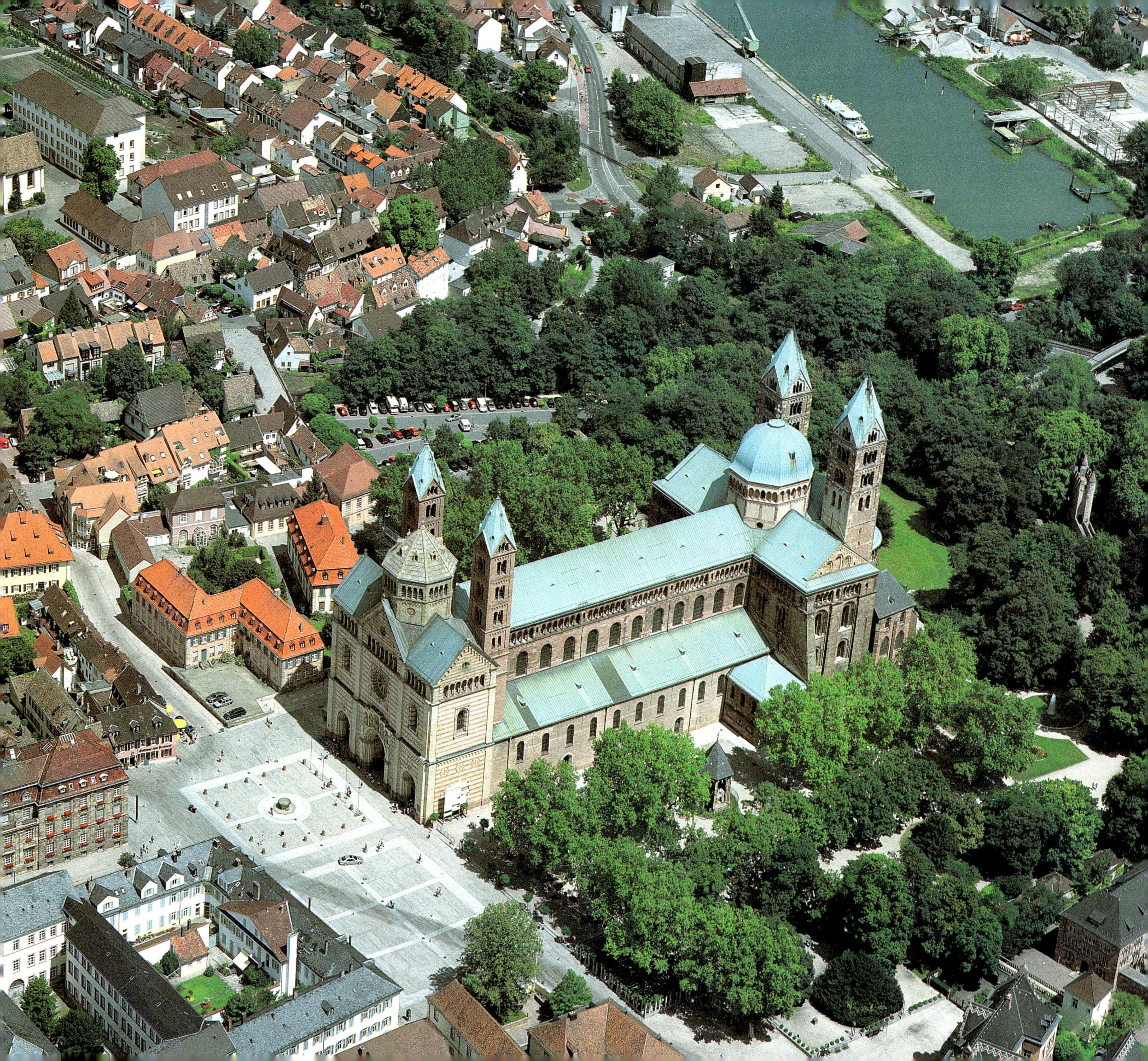

*Majestätisch reckt sich der Dom zu Speyer aus dem Grün seiner Umgebung empor. Mit jedem Bauabschnitt – um 1030 begann der erste – hatte man die Pläne verändert und die Dimensionen des Gotteshauses wachsen lassen, vor allem in der Länge und Höhe. So galt er bei seiner Vollendung als das größte Bauwerk seiner Zeit. In der zweiten Bau- oder Umbau-Phase – nach 1080 bis 1106 – wurden unter anderem die Türme aufgesetzt. Außen kamen schmückende Elemente hinzu: die kräftige Gliederung des Blendbogensystems, vor allem aber die Zwerggalerien, wie man sie häufig in der Lombardei, etwa am Dom von Modena, findet (nächste Doppelseite).*

## Der Dom zu Speyer

Benediktinische Zucht und kaiserliches Machtbewusstsein, so heißt es, prägten die Bauten der frühen Salier. Eindrucksvoll beweist dies der Dom St. Maria und St. Stephan. An der Stelle einer merowingischen Domkirche begann Konrad II. um 1030 mit seinem Bau. Rund drei Jahrzehnte später folgte die Schlussweihe. Noch während der Bauarbeiten wurden der Stifter, seine Gemahlin Gisela und beider Sohn Heinrich III. in dem neuen Gotteshaus bestattet. Später wählten auch die Staufer und Habsburger den Speyrer Dom als Grablege.

Kaiser Konrad II. hatte den Bau über einem kreuzförmigen Grundriss anlegen lassen: als dreischiffige, flach gedeckte Pfeiler-Basilika mit mächtigem Westbau, ausladendem Ost-Querschiff und tonnengewölbtem Chorquadrat. Damit schloss sich die rheinische Baukunst an die Errungenschaften der großen Dome und Abteikirchen in Frankreich an.

Nach 1080 ließ Konrads Enkel, Heinrich IV., den monumentalen frühromanischen Skelettbau umgestalten. Man unternahm das Wagnis, die hohen Kirchenschiffe einzuwölben. Zugleich wurde der abschließende gerade Chor mit einer großen, halbrunden Apsis ausgestattet. Auch das Äußere wurde in der zweiten, bis in das Jahr 1106 dauernden Bauphase reich geschmückt.

Mit seinen vier mächtigen Türmen, zwei Kuppeln und dem über 130 Meter langen massigen Mittelbau flößt der Speyrer Dom noch heute Ehrfurcht ein. Als er errichtet wurde, galt er als das gewaltigste Bauwerk der gesamten christlichen Welt. Im Pfälzischen Erbfolgekrieg sank es unter dem Angriff französischer Truppen jedoch in Trümmer. Nach dem Wiederaufbau fügte ihm die Französische Revolution von 1789 kräftige Schäden zu: Die Innenausstattung wurde komplett herausgerissen, das Langhaus als Lager und Viehstall genutzt.

Erst im 19. Jahrhundert ging man erneut daran, den Dom wiederherzustellen. Chor, Querhaus, das Vierungsgewölbe, die südliche Seitenschiffwand, der untere Teil der Vorhalle sowie die fünf östlichen Pfeilerpaare im Langhaus stammen noch aus dem ursprünglichen romanischen Bau. 1981 wurde der Dom zu Speyer als Hauptwerk romanischer Baukunst in Deutschland in die Welterbe-Liste der UNESCO aufgenommen.

## The Cathedral of Speyer

It has been stated that the buildings of the early Salians are characterized by Benedictine discipline as well as an awareness of imperial power. The cathedral St. Maria and St. Stephan is an impressive example. Construction on the site of a former Merovingian cathedral church began under Konrad II, and the structure was consecrated about three decades later. The donor, his spouse Gisela and their son Heinrich III were interred in the cathedral while it was still under construction, and even after them, it was the preferred burial-place of Staufer and Habsburg royalty.

Emperor Konrad II commissioned the church to be built over a cross-shaped floor plan – a flat-roofed basilica with three aisles, the nave resting on pillars, an elongated transept and a chancel square spanned by a barrel vault. The architecture on the Rhine had joined rank with the achievements of the great French cathedrals and abbeys.

After 1080, Konrad's grandson, Heinrich IV, had the monumental Early Romanesque skeleton building redesigned, undertaking the risk of inserting vaults into the soaring aisles as well as adding a large, semicirular apse to the end of the rectilinear chancel. The exterior, too, was richly decorated in this second phase of construction, which lasted until 1106.

With its four mighty towers, two cupolas and the long, massive nave, the Speyer cathedral is still an awe-inspiring building. When it was built, it was considered the most formidable structure in the Christian world. Ruined in the Palatine war of Succession by French troups, it was rebuilt and then again damaged in the French Revolution in 1789: Its interior was destroyed, the nave used as a cowshed.

It was not until the 19th century that the cathedral was reconstructed. Chancel, transept and the central dome, the southern wall of the side aisle, the lower part of the narthex as well as the five eastern twin pillars in the nave still date back to the original Romanesque building. In 1981, the Speyer cathedral was accepted to the UNESCO World Heritage Program as the most important Romanesque building in Germany.

*The Speyer cathedral majestically towers over its green surroundings. The plans to the church were altered with each construction phase – the first began in 1030 –, ever expanding the building's length and height. At the date of its completion, it was considered the largest building in its time. The towers, among other parts, date back to the second building or renovation phase – after 1080 to 1106. Façade ornaments were also added, for instance the distinctively structured blind arch system, and, above all, the dwarf galleries often seen in Lombardy, as at the cathedral of Modena, for example (overleaf).*

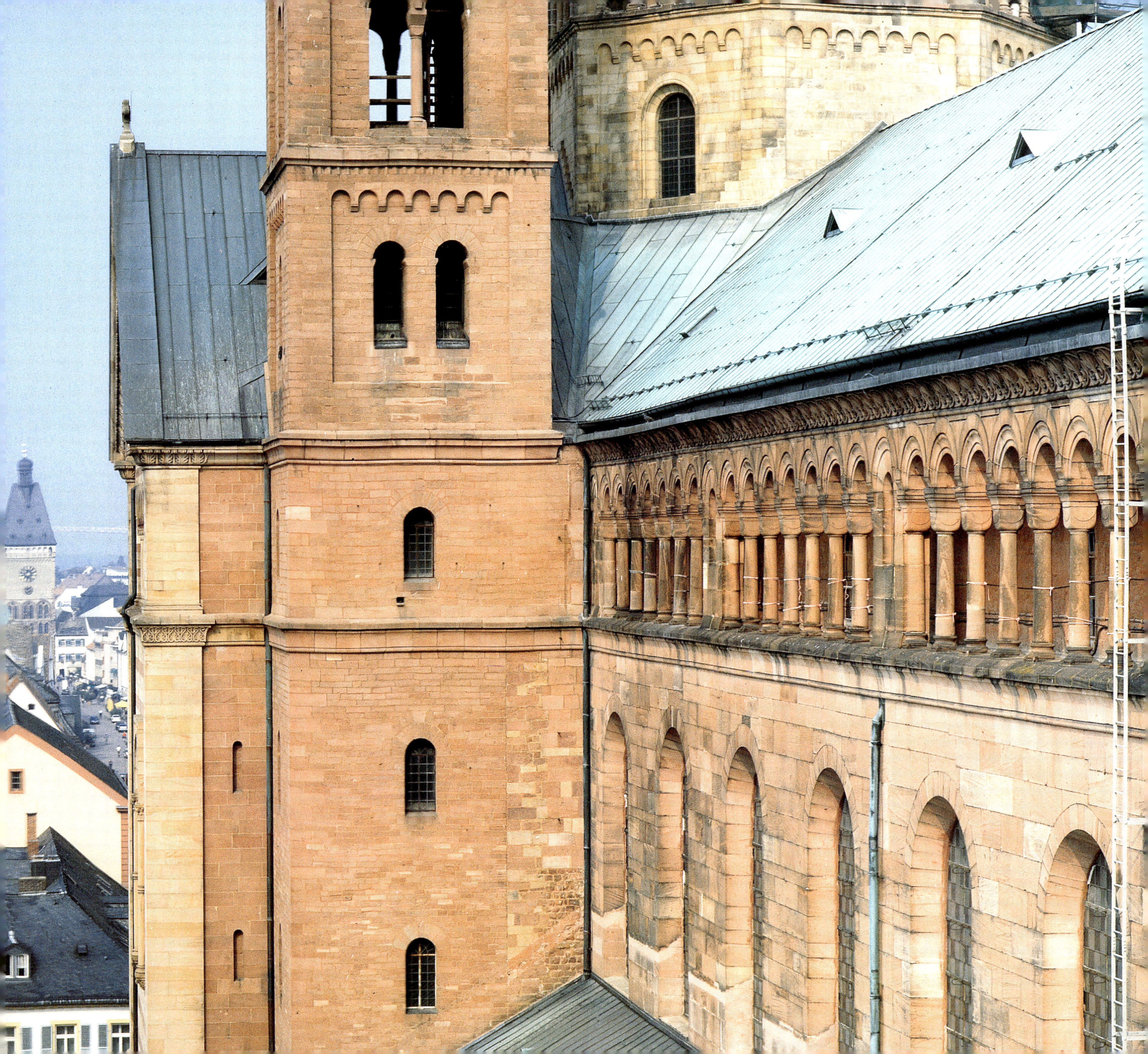

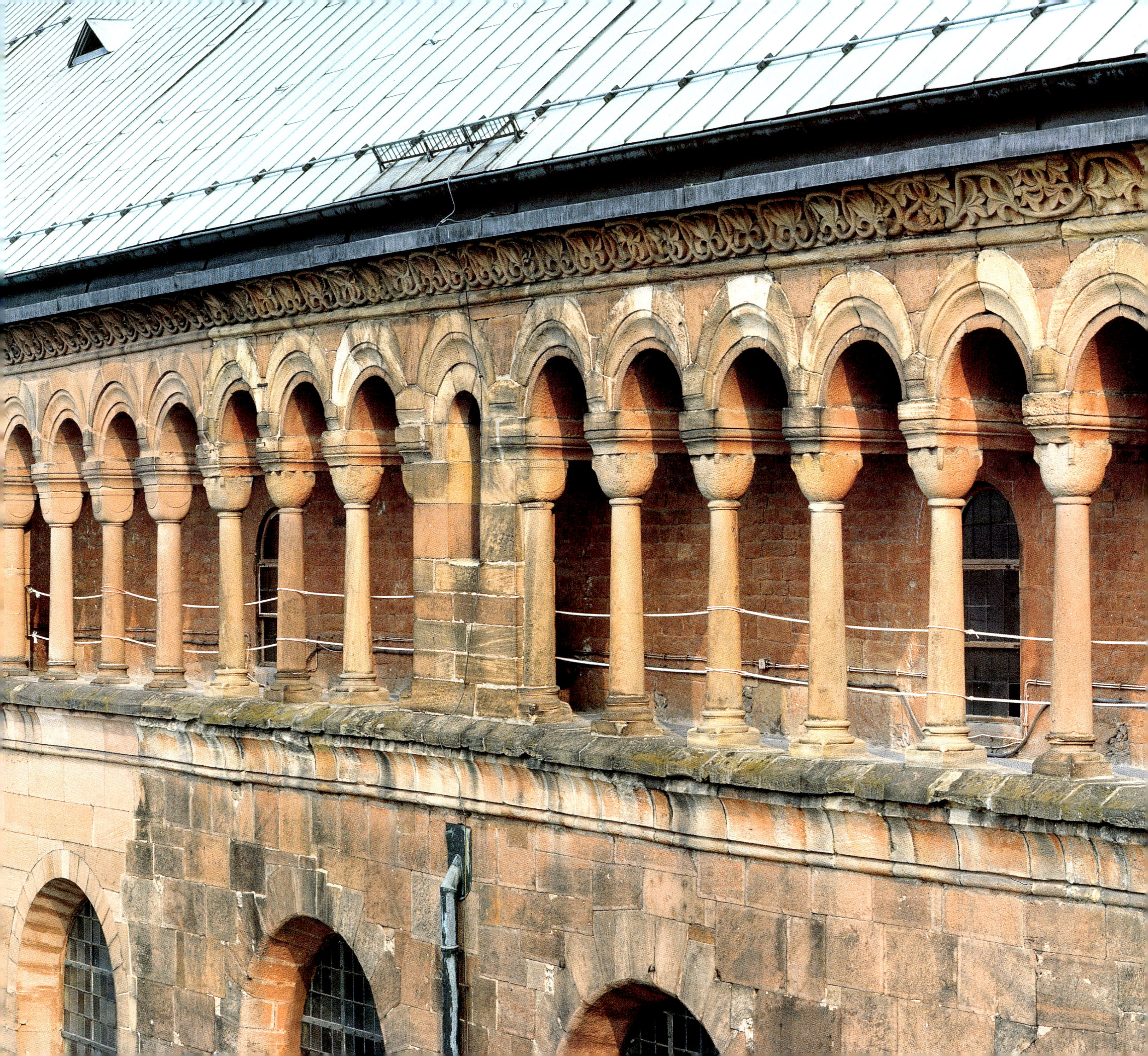

Himmelan stürmt die Vierungskuppel im Speyrer Dom, sie stammt noch aus der frühromanischen ersten Bauzeit (links). Die gewaltige Höhe des Kaiserdoms wird unterstrichen durch seine Lage rund 10 Meter über dem Rhein (ganz rechts). Die umfangreichen Steinmetzarbeiten besonders der zweiten Bauphase schmückten auch die Umrahmung der Portale (rechts oben). Das Denkmal für Kaiser Rudolf von Habsburg (rechts unten), der 1291 in Speyer verstarb, wurde von Ludwig von Schwanthaler 1843 geschaffen. Es erinnert an zweierlei: Nach den Saliern ließen sich einige Kaiser und Könige aus den Reihen der Staufer und Habsburger in Speyer bestatten. Und noch im 19. Jahrhundert gehörten große Teile der Pfalz zum Königreich Bayern; König Ludwig I. fand für den von ihm geförderten Bildhauer also reichlich Betätigung, über München und die Walhalla hinaus.

The central dome of the cathedral at Speyer reaches up into the heavens, dating back all the way to the Romanesque construction phase (left). The lofty height of the imperial cathedral is enhanced by its position about 10 meters above Rhine level (very right). The portals are richly embellished with masonry, mainly dating to the second construction phase (top right). In 1843, Ludwig von Schwanthaler created the memorial to Emperor Rudolf von Habsburg (bottom right), who died at Speyer in 1291. This serves as a reminder both of the preference of some emperors and kings of the Staufer and Habsburg dynasties for Speyer as a burial-place, and of the fact that large parts of the Palatinate belonged to the Kingdom of Bavaria well into the 19th century. King Ludwig I seems to have found enough work for his preferred sculptor beyond Munich and the Valhalla.

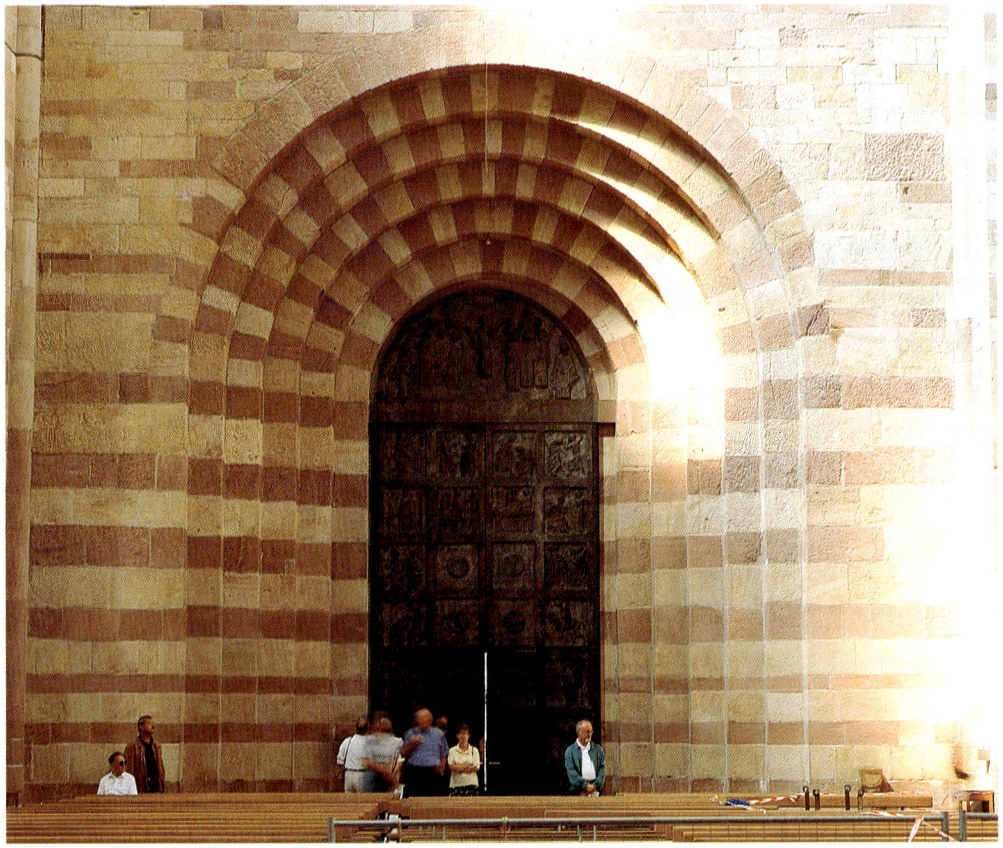

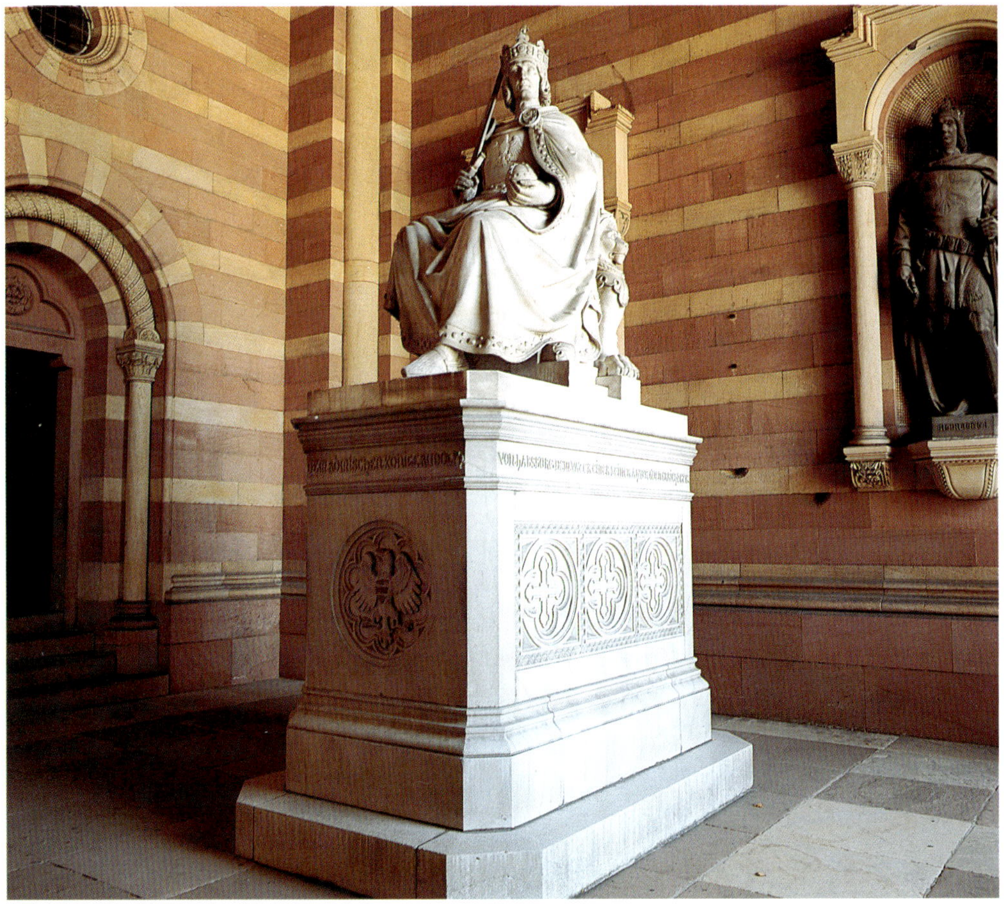

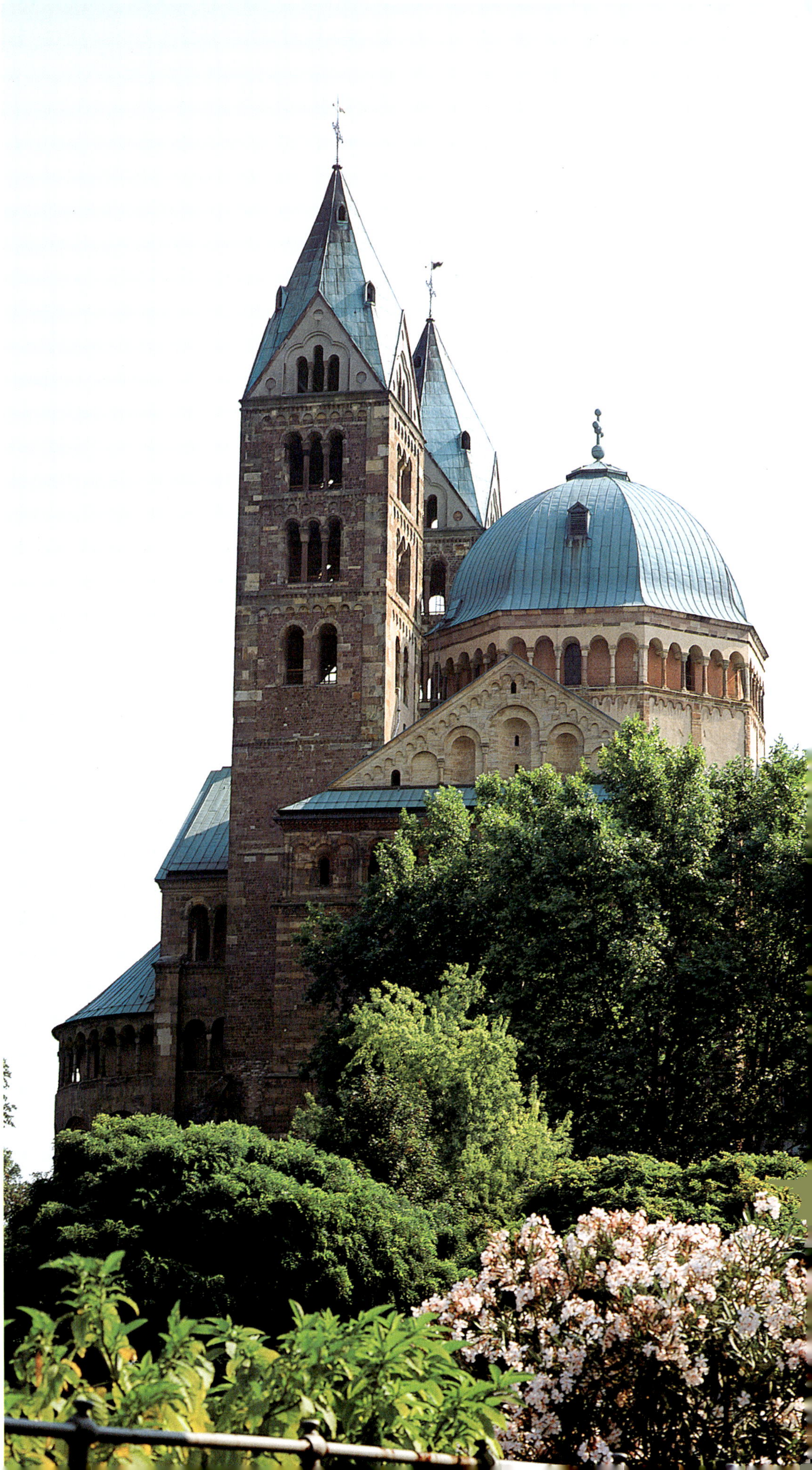

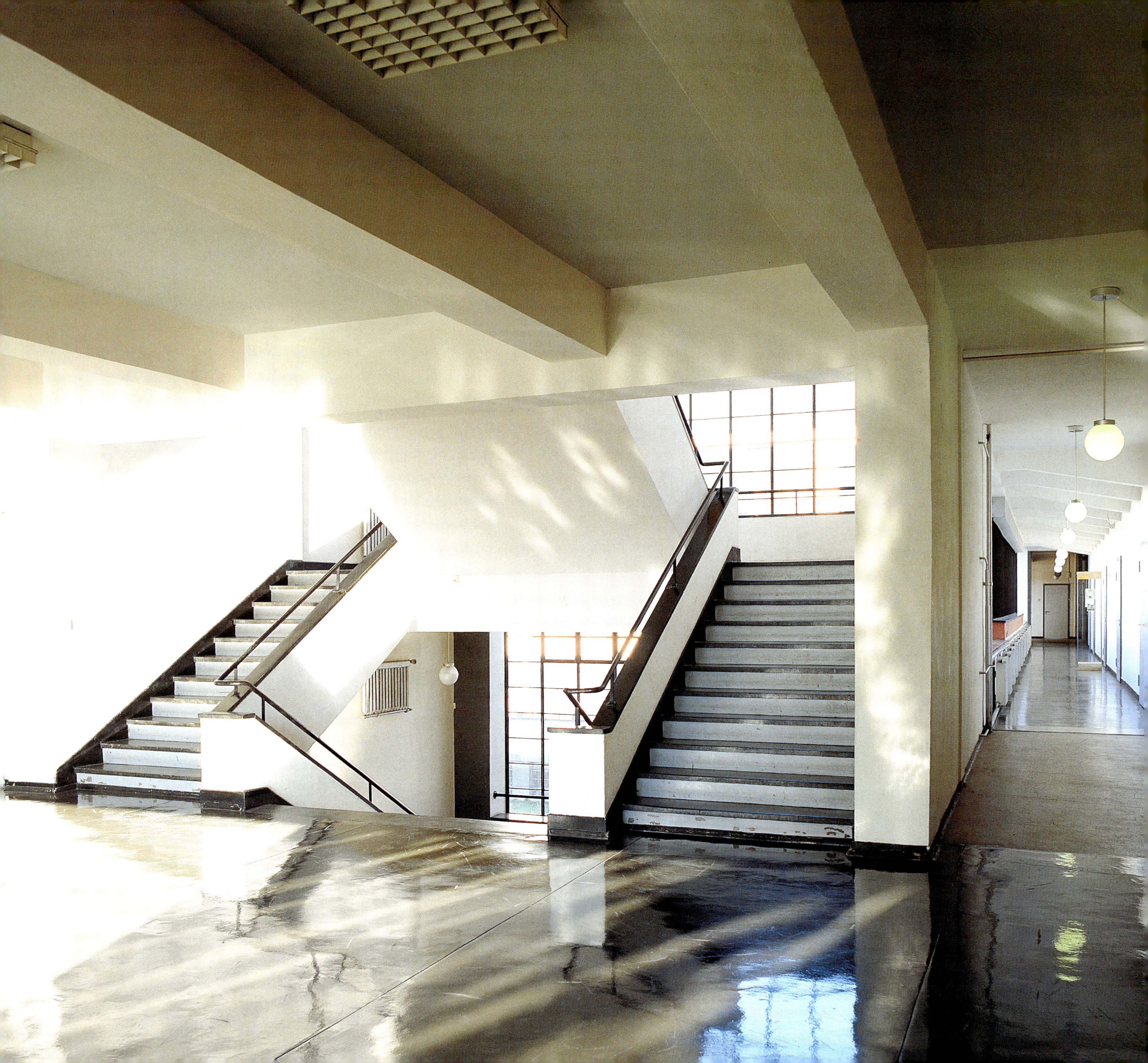

*Transparenz und Funktionalität kennzeichnen die Architektur des Bauhauses. Dies wird bereits in der Eingangshalle mit Treppenhaus, dem zentralen Zugang, deutlich. Im neuen Dessauer Domizil der interdisziplinären Ausbildungsstätte führen die verschiedenen Gebäudeflügel das avantgardistische Credo der Bauhausphilosophie aufs Schönste vor Augen (nächste Doppelseite).*

## Das Bauhaus in Dessau

Als kleine Welt für sich präsentierte sich das 1919 von Walter Gropius in Weimar gegründete Bauhaus in seinem neuen Dessauer Domizil von 1926 an. Fast alle Bereiche des täglichen Lebens, vom Wohnen, Essen, Arbeiten und Lernen bis zu Unterhaltung und Sport umfasste der von Gropius entwickelte lichte, asymmetrische Dreiflügelbau. Seine Einweihung am 4. Dezember 1926 geriet zu einem Fest, mit mehr als 1 000 Gästen. Entstanden war ein neuer Hort für die Ausbildung sozial engagierter und kreativer Gestalter, die auch disziplinübergreifend arbeiten können.

Mit dem Dessauer Bauhausgebäude schrieb Gropius seine 1911 bei der Errichtung der Faguswerke in Alfeld a. d. Leine erstmals umgesetzte Philosophie fort, eine Architektur konsequent aus ihrer Bestimmung und den technischen Bedingungen von Material und Konstruktion heraus zu entwickeln, ohne die einzelnen Teile „symbolisch" zu erhöhen. Deutlich waren daher alle Funktionsbereiche voneinander abgegrenzt. In einem Flügel waren die Technischen Lehranstalten (Gewerbliche Berufsschule) untergebracht mit Unterrichtsräumen und Bibliothek. Im 1. und 2. Obergeschoss führte eine auf 4 Pfeilern über die Zufahrtstraße gespannte Brücke zum 3-geschossigen Flügel der Werkstätten und Lehrräume des Bauhauses, mit seiner berühmten Glasvorhangfassade. In der Brücke befanden sich die Verwaltung, die Architekturabteilung sowie Gropius' privates Bauatelier. Ein Zwischentrakt im Erdgeschoss, in dem Aula, Bühne und Mensa untergebracht waren, verband die einzelnen Flügel mit dem Atelierhaus. Es barg auf seinen 5 Etagen 28 Studenten-Wohnateliers sowie Bäder und einen Gymnastikraum.

Nur 5 Gehminuten vom Bauhausgebäude entfernt ließ Gropius in einem Fichtenwäldchen die „Meisterhäuser" errichten für den Direktor und die wichtigsten Bauhaus-Lehrkräfte. Ihre Namensreihe reicht von Kandinsky über Klee, Feininger, Meyer, Schlemmer, Itten und Moholy-Nagy bis hin zu Mies van der Rohe. Bei einem Fliegerangriff im März 1945 brannte das Dessauer Bauhausgebäude völlig aus. Nach ersten Wiederherstellungen 20 Jahre später wurde es zwischen 1976 und 1978 vorzüglich restauriert.

## The Bauhaus at Dessau

The Bauhaus, founded in 1919 by Walter Gropius at Weimar and after 1926 in its new domicile at Dessau, presents itself as a little world of its own. The airy asymmetrical structure with three wings designed by Gropius incorporated almost all areas of daily life, from living, dining and learning to entertainment and sports. Its inauguration on December 4, 1926, was a festive event with more than 1,000 guests. It marked the beginning of a new refuge for the education of creative designers committed to a social cause, with the possibility for interdisciplinary work.

The Dessau Bauhaus area is a continuation of Gropius' philosophy, first implemented in 1911 with the construction of the Fagus plant at Alfeld on the Leine, to develop architecture directly from its purpose and the technical properties of material and construction, without symbolic elevation of individual parts. Thus, all functional areas remained distinctly separate. One wing housed the technical college (trade school) including classrooms and library. From the first and second story, a bridge resting on four pillars leads across the driveway to the three-story wing of the Bauhaus workshops and classrooms with its famous glass curtain façade. The bridge featured administrative offices and the architectural department as well as Gropius' private building studio. A ground floor structure connecting the wings and the studio building contained the auditorium, stage and cafeteria. The five-story studio building included 28 studio apartments, baths and a gym. Only five minutes away, in a pine grove, Gropius had "master houses" built for the dean and other important Bauhaus faculty, an illustrous list of names that includes Kandinsky, Klee, Feininger, Meyer, Schlemmer, Itten, Moholy-Nagy and Mies van der Rohe. The Bauhaus building was gutted by fire in an air raid in March 1945. After first reconstruction measures more than 20 years later, it was superbly restored in the years between 1976 and 1978.

*Bauhaus architecture is characterized by transparency and functionality, especially evident in the foyer with its staircase. The new Dessau home of the interdisciplinary institute of learning with its separate wings beautifully illustrates the avantgarde credo of the Bauhaus philosophy (overleaf).*

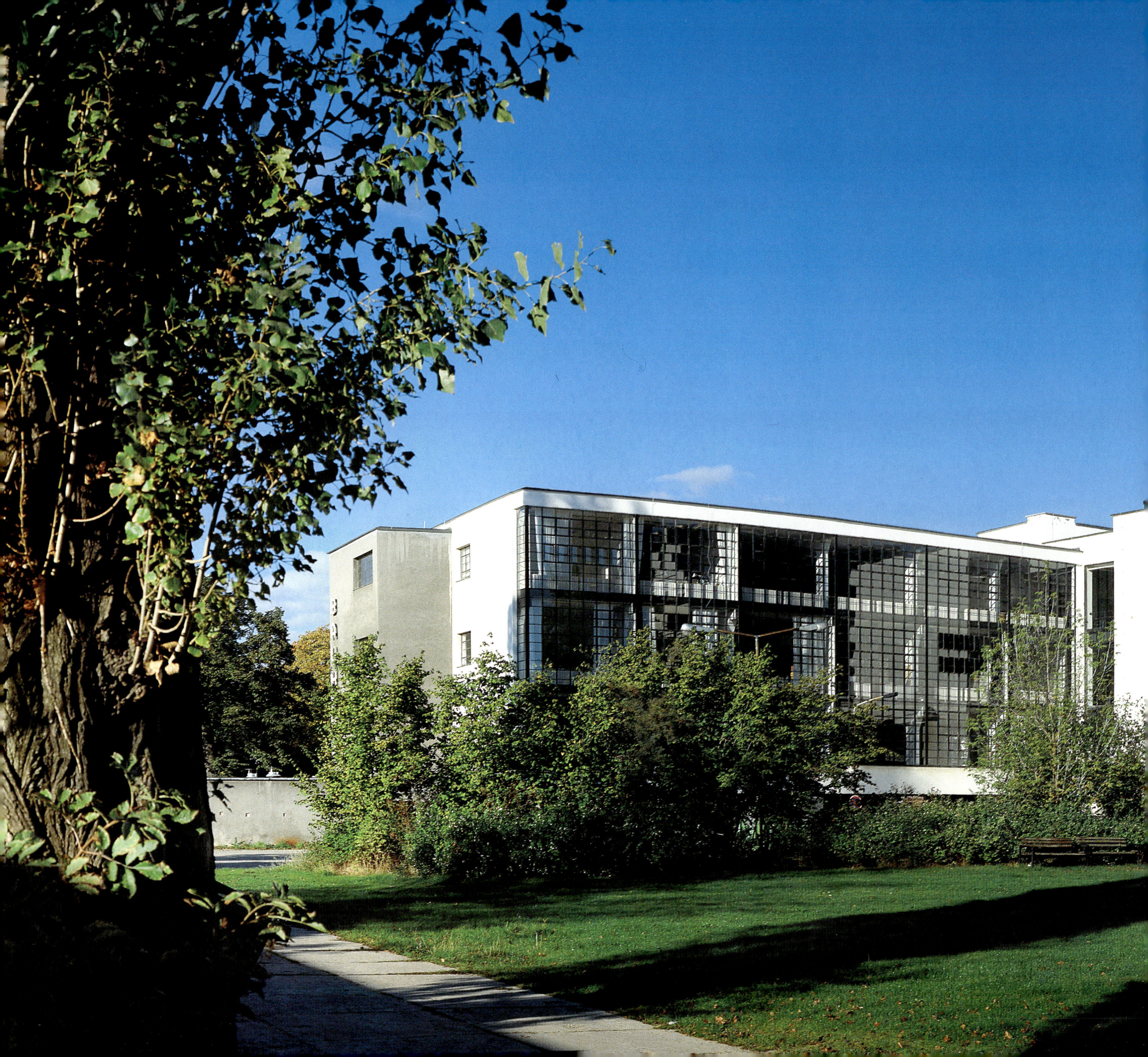

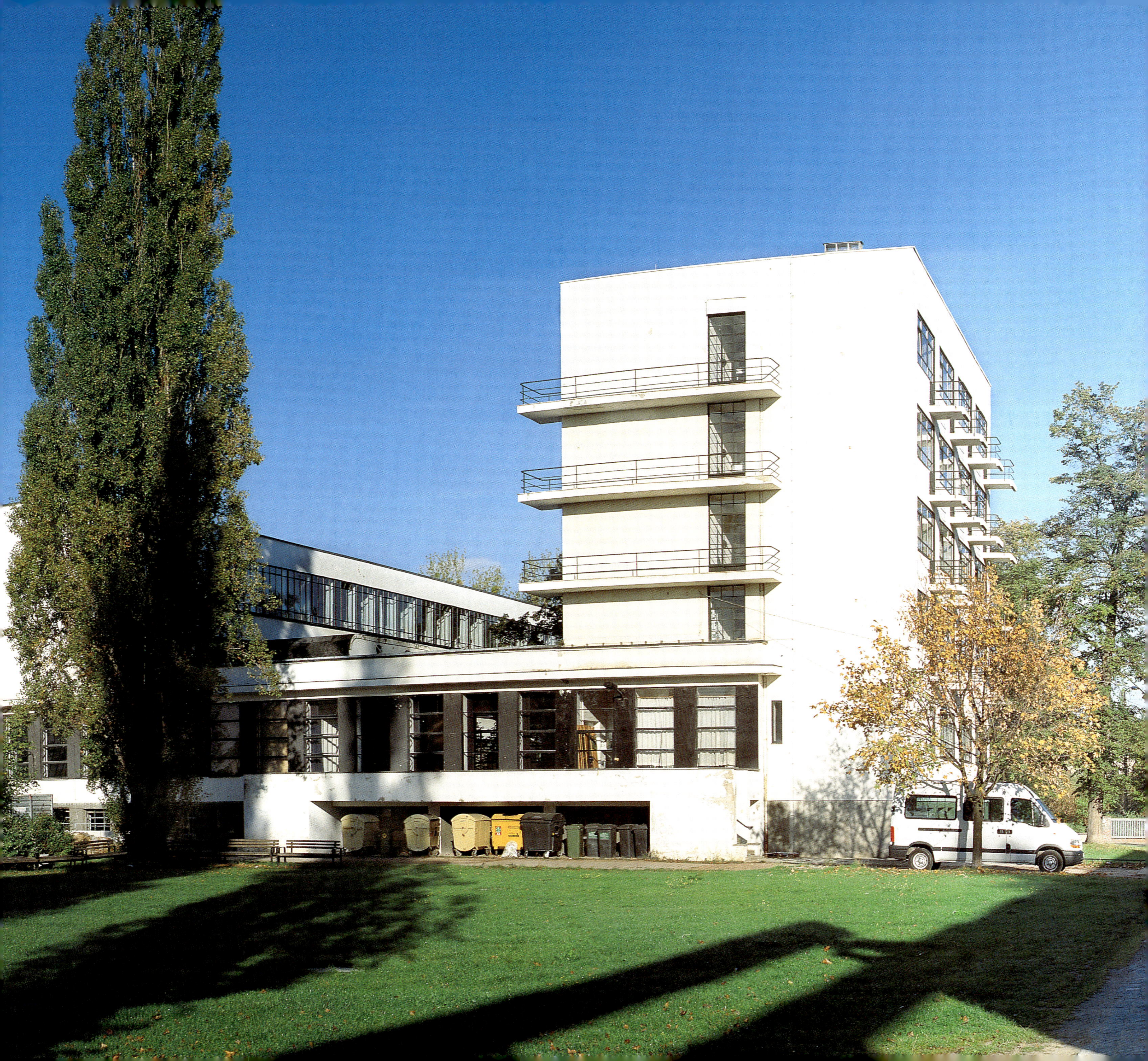

*Berühmt für seine Glasfassade ist der Werkstättentrakt, in dem Arbeits-, Lehr- und Ausstellungsräume für die verschiedenen Abteilungen des Bauhauses untergebracht waren.*
*Beim Blick aus den Werkstätten (unten) fällt die Verwendung von Stahlbeton auf, eines mehr als 70 Jahre später immer noch sehr modernen Baustoffs.*

*The workshop building, which housed workshops, classrooms and exhibition halls for the various Bauhaus divisions, is famous for its glass façade. A view from the workshops (below) reveals the use of reinforced concrete, a material that is still up-to-date more than 70 years later.*

Das Dessauer Bauhaus setzte von seinen Weimarer Anfängen bis zur Auflösung 1933 in Berlin revolutionäre Ideen der Baugestaltung und Stadtplanung durch. Walter Gropius selbst schrieb 1930: „entscheidend für die beurteilung eines bauwerks bleibt die feststellung, ob der architekt und ingenieur mit einem geringsten aufwand an zeit und material ein instrument geschaffen hat, das funktioniert, d. h. dem geforderten lebenszweck vollendet dient ..."

The Bauhaus at Dessau is the cradle of Modernist architecture and design. From its beginnings at Weimar to its dissolution in 1933 in Berlin, the Bauhaus implemented revolutionary ideas in building design and urban planning. In Walter Gropius' own words (1930): "the decisive factor in judging a piece of architecture is the observation as to whether the architect and engineer, with the smallest requirement of time and material, has created an instrument that works, i.e. that fully serves the intended purpose, a purpose which may be based on spiritual as well as material demands."

In unmittelbarer Nähe zum neuen Dessauer Bauhausgebäude entstanden zeitgleich die so genannten Meisterhäuser für die wichtigsten Lehrer: geometrisch-klare Doppelanlagen, die im Zweiten Weltkrieg zum Teil unwiederbringlich zerstört und bis heute nicht alle rekonstruiert oder erst nach dem Krieg zweckentfremdet und entstellt wurden. Oben links das Wohnhaus von Lyonel Feininger, unten rechts der Treppenaufgang darin, unten links das puristische Schlafzimmer von Frau Feininger, mit Möbeln nach original Bauhaus-Entwürfen; und oben rechts zeigt sich das Haus Kandinsky/Klee seit jüngster Zeit wiederhergestellt.

The so-called master houses in the immediate vicinity of the Bauhaus building were built at the same time: twin structures in a clear geometric design to house important faculty members. Some of the buildings were irretrievably destroyed in World War II and have not yet been reconstructed, others were disfigured and used for other purposes after the war. Above left, the domicile of Lyonel Feininger, below right its staircase, below left the puristic bedroom of Mrs. Feininger, with furniture from original Bauhaus designs; and above right the Kandinsky/Klee house, newly reconstructed.

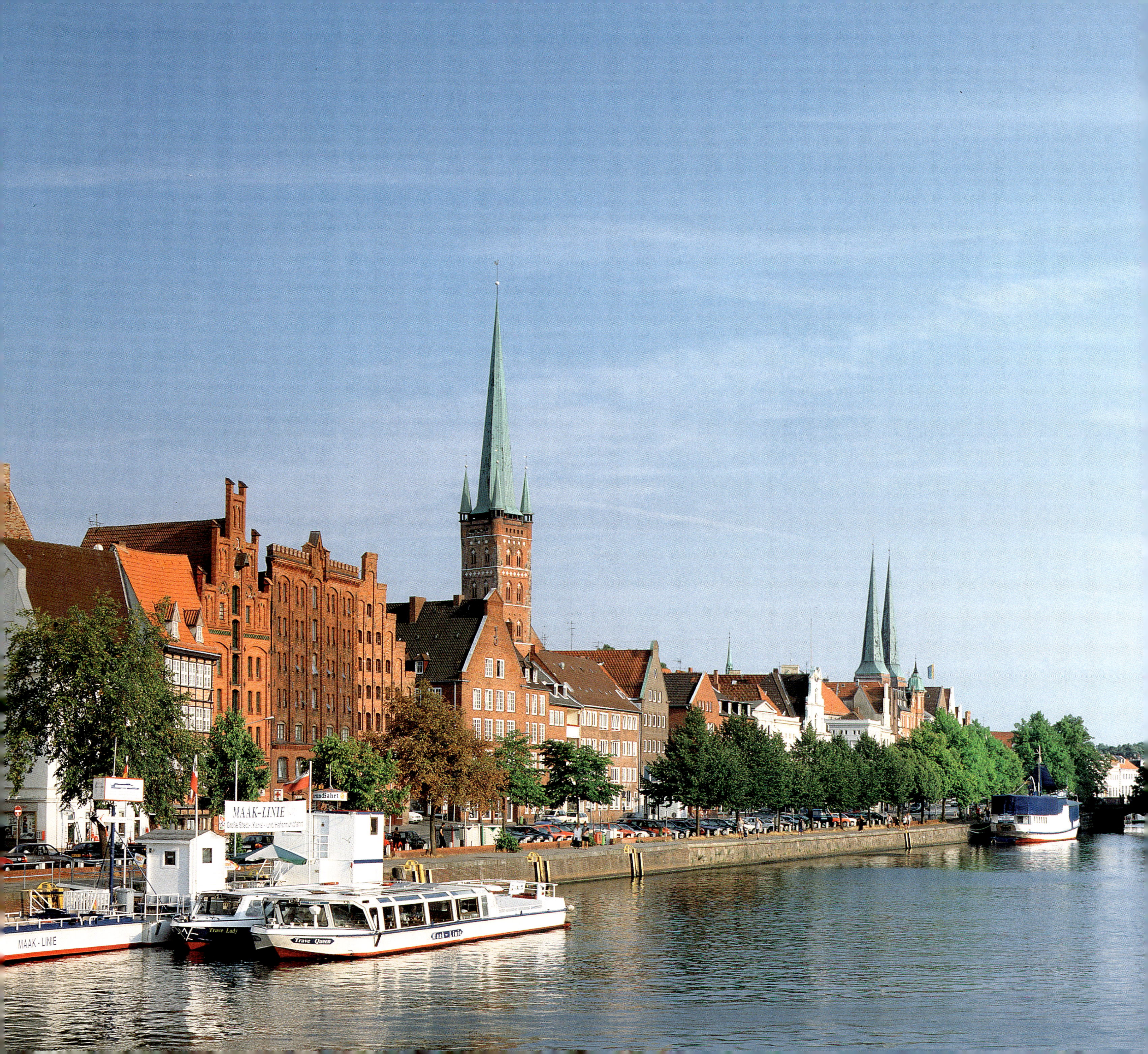
MAAK-LINIE
MAAK - LINIE
Trave Lady
Trave Queen

*Lübeck, „Königin" der Hanse, im 14. und 15. Jahrhundert unangefochtene Nummer eins im Ostseehandel, von einer heute ganz beschaulich wirkenden Seite: Über die Stadttrave hinweg, auf deren meerwärts gewandtem Teil namens Untertrave die Hansekoggen ankerten, sieht man eines der Wahrzeichen, den Turm von St. Petri. Die Kirche dient heute als Versammlungs- und Ausstellungsraum, ihr Turm gewährt einen ausgezeichneten Überblick über die Altstadt.*
*Nächste Doppelseite: Die durch Salzhandel mit dem „weißen Gold" aus Lüneburg reich gewordene Stadt hatte einst einen westlichen Zugang, den jeder kennt: das Holstentor. Optisch flankiert wird es – jenseits der hier nicht sichtbaren Holstenbrücke über die Stadttrave – von St. Petri (rechts) und der hochgotischen Marienkirche (links), die lange Zeit Vorbild für die Gotteshäuser der Hansestädte war.*

# Lübeck

Als Hort der Backsteingotik und planerisches Exempel für die hanseatische Städtefamilie im Ostseeraum gebührt Lübeck ein wichtiges Kapitel in der europäischen Baugeschichte. 1157, nur 15 Jahre nach ihrer Gründung, durch einen Brand völlig vernichtet, wurde die „Stadt der sieben Türme" 1159 unter Heinrich dem Löwen am selben Platz neu angelegt. Den Kern der exakten Neuplanung bildete ein 1 000 Meter breites und 1 600 Meter langes Areal auf einer Halbinsel zwischen Trave und Wakenitz. Zwei durch die Hauptstraßenachse verbundene Torbauten begrenzten es im Süden und Norden.

Jeder Stand hatte sein Viertel. Der doppeltürmige Dom im Süden, 1266 als erster monumentaler Backsteinbau im weiten Umkreis begonnen, markierte den bischöflichen Bereich. Im Norden am Koberg mit der St.-Jakobi-Kirche waren die Fischer und Seefahrer zu Hause, im Osten das Kleingewerbe und die Handwerker. Im Westen standen die Kontor- und Wohnhäuser der wohlhabenden Kaufleute. Die Aufreihung gleichartiger Giebelhäuser und Dachwerke machen diese gesellschaftliche und wirtschaftliche Differenzierung noch heute anschaulich. Besonders deutlich zeigt sie sich zudem in der Anordnung der „Gangbuden". Dies waren Werkstätten auf dem rückwärtigen Grundstück der Kaufmannshäuser, zu denen ein enges Netz von „Gängen" führt.

Die UNESCO erkannte mit Lübeck 1987 erstmals eine ganze nordeuropäische Altstadt als Weltkulturerbe an, einschließlich der wichtigsten Bauwerke und Stadtviertel: Es gehören unter anderen dazu das Heiligen-Geist-Hospital, die Baublöcke zwischen Glockengießer- und Aegidienstraße, das Viertel der Patrizierhäuser des 15. und 16. Jahrhunderts zwischen Petrikirche und Dom, das trutzige Holstentor und die alten Salzspeicher am linken Traveufer, nicht zuletzt die doppeltürmige Hauptpfarrkirche St. Marien, die 1942 ausbrannte, aber Mitte der 50er Jahre restauriert wurde. Ebenfalls in der Altstadt steht die turmlose Katharinenkirche. Sie ist die einzige erhaltene Klosterkirche der Stadt. Ihr Inneres birgt eines der kostbarsten Kunstwerke Lübecks: Jacopo Tintorettos Gemälde „Die Auferweckung des Lazarus".

# Lübeck

A haven of the brick Gothic style and the planning model for the Hanse cities on the Baltic, Lübeck represents an important chapter in the history of building in Europe. Ravaged by a fire in 1157, only 15 years after its foundation, the "City of the Seven Towers" was rebuilt on the same site under Heinrich der Löwe in 1159. The core of the detailed new plan was an area of 1,000 meters in width and 1,600 meters in length on a peninsula between the Trave and Wakenitz rivers. Two gate structures in the south and in the north were connected by a main thoroughfare. The quarters were assigned to the different estates. The cathedral with its twin towers in the south, begun in 1266 as the first monumental brick structure, marked the bishopric. In the north, the Koberg with its St. Jakobi church was home to the fishermen and seafarers, the eastern quarter to craftsmen and small industries. The west featured the office and residential buildings of wealthy tradesmen. Long rows of houses with similar gable structures and roofs still testify to these social and economic differences today, and they are also indicated in the arrangement of the "passage booths", workshops on the premises behind the tradesmen's houses which were accessed by means of a separate network of passageways.

Lübeck was the first old town in Northern Europe to be accepted into the UNESCO World Heritage Program as a whole, most important buildings, residential areas and all. Among them are the Heiligen-Geist-Hospital, the blocks of houses between the Glockengießer and Aegidienstraße streets, the patrician quarter with its houses from the 14th and 16th centuries between Petrikirche church and the cathedral, the fierce-looking Holstentor and the old salt storehouses on the left bank of the Trave as well as the main parish church St. Marien with its twin towers, which was gutted by fire in 1942 but restored in the mid-fifties. The towerless Katharinenkirche church, also in the old town, is the city's only preserved monastery church and home of one of Lübeck' most precious works of art: Jacopo Tintoretto's painting "The Awakening of Lazarus".

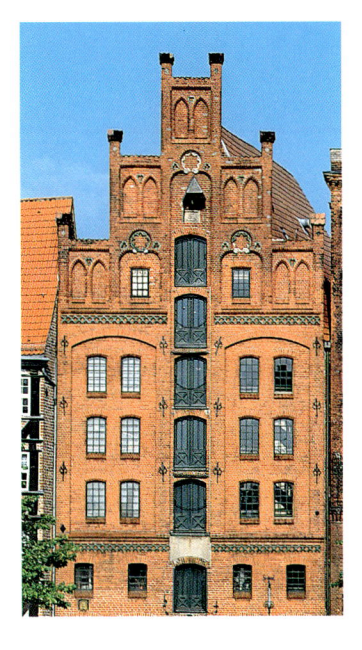

*Lübeck, the "queen" of the Hanse cities, and in the 14th and 15th centuries the uncontested number one in the Baltic trade, from quite a peaceful angle: A view across the Stadttrave, whose seafront channel named Untertrave was the anchoring site for the Hanse cogs, onto one of the city's landmarks: the tower of St. Petri's. Today, the church serves as an exhibition and assembly hall, and its steeple affords an excellent view onto the old town.*
*Overleaf: The western entrance to the city, which grew rich from its trade with the "white gold" from Lüneburg, is quite famous: the Holstentor gate. It is framed – beyond the hidden Holstenbrücke bridge across the Stadttrave – by the spires of St. Petri's (right) and the High Gothic Marienkirche church (left), for a long time the model for the churches of the Hanse cities.*

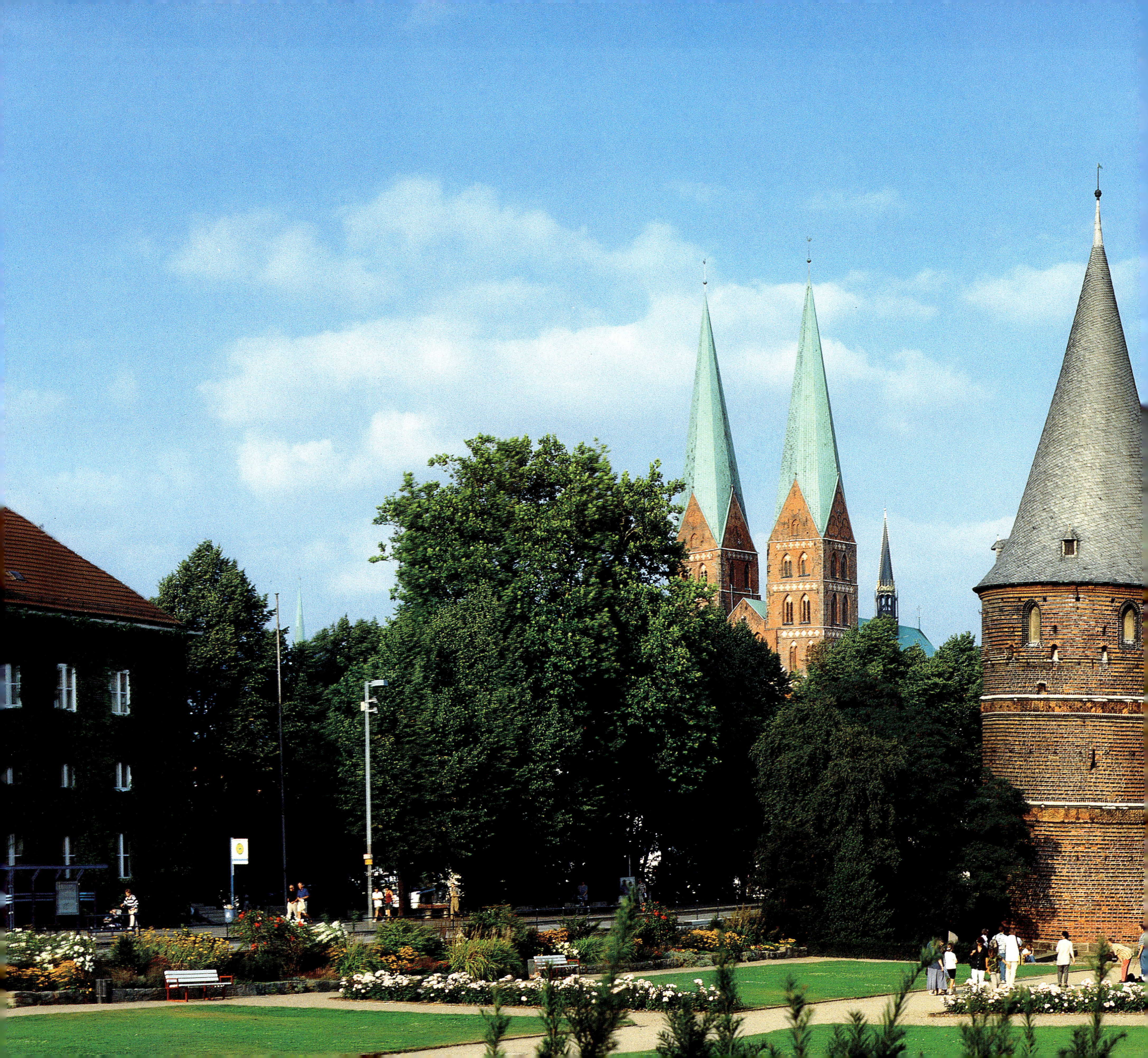

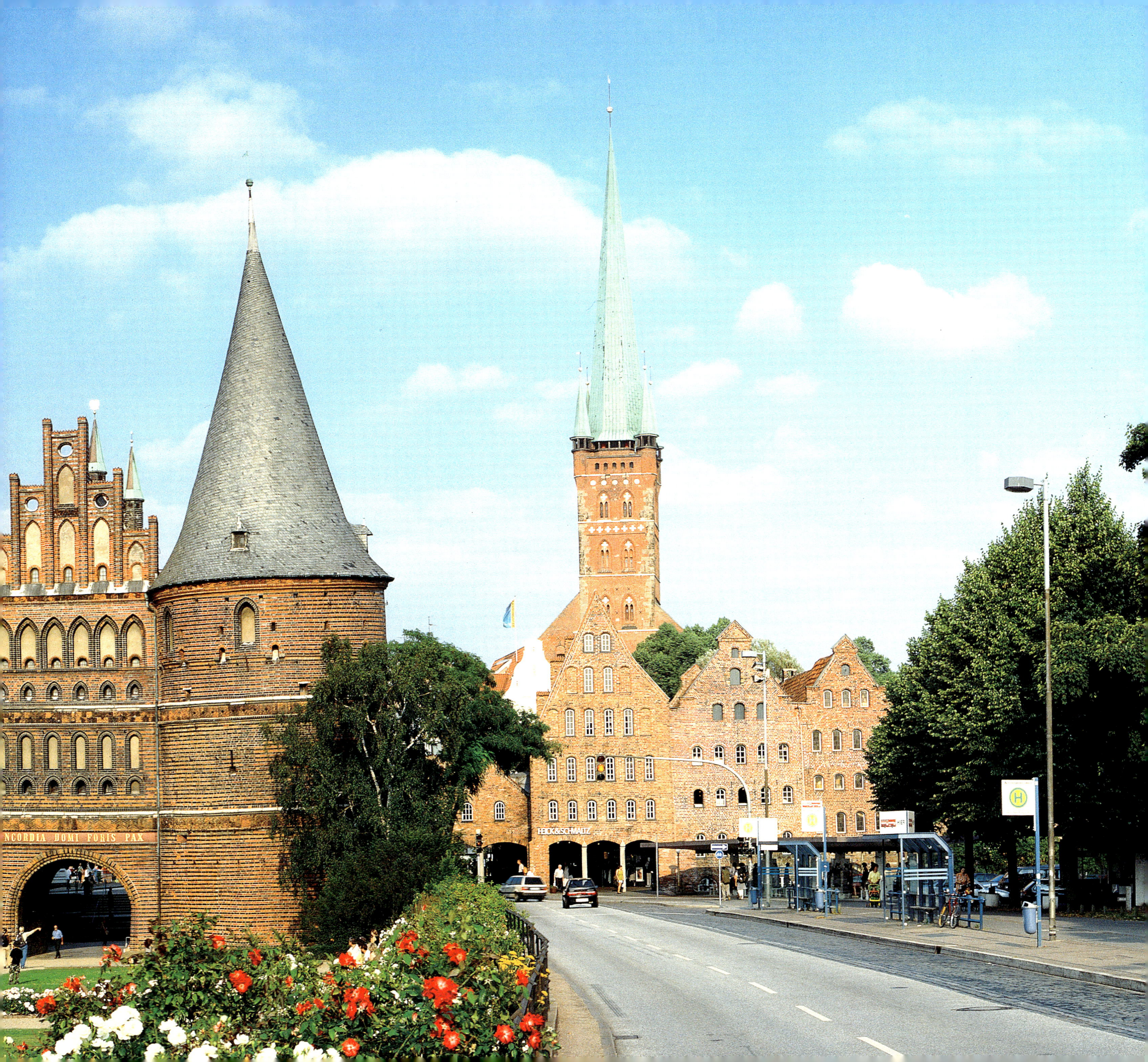
NCORDIA DOMI FORIS PAX
HEICK&SCHMALTZ

*Oben: Unterschiedliche Brücken verbinden das reizvolle Eiland, auf dem Lübeck liegt, mit dem Festland. Der Fußgängersteg überspannt die Obertrave, den Teil des Lübecker Hafens, den einst die Schuten der Stecknitz-Kanal-Schiffer ansteuerten. Ihre Fracht von Lüneburg her – wir wissen es bereits – war Salz, bestimmt für die Salzspeicher nahe dem Holstentor. Die Silhouette prägen auch von hier aus Petrikirche (vorne) und Marienkirche. Unten rechts zeigt sich das Renaissance-Rathaus elegant-filigran mit seinen Spitztürmen und kuriosen Windlöchern, eine ideale Kulisse für den Marktplatz. Und links unten ist ein Detail aus der Hafenfront zu sehen.*

*Top: An assortment of bridges connect the charming island on which Lübeck resides with the mainland. The pedestrian bridge spans the Obertrave, the part of the Lübeck harbor formerly used by the barges of the Stecknitz canal boatmen. As indicated before, their freight from Lüneburg was salt, meant for the salt storehouses near the Holstentor gate. The skyline here is again dominated by the Petrikirche (foreground) and Marienkirche steeples. Bottom right, the elegant filigree-like Renaissance city hall, with its turrets and peculiar wind holes, an ideal backdrop for the market-place. Bottom left, a harbor front detail.*

Oben bannt die eigenwillige, fünftürmige Front des Heiligen-Geist-Hospitals den Blick. Wohlhabende Kaufleute hatten es im 13. Jahrhundert für Kranke und Arme gestiftet, bis nach 1960 wohnten hier alte Menschen, jetzt wird der ehrwürdige Bau anders genutzt.
Der Speicher am Hafen (unten links) weist ebenso darauf hin, woher Lübecks große Bedeutung rührte, wie der prächtige Eingang des Hauses der Schiffergesellschaft von 1535 (unten rechts) an der Ecke Breite Straße/Engelsgrube.

Above, the unusual front of the Heiligen-Geist-Hospital with its five towers is a delight for the eye. It was endowed by well-to-do tradesmen for the poor and the sickly in the 13th century, and remained an old folks' home until 1960. Today, the time-honored building is used for different purposes. Both the storehouse at the harbor (bottom left) and the splendid entranceway to the house of the boatsmen's guild from 1535 (bottom right) on the corner of Breite Straße and Engelsgrube indicate the source of Lübeck's might.

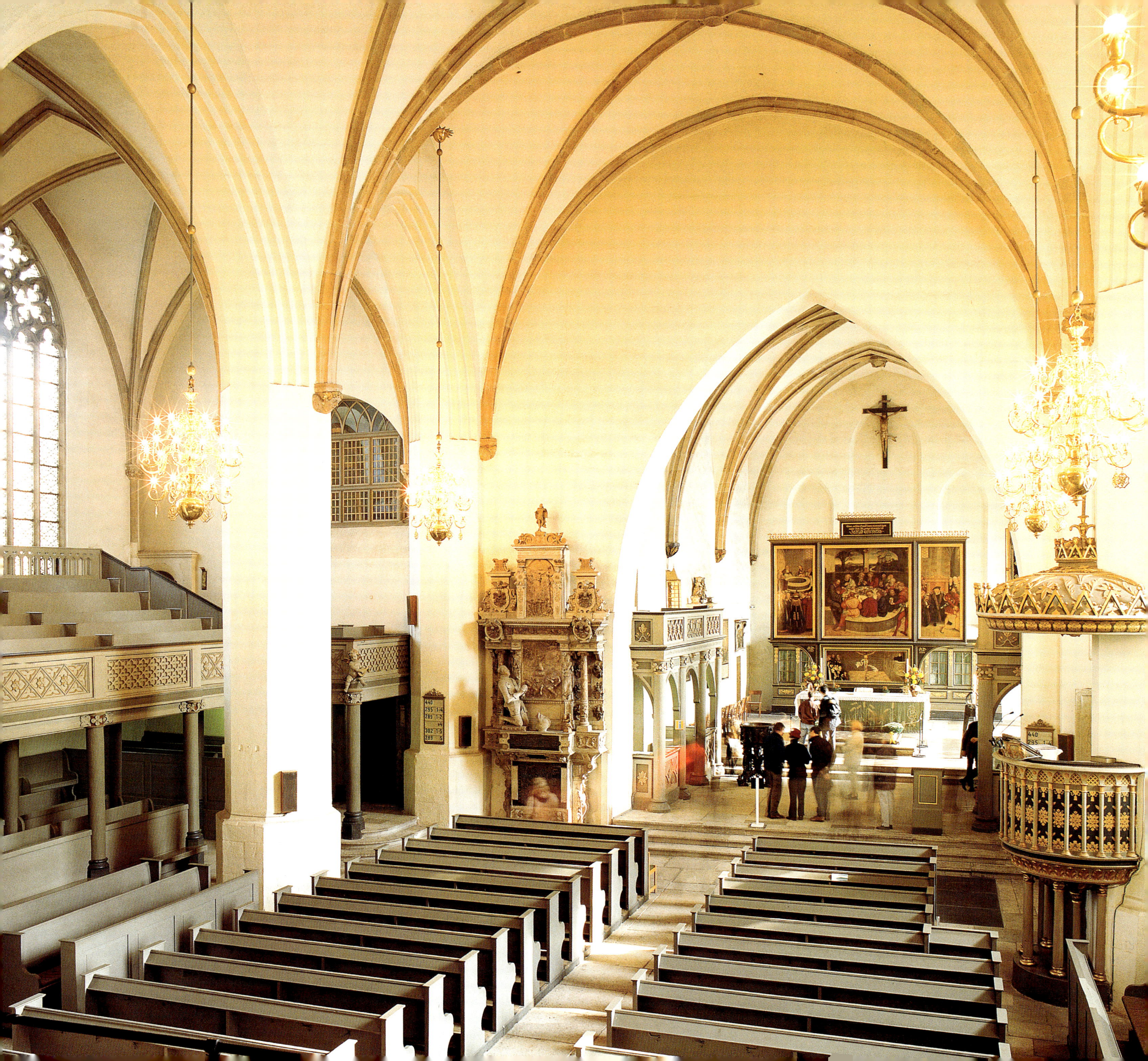

*Links zeigt sich die Stadtkirche St. Marien zu Wittenberg als gotisches Bauwerk in reiner Form, mit einem wunderbaren Flügelalter von Lucas Cranach d. Ä. und d. J. Martin Luther hatte mehr als 30 Jahre hier das Predigeramt inne, hielt in ihren Mauern berühmte Predigten und führte neue Gottesdienstformen ein. Seit Luthers Tod wurde die Kirche fast nicht mehr verändert. Nächste Doppelseite: Den weiträumigen Marktplatz der Lutherstadt Wittenberg flankiert das schöne und beeindruckende Rathaus (links), ein Renaissance-Bau. Auf dem Platz links wird der große Humanist, Theologe und Reformator Philipp Melanchthon seit 1860 mit einem Denkmal von Friedrich Drake gewürdigt. Keinen Steinwurf entfernt, näher zur Stadtkirche (hinter der Häuserreihe) hin, wurde für Martin Luther bereits 1821 ein Standbild aufgestellt (auch Bild rechts). Geschaffen hat es Gottfried Schadow, der viele klassizistische Werke hervorbrachte, unter anderem die Quadriga mit Viktoria auf dem Brandenburger Tor in Berlin.*

# Luthergedenkstätte Wittenberg

Lucas Cranach d. Ä. wirkte in Wittenberg als kurfürstlicher Hofmaler und seine beiden Söhne erblickten hier das Licht der Welt. Doch seine Berühmtheit verdankt die sächsisch-anhaltinische Stadt am Südrand des Fläming nicht der Kunst, sondern der Reformation. An der Wittenberger Schlosskirche, so heißt es, schlug der ehemalige Augustinermönch Martin Luther am 31. Oktober 1517 seine 95 Thesen an. Fünf Jahre zuvor hatte man Luther in diesem Gotteshaus, das zugleich die Kirche der von Kurfürst Friedrich III. anno 1502 gegründeten Wittenbergischen Universität war, zum Doktor der Theologie promoviert. Besondere Bedeutung hat die Schlosskirche auch als Begräbnisstätte Luthers und seines Schülers Philipp Melanchthon. 1760 bei einem Brand zerstört, wurde sie zunächst in barocker Manier wiedererbaut. Mitte des 19. Jahrhunderts bekam sie ihr mittelalterliches Aussehen weitgehend zurück. Auf den Flügeln ihres Portals sind Luthers Thesen in Gutenberg'schen Minuskeln zu lesen.

Die Reformation wurde auch in der Stadtkirche St. Marien vorangetrieben, Wittenbergs ältestem Gebäude, an der Luther lange wirkte. Außerdem legte er in der Marienkirche die Mönchskutte ab, um die ehemalige Nonne Katharina von Bora zu heiraten. Die gotische Stadtkirche war aber auch ein Schauplatz der Radikalisierung der reformerischen Tendenzen, unter anderem des Bildersturms vom 6. Februar 1522.

In unmittelbaren Nachbarschaft von St. Marien steht das Rathaus aus dem 16. Jahrhundert. Nur wenige Schritte vom Marktplatz findet man auch das Haus Melanchthons. Kurfürst und Universität ließen es 1536 für den Theologen errichten. Luthers langjähriges Wohnhaus war das ehemalige Klostergebäude der Augustiner-Eremiten. Nach der Auflösung des Ordens stellte der Kurfüst dem Reformator das spätgotische Gebäude als Domizil zur Verfügung. Hier entstanden seine wichtigsten Werke. In das Auditorium des Hauses strömten die Studenten zu den Vorlesungen Luthers und Melanchthons. Die getäfelte Lutherstube war der Ort der „Tischgespräche". Schon im 16. Jahrhundert galt sie als hoch geachtete Gedächtnisstätte. Sie ist nahezu unverändert erhalten.

# The Wittenberg Luther Memorial

Lucas Cranach the Older was the court painter of the Wittenberg elector, and his two sons were born there. Yet, the fame of the town in Saxony-Anhalt on the southern edge of the Fläming mountains is not founded on art but on the Reformation. Legend has it that it was the door to the Wittenberg palace church on which the former Augustine monk Martin Luther nailed his 95 theses on October 31, 1517. Five years earlier, Luther had received his doctor of theology degree in the same church, which also functioned as the church of the Wittenberg university founded in 1502 by Elector Friedrich III. The church is the burial-place of Luther and his student Philipp Melanchthon. Destroyed by fire in 1760, it was first rebuilt in the Baroque style, but was returned to much of its medieval aspect in the middle of the 19th century. Luther's theses are inscribed on the wings of its portals in Gutenberg-type minuscules.

The Reformation was also advocated at the town church St. Marien, Wittenberg's oldest building and for a long time Luther's sphere of activity. Here he dropped his monk's habit in order to marry the former nun Katharina von Bora. The Gothic town church was also a site of the increasingly radical reform tendencies such as the iconoclast raids of February 6, 1522.

The city hall right next to St. Marien's dates back to the 16th century. Melanchthon's house is only a few steps away from the market-place. It was commissioned by the elector and the university for the theologian in 1536. Luther's long-time residence was the former monastery building of the Augustine hermits. After the dissolution of the order, the Late Gothic structure was made available as a residence by the elector. Luther's most important works were written there, and students flocked to the auditorium of the house to listen to Luther's and Melanchthon's lectures. The famous "Dinner Talks" took place at the Luther Room. A highly revered memorial site as early as the 16th century, it has been preserved almost unchanged.

*Left, the town church St. Marien at Wittenberg presents itself in its true Gothic splendor, with a wonderful winged altarpiece by Lucas Cranach the Older and the Younger. Martin Luther preached there for more than 30 years, including a number of his famous sermons, and introduced new forms of worship. The church has hardly been changed since Luther's death.*
*Overleaf: The stunningly beautiful city hall (left), a Renaissance structure, overlooks the sizable market-place of the Luther town Wittenberg. Since 1860, the great humanist, theologian and reformer Philipp Melanchthon has been immortalized in a monument by Friedrich Drake on the square to the left. A stone's throw away, towards the town church (behind the row of houses), a monument to Martin Luther was erected as early as 1821 (see top). It was conceived by Gottfried Schadow, who created a number of Classicist works, among the quadriga with its Victoria on the Berlin Brandenburg Gate.*

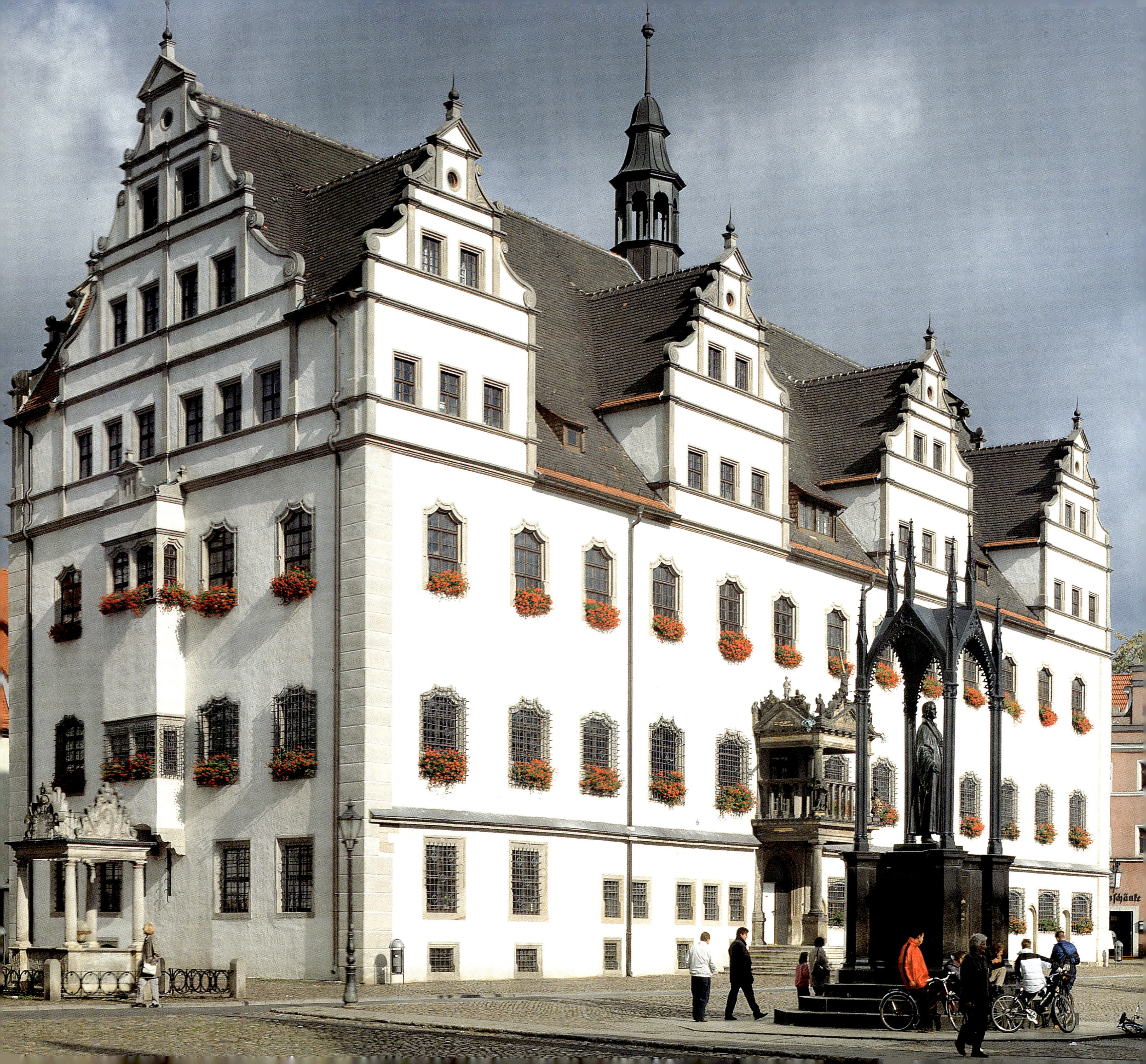
schänke

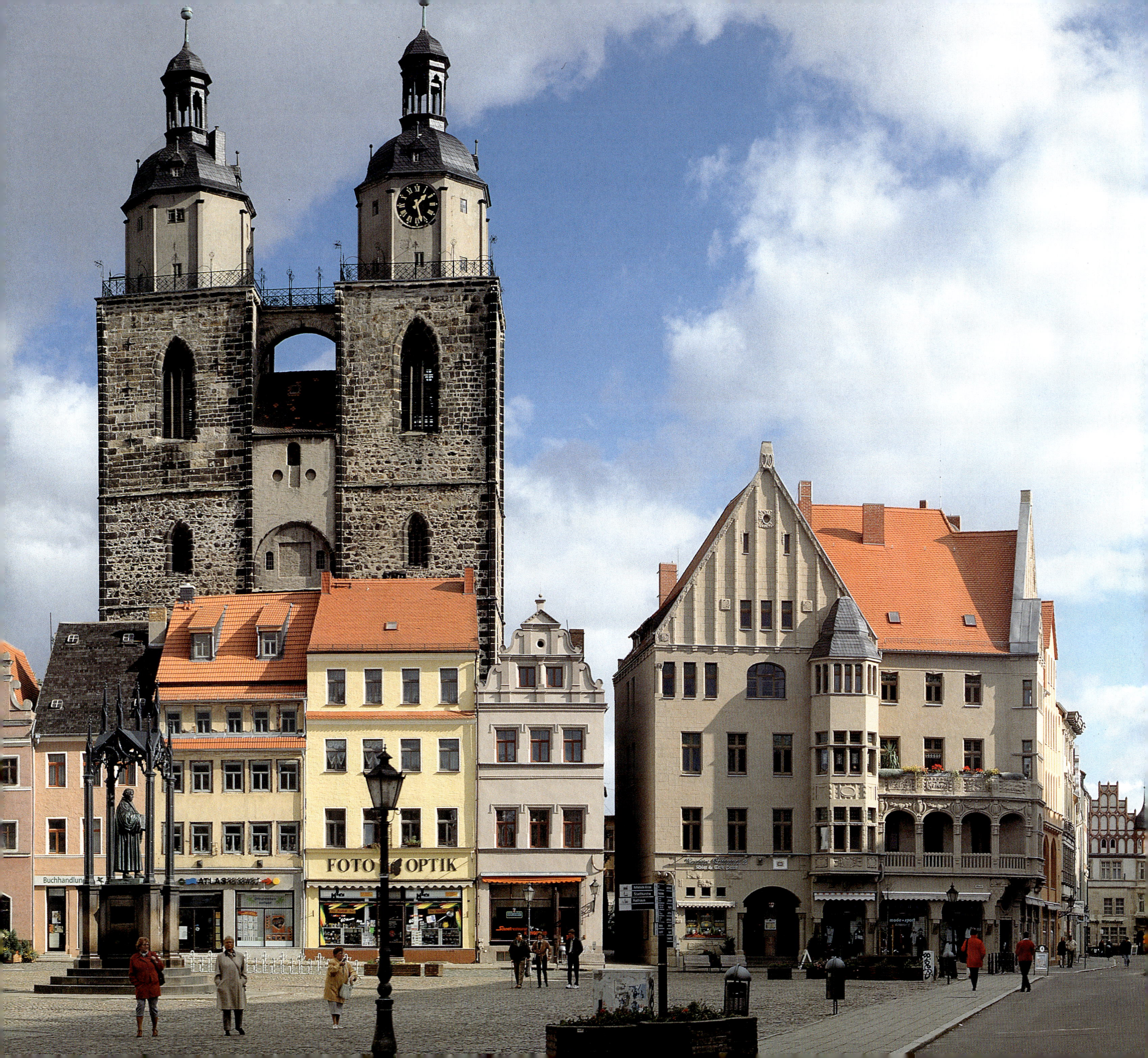
FOTO OPTIK

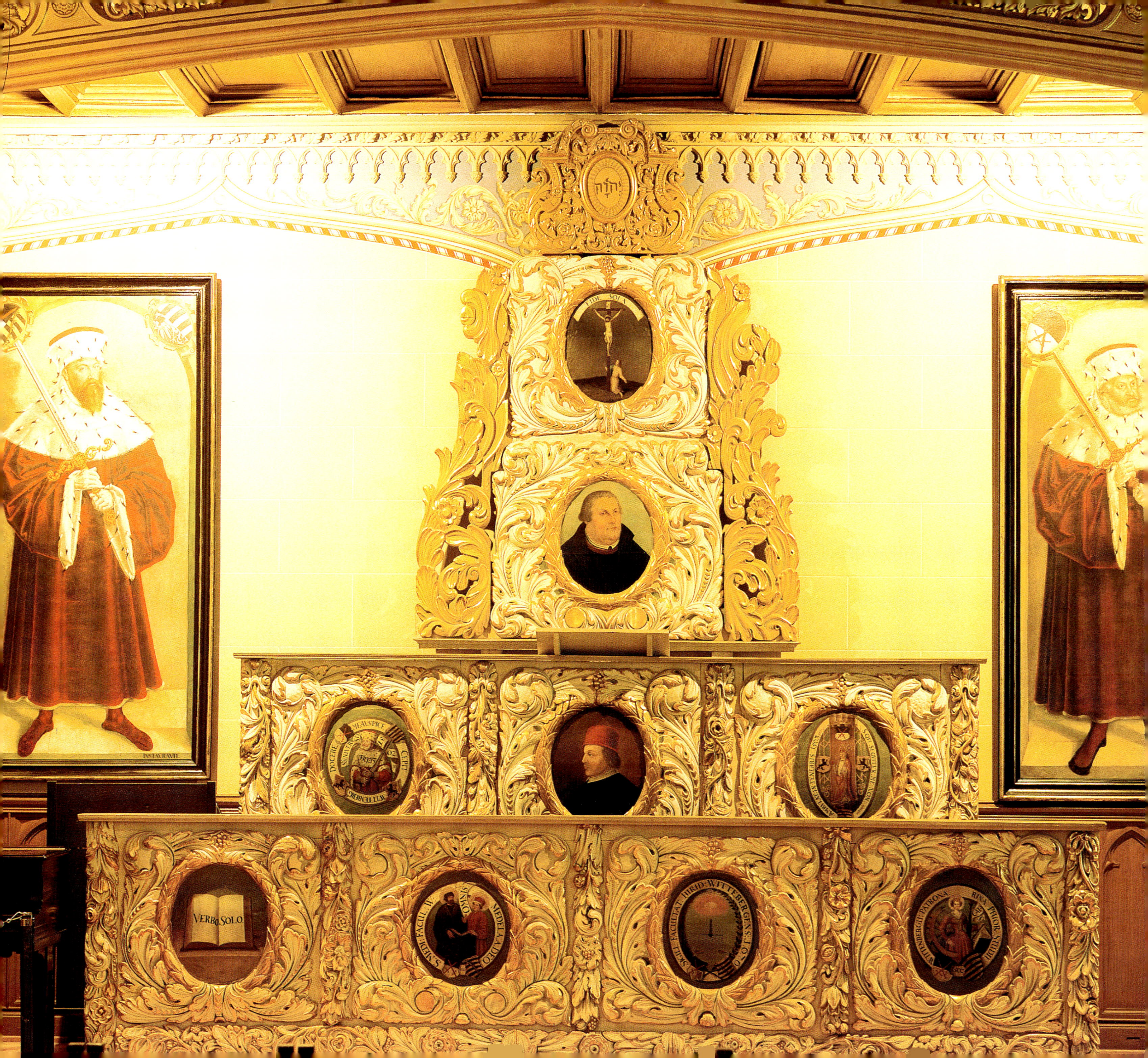
FIDE SOLA
VERBO SOLO

*Einer sagenhaften Überlieferung nach soll Graf Ludwig der Springer im Jahre 1067 den Wartberg südlich des Flusses Hörsel mit den Worten „Wart Berg, du sollst mir eine Burg werden!" in Besitz genommen haben. 1080 stand die Burg nachweislich hier. Noch aus der Romanik stammt der Palas (links, unter dem Turm).*
*Goethe besuchte die Burg 1777 und war begeistert. Damals sah die Wartburg allerdings ganz anders aus, war stark verfallen. Ludwig Bechstein, der Sammler von Sagen und Märchen bezeichnete sie 1838 als den „Zentralstern der thüringischen Geschichte". Danach fanden zweimal größere Restaurierungen und Neugestaltungen statt: In der ersten Phase von 1838 bis 1889 zogen viele romantische Elemente ein, wurde außen am Vogtei-Bau beispielsweise ein gotischer Erker aus Nürnberg angefügt (rechts). Innen schuf Moritz von Schwind den bekannten Freskenzyklus mit Themen wie dem Sängerkrieg und der Elisabeth-Legende. Die zweite Phase von 1952 bis 1983, dem Lutherjahr, machte die Burg vollends zu einem Museum, das Jahr für Jahr Abertausende anzieht.*

# Die Wartburg

Wie ein Vorposten erhebt sich die Wartburg über der später entstandenen Stadt Eisenach. Errichtet sicher vor 1080, wählten die Landgrafen von Thüringen sie für lange Zeit zu ihrem Sitz. Das Welterbe-Komitee bezeichnete die Wartburg als ein „hervorragendes Denkmal der Periode der Lehnsherrschaft in Mitteleuropa". Im mittelalterlichen abendländischen Feudalismus delegierte der König oder Kaiser als oberster Lehnsherr Befugnisse an Kronvasallen, an Herzöge, Reichsäbte, Bischöfe – auch an die Thüringer Landgrafen.

Zu einem nationalen Symbol geriet die Wartburg durch unterschiedliche Ereignisse. Dazu zählt als Erstes der sagenhafte „Sängerkrieg", ein Wettstreit der Troubadoure, der um 1206/1207 auf der Wartburg stattgefunden haben soll. Belegt ist, dass sich Wolfram von Eschenbach 1203 länger am Hof des Landgrafen Hermann I. auf der Wartburg aufgehalten und dabei wohl einen Teil des „Parzival" verfasst hat. Walther von der Vogelweide „pries" Hermanns Mäzenatentum für die großen Minnesänger und Epiker: „Der lantgrave ist so gemuot, / daz er mit stolzen helden sin habe vertuot." Und Richard Wagner setzte das dankbare Thema in seiner Oper „Tannhäuser" um.

Martin Luther wurde auf dem Rückweg von dem Reichstag zu Worms, auf dem man ihn mit Acht und Bann belegte, am 4. Mai 1521 von seinem Landesherrn Herzog Friedrich dem Weisen in einem fingierten Überfall dem Zugriff anderer Mächte entzogen und auf die Wartburg gebracht. Dort hat er innerhalb 10 Wochen das Neue Testament aus dem Griechischen übersetzt. Dass er damit zu einem wichtigen Erneuerer der deutschen Sprache wurde und gleichzeitig einen wahren Bestseller schuf, stellte sich bald heraus.

Jahrhunderte später ging von der Wartburg ein früher Anstoß zur Einigung der von Napoleon reichlich durcheinander gewirbelten deutschen Länder aus: Im Juni 1815 war der Bund der Studenten gegründet worden, am 18. Oktober 1817 zogen über 400 Burschenschaftler los, hinauf zur Burg, hinter der schwarz-rot-goldenen Fahne der Jenaer Studenten. – Die Geschichte wird weisen, welche Einheit die dauerhaftere sein wird, die von 1871 oder von 1990.

# The Wartburg

Wartburg Castle is towering above the northwestern foothills of the Thüringer Wald mountains like an outpost overlooking the town Eisenach, which is much its junior. Built in 1080, the Wartburg for a long time served as the seat of the landgraves of Thuringia. In 1999, the World Heritage Committee described it as "an outstanding reminder of the feudal system in Central Europe". Under the occidental feudalist system of the Middle Ages, the king or emperor as the highest feudal lord delegated powers to his crown vassals, among them dukes, imperial abbots, bishops – and the landgraves of Thuringia.

A number of events turned the Wartburg into a national symbol: First, the legendary "singers' contest", a competition of minstrels said to have taken place on the Wartburg in 1206/07. Wolfram von Eschenbach apparently did stay at the court of Landgrave Hermann I for a longer period of time in 1203 and seems to have written part of his "Parzival" epic there. Walther von der Vogelweide also "praised" Hermann as a sponsor for the great minstrels and epic poets: "It seems the landgrave's inclination/to squander his wealth with heroes of station". And Richard Wagner took up the popular theme in his opera "Tannhäuser".

On May 4, 1521, on his way back from Worms after having been excommunicated at the imperial diet, Martin Luther was taken into custody by his sovereign Duke Friedrich in a simulated attack on his party and brought to the Wartburg. There, in the course of ten weeks, he translated the New Testament from the Greek, and it soon turned out that he had created a true bestseller, at the same time providing new momentum to the development of the German language.

Centuries later, an early impulse for the reunification of the German states, all in a jumble since Napoleon, originated from the Wartburg: In June 1815, the fraternity "Bund der Studenten" was founded, and on October 18, 1817, more than 400 of its members marched up to the castle behind the flag of the Jena students. – History will prove which unity will last longer, that of 1871 or of 1990.

*According to legend, in 1067 Count Ludwig der Springer took possession of the Wartberg mountain south of the Hörsel river with the following words: "Wait, rock, you will become my castle". By 1080, the Wartburg ["Wait-Castle"] had been erected at the site. The living quarters (left, gables and tower) still date back to the Romanesque period.*
*Goethe visited the castle in 1777 and was in raptures, even if the castle at that time looked very different, quite dilapidated that is. Ludwig Bechstein, collector of legends and fairytales, called it "the shining star of the history of Thuringia". After that, the castle underwent two great refurbishments. In the first, from 1838 to 1889, a number of Romantic elements were added, and the bailiff's building received a Gothic oriel from Nuremberg (above). Moritz von Schwind created the well-known fresco cycle with topics such as the singer's contest and the legend of St. Elizabeth in the inside. In the second phase from 1952 to 1983, the Luther anniversary year, the castle was finally styled into a museum, drawing thousands of visitors each year.*

*Vom Turm der Wartburg schweift der Blick über die Burganlage, die sich um zwei Höfe gruppiert und alles in allem unserem Idealbild einer Burg aus dem Mittelalter zu entsprechen vermag. Von der Burg aus, die auf dem letzten Ausläufer des Thüringer Walds liegt, ist es nur ein Katzensprung zum berühmten Rennsteig. Er gilt als der am meisten begangene Fernwanderweg Deutschlands. Nah ist es auch zur Stadt Eisenach – und zur geographischen Mitte Deutschlands, wie eine Deutschlandkarte leicht zeigt. Und angesichts eines Bilds aus dem Sommer, nicht Februar wie hier, würde uns Thüringens Anspruch „grünes Herz Deutschlands" zu sein, sofort einleuchten.*

*The tower of the Wartburg affords a view over the entire castle complex, which is organized around two courtyards and comes pretty close to what is commonly pictured as an ideal medieval castle. From the castle, which rests on the outer foothills of the Thüringer Wald mountains, it is not very far to the famous "Rennsteig", the most popular long-distance hiking path in Germany. The town Eisenach, too, is not far away, and neither the geographical center of Germany, as may easily be gathered from a map. Looking at a summer picture instead of this shot from February, would immediately substantiate Thuringias's claim to the title "the green heart of Germany".*

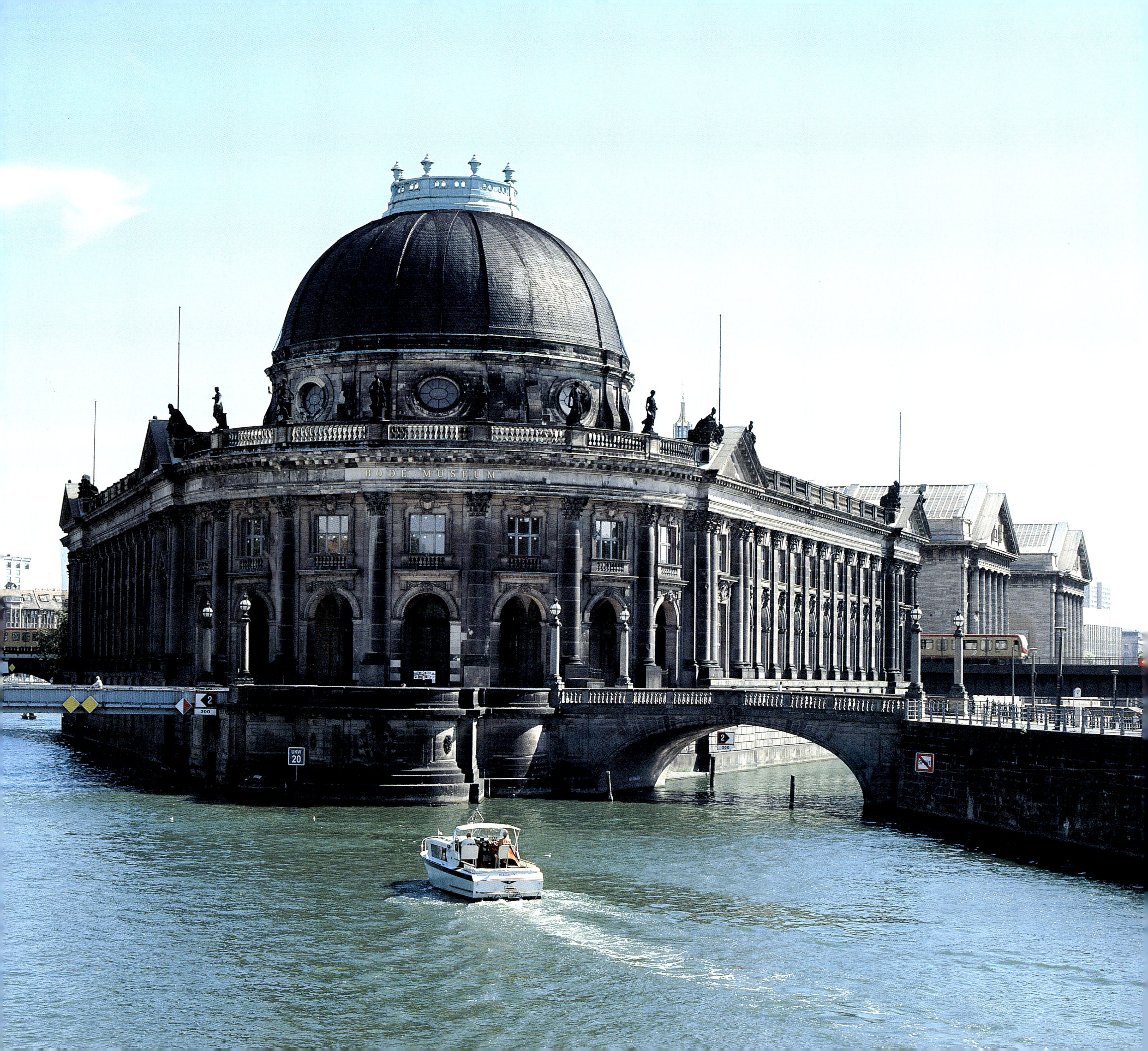
BODE MUSEUM
UKW
20

## Die Berliner Museumsinsel

Angesichts des Baubooms in der lange geteilten Stadt ist es als Ansporn und Versprechen zu sehen, wenn mit der Berliner Museumsinsel ein zurzeit nur in Teilen zugängliches, gleichwohl „einzigartiges Ensemble von Museumsbauten" gewürdigt wird. Weiter heißt es in der Begründung des Welterbe-Komitees, hier werde „die Entwicklung modernen Museums-Designs über mehr als ein Jahrhundert illustriert" – und das in unmittelbarer Nachbarschaft.

Einzeln betrachtet lässt sich dies untermauern: Geplant war das Alte Museum schon Ende des 18. Jahrhunderts, erbaut wurde es dann mustergültig klassizistisch 1824 bis 1828 von Karl Friedrich Schinkel. Als eines der ersten öffentlichen Museen überhaupt beherbergt es Kleinkunst der griechischen und römischen Antike: Skulpturen, Bronzearbeiten, Gläser und Schmuck.

Auf den Architekten Friedrich August Stüler (1800–1865), der auch die Burg Hohenzollern wieder aufgebaut hat, geht das Neue Museum zurück. Errichtet 1843 bis 1855, sollte es einen Überblick über die Kunstgeschichte der Welt vermitteln. Es wurde im Zweiten Weltkrieg stark zerstört und wird derzeit renoviert.

Auch die Alte Nationalgalerie wurde von Stüler entworfen und von Johann Heinrich Strack 1866 bis 1876 streng klassizistisch ausgeführt. Ihre Sammlung internationaler und deutscher Malerei und Bildhauerei reicht vom späten 18. Jahrhundert bis in die Moderne: von Constable über Manet bis Picasso oder Rodin. Voraussichtlich bis 2001 ist die Galerie geschlossen, einige Exponate sind solange im Alten Museum zu sehen.

Unter dem Dach des Bode-Museums, 1897 bis 1904 erbaut, ist Raum für mehrere Museen und Sammlungen, doch auch dieser große Komplex wird noch umgebaut.

Die großen, monumentalen Stücke der Antikensammlung finden angemessenen Platz im jüngsten Bau des Quintetts, dem Pergamonmuseum, das bis 1930 errichtet wurde. Der Zeus-Altar aus der kleinasiatischen Stadt Pergamon füllt allein einen Raum, galt als eines der sieben Weltwunder und ist ein Publikumsmagnet.

Wenn die Gelder wie geplant fließen, können sich wohl bis 2010 alle fünf Museen im alten Glanz zeigen.

## The Berlin Museum Island

Vicious tongues say that building is the only thing going on in Berlin ... and now the UNESCO even entered a permanent construction site into the World Heritage List: the Museum Island. Five museal structures, designated a "unique ensemble that illustrates the development of modern museum architecture over more than a century" by the committee, stand side by side, enclosed by two channels of the Spree river.

The individual buildings lend substance to this evaluation: The "Altes Museum" was in planning as early as the end of the 18th century and was finally built as one of the first public museums in an exemplary Classicist style from 1824 to 1828 by Karl Friedrich Schinkel. It houses small artefacts from Greek and Roman Antiquity: sculptures, bronzes, glyptographs, glassware and gold and silver jewelry.

The "Neues Museum" was conceived by the architect Friedrich August Stüler (1800–1865), who also rebuilt the Hohenzollern Castle. It was erected between 1843 and 1855 and was intended to give an overview over the history of art around the world. Heavily damaged in World War II, it is currently being renovated.

The Alte Nationalgalerie was also designed by Stüler and built under Johann Heinrich Strack from 1866 to 1876 in a strictly Classicist style. Its collection of international and German paintings and sculptures includes works from the 18th century to Modernism, from Constable to Manet to Picasso or Rodin. The gallery will probably be closed until 2001, some pieces are now to be admired in the Altes Museum.

The Bode-Museum, built in 1897 to 1904, has room for a number of museums and collections, but momentarily is also under construction.

The large, monumental pieces of the Antiquity Collection are appropriately found in the youngest structure of the quintet, the Pergamonmuseum, which opened its doors in 1930. The Zeus altar from the town of Pergamon in Minor Asia, always drawing large crowds, fills an entire hall by itself and belonged among the Seven Wonders of the World in Antiquity.

If the funds are available as planned, all five museums will be accessible in their old splendor by 2010.

---

*Zwischen Spree (links) und Spreekanal (rechts) wird von Nordwesten her gesehen die äußerste Spitze der Spreeinsel, des Berliner Werders, von einem mächtigen, dreieckigen Bau beherrscht: dem Bode-Museum. Ernst von Ihne hat es im Stil des wilhelminischen Barock errichtet. Mit vier weiteren Museen gleich nebenan kann die Museumsinsel aufwarten: Altes Museum, Neues Museum, Alte Nationalgalerie und Pergamonmuseum. Nach Abschluss der laufenden Sanierungsarbeiten – die teilweise noch durch Kriegsschäden bedingt sind – werden wieder Sammlungen des Museums für Spätantike und Byzantinische Kunst, von Skulpturen, etwa einer halben Million Münzen oder auch eine Kindergalerie die Besucher ins Bode-Museum locken – und ein Café unter der lichtdurchfluteten Kuppel.*

*Oben: Wer selbst sehen will, wo der Pergamon- oder Zeus-Altar 1878 bis 1886 freigelegt wurde, muss Bergama besuchen. Die heutige Stadt im Westen der Türkei steht zum Teil auf dem Boden des antiken Pergamon, der Hauptstadt des gleichnamigen hellenistischen Reiches. Es bestand im 3. und 2. Jahrhundert v. Chr., ehe Rom die Macht übernahm und im Jahre 129 v. Chr. seine Provinz Asia errichtete.*

*Seen from the northwest, the outer point of the Spree island Berlin Werder between the Spree river (far left) and the Spree canal (right) is dominated by a mighty triangular structure – the Bode-Museum. It was built in the Wilhelminian Baroque style according to plans by Ernst von Ihne. The island offers four other museums in close proximity: Altes Museum, Neues Museum, Alte Nationalgalerie and Pergamonmuseum. After the refurbishment measures, which are partially still due to damages from the war, the Bode-Museum once more will display its collections of Late Antiquity and Byzantine art, sculptures, about half a million coins and a children's gallery, as well as a café under a glass dome.*

*Above: Those who would like to see the original site of the Pergamon or Zeus altar, excavated from 1878 to 1886, must go to Bergama. The town in Western Turkey is partially built onto the site of Ancient Pergamon, the capital of the Hellenistic empire of the same name in the 2nd and 3rd centuries B.C., before Rome came to power establishing its province Asia in 129 B.C.*

# Orts-, Personen- und Sachregister

Aachen, Dom (Münster), Pfalzkapelle 35 ff.
Alte Nationalgalerie > Berlin 131
Altes Museum > Berlin 131
Amphitheater > Trier 63 ff.
Anna Amalia (1739–1807), Herzogin von Weimar 97 ff.
(Herzogin-)Anna-Amalia-Bibliothek > Weimar 97 ff.
Arnold von Trier, Erzbischof 7
Augustiner-Eremiten > Wittenberg 121 ff.
Augustusburg, Schloss > Brühl 57 ff.
Auwera (Auvera), Johann Wolfgang van der (1708–1756), Hofbildhauer in Würzburg 13

Babelsberg in Potsdam 75, 83
Backsteingotik, Lübeck 115 ff.
Bamberg 19 ff.
Bamberger Reiter 23
Barock 13, 19, 57 ff., 63 ff.
Barock, wilhelminischer 131
Barbarathermen > Trier 63 ff.
Barbarossa > Friedrich I. 35
Basilika (Palastaula) in Trier 63 ff.
Bauhaus in Dessau 109 ff.
Bechstein, Ludwig (1801–1860), deutscher Schriftsteller 127
Belvedere in Weimar 97 ff.
Benediktiner 85, 103
Bergama, türkische Stadt > Pergamon 131
Berlin, Museumsinsel 131
Bernward (um 960–1022), hl., Bischof von Hildesheim 69 ff.
Bildergalerie > Potsdam 75 ff.
Bode-Museum, Berlin 131
Boffrand, Germain (1667–1754), französischer Baumeister 13
Bora, Katharina von (1499–1552), Ehefrau Martin Luthers 121
Bossi, G. Antonio († 1764), italienischer Stuckator 13
Brühl, Schlösser Augustusburg und Falkenlust 57 ff.
byzantinische Kunst 131

Carlone, Carlo, italienischer Maler 57
Cecilienhof in Potsdam 75, 83
Charlottenhof > Potsdam 75 ff.
Chinesisches Teehaus in Potsdam 75
Cotte, Robert de (1656–1735), französischer Baumeister 13
Cranach, Lucas d. Ä. (1472–1553), deutscher Maler, Zeichner und Kupferstecher 97, 121
Cranach, Lucas d. J. (1515–1586), deutscher Maler und Zeichner 121
Cuvilliés, François de (1695–1768), französisch-deutscher Baumeister 57, 61

Dessau, Bauhaus 109 ff.
Deutsches Nationaltheater > Weimar 97 ff.
Dientzenhofer, Johann Leonhard (1660–1707), bayerischer Baumeister 19, 23
Dioskuren-Denkmal > Weimar 97 ff.
Dom und St. Michael > Hildesheim 69 ff.
Doppelkirche, Dom und Liebfrauen in Trier 63 ff.
Drake, Friedrich (19. Jh.), deutscher Bildhauer 121 ff.

Eisenach 127 ff.
Eisleben, Lutherstadt 125
Eozän, zweitälteste Serie des Tertiärs > Messel 53 ff.
Ettersburg > Weimar 97 ff.

Falkenlust, Schloss in Brühl 57 ff.
Feininger, Lyonel (1871–1956), deutsch-amerikanischer Maler und Graphiker 109, 113
Friedenskirche in Potsdam 75, 79
Friedrich I. Barbarossa (1122–1190, Rotbart), deutscher Kaiser 35
Friedrich II., der Große (1712–1786), preußischer König 75 ff.
Friedrich III., der Weise (1463–1525), sächsischer Kurfürst 121, 127
Fürstengruft > Weimar 97 ff.

Gerard (Gerhard), Meister († 1271), deutscher Steinmetz 91
Girard, Dominique, Gartenarchitekt im Barock 57
Gisela (um 990–1043), Gattin Kaiser Konrads II. > Speyer 103 ff.
Glienicke, Schloss > Potsdam 75 ff.
Goethe, Johann Wolfgang von (1749–1832), deutscher Dichter 97 ff., 127
Goethe- und Schillerarchiv > Weimar 97 ff.
Gontard, Karl von (1731–1791), deutscher Baumeister 75, 83
Goslar, Kaiserpfalz, Dom, Altstadt, Rammelsberg 41 ff.
Gotik 7, 19, 63 ff., 88 f., 91 ff., 115 ff.
Gropius, Walter (1883–1969), deutsch-amerikanischer Architekt 109 ff.

Hanse > Lübeck 115 ff.
Heiligen-Geist-Hospital in Lübeck 115, 119
Heinrich I. (um 875–936), deutscher König 29 ff.
Heinrich III. (1017–1056), deutscher König/ Kaiser > Goslar, Speyer 41, 103
Heinrich IV. (1050–1106), deutscher König/ Kaiser 103
Heinrich der Löwe (um 1129–1195), Herzog von Sachsen u. Bayern 115
Herder, Johann Gottfried von (1744–1803), deutscher Philosoph, Theologe und Dichter 97, 100
Hermann I. (1155–1217), Landgraf von Thüringen 127

Hesse, Hermann (1877–1962), deutscher Dichter und Nobelpreisträger 7
Hildebrandt, Johann Lucas von (1668–1745), österreichischer Baumeister 13
Hildesheim, Dom und St. Michael 69 ff.
Hölderlin, Friedrich (1770–1843), deutscher Dichter 7
Historischer Friedhof > Weimar 97 ff.
Holstentor in Lübeck 115 ff.

Ihne, Ernst Eberhard von (1848–1917), deutscher Baumeister 131
Ilmpark > Weimar 97 ff.
Itten, Johannes (1888–1967), schweizerischer Maler und Kunstpädagoge > Bauhaus Dessau 109 ff.

Justinian I. (482–565), (römischer) Kaiser > Aachen 35 ff.

Kaiserthermen > Trier 63 ff.
Kaiserthron > Königsstuhl
Kandinsky, Wassily (1866–1944), russischer Maler und Graphiker 109, 113
Karl August (1757–1828), Herzog/ Großherzog von Sachsen-Weimar-Eisenach 97 ff.
Karl der Große (747–814), römischer Kaiser 35, 39, 85
karolingische Kunst 35, 85, 88 f.
Kepler, Johannes (1571–1630), deutscher Astronom 7
Klee, Paul (1879–1940), deutsch-schweizerischer Maler und Graphiker 109, 113
Knobelsdorff, Georg Wenzeslaus von (1699–1753), deutscher Baumeister 75
Köln, Dom 91 ff.
Königsstuhl (Thron) in Aachen 39, in Goslar 41
Konrad II. (um 990–1039), deutscher König/ Kaiser 103

Lenné, Peter Joseph (1789–1866), deutscher Gartenbaumeister 75
Lettner > Chorschranke in Maulbronn 10
Leveilly, Mich(a)el, Kurkölner Baumeister 57, 61
Lochner, Stephan (1400–1451), deutscher Maler 91
Lorsch, Kloster 85 ff.
Lübeck, Hansestadt 115 ff.
Ludwig der Springer, thüringischer Graf 127
Luther, Martin (1483–1546), deutscher Reformator 121 ff., 127

Marienkirche in Lübeck 115 ff.
Marmorpalais in Potsdam 75, 83
Mathilde, Gattin Heinrichs I., Mutter Ottos I. > Quedlinburg 29 ff.

Maulbronn, Kloster 7 ff.
Meister Gerard(us) > Köln 91 ff.
Meisterhäuser, Bauhaus Dessau 109, 113
Melanchthon (Schwarzerd[t]), Philipp (1497–1560), deutscher Humanist und Reformator 121 ff.
Messel, Grube 53 ff.
Meyer, Hannes (1889–1954), schweizerischer Architekt > Bauhaus Dessau 109 ff.
Mies van der Rohe, Ludwig (1886 bis 1969), amerikanisch-deutscher Architekt > Bauhaus Dessau 109 ff.
Moholy-Nagy, László (1895–1946), ungarischer Künstler > Bauhaus Dessau 109 ff.
Museumsinsel Berlin 131

Neuer Garten > Potsdam 75 ff.
Neues Museum > Berlin 131
Neues Palais in Potsdam 75, 79 ff.
Neumann, Balthasar (1687–1753), Baumeister 13 ff., 57
Nikolaus von Verdun (sicher bis 1208), lothringischer Goldschmied und Emailleur 91

Ölschiefer > Messel 53 ff.
Orangerie in Potsdam 75, 79
Otto I., der Große (912–973), deutscher König und Kaiser 29
Otto III. (980–1002), deutscher König und Kaiser 29
ottonische Kunst 35

Pergamon > Bergama, türkische Stadt in Kleinasien 131
Pergamon- oder Zeus-Altar > Berlin 131
Pergamonmuseum > Berlin 131
Persius, Ludwig (1803–1845), deutscher Baumeister 75
Petrikirche in Lübeck 115 ff.
Pfaffenwinkel, Oberbayern 47
Pfaueninsel in Potsdam/Berlin 75, 83
Porta Nigra in Trier 63
Potsdam 75 ff.

Quedlinburg 29 ff.

Rammelsberg, Goslar 41 ff.
Rathaus in Lübeck 115, 118
Rathaus in Wittenberg 121 ff.
Ravenna 35
Renaissance 11, 118, 121
Riemenschneider, Tilman (um 1460–1531), deutscher Bildschnitzer und Bildhauer 17
Röchling, Carl und Hermann, deutsche Unternehmer 25
Römische Bäder > Potsdam 75 ff.
Römisches Haus in Weimar 97, 101
Rokoko 13, 47 ff., 57 ff.
Romanik 10, 19, 63 ff., 103 ff., 127
Rudolf I. von Habsburg (1210–1291) > Speyer 103 ff.

Salier, fränkisches Adelsgeschlecht > Speyer 103
Sankt Marien, Dom (Münster) in Aachen 35
Sankt Marien, Stadtkirche in Wittenberg 121 ff.
Sankt Servatii, Stiftskirche in Quedlinburg 29, 33
Sanssouci, Schloss, Potsdam 75 ff.
Schadow, Gottfried (1764–1850), deutscher Bildhauer 121 ff.
Schiffergesellschaft, Haus der, in Lübeck 119
Schiller, Friedrich von (1759–1805), deutscher Dichter 97 ff.
Schillerhaus in Weimar 97, 101
Schinkel, Karl Friedrich (1781–1841), deutscher Baumeister 75, 131
Schlaun, Johann Conrad (1695–1773), deutscher Baumeister 57
Schlemmer, Oskar (1888–1943), deutscher Maler und Bildhauer > Bauhaus Dessau 109 ff.
Schönborn, Johann Philipp Franz von, Fürstbischof von Würzburg 13
Schönborn, Lothar Franz von, Fürstbischof von Bamberg 19
Schwanthaler, Ludwig von (1802 bis 1848), bayerischer Bildhauer 106
Schwarzerd(t), Philipp > Melanchthon 121 ff.
Schwind, Moritz von (1804–1871), österreichisch-deutscher Maler und Zeichner > Wartburg 127 ff.
Seitz, Johann, deutscher Baumeister 63
Sinterung (von Eisenerz) 25
spätantike Kunst 35, 131
Speyer, Dom 103 ff.
staufische Kunst 35
Steingaden, Wieskirche 47
Strack, Johann Heinrich (1805–1880), deutscher Architekt 131
Stüler, Friedrich August (1800–1865), deutscher Architekt 131

Tertiär, System im jüngsten Erdzeitalter > Messel 53 ff.
Tiepolo, Giovanni Battista (1696–1770), italienischer Maler 13
Trier 63 ff.
Trockengasreinigung 25

Völklingen, Alte Hütte von V. 25 ff.

Wagner, Peter (1730–1809), deutscher Bildhauer 17
Wagner, Richard (1813–1883), deutscher Komponist 127
Walther von der Vogelweide (um 1170–1230), mittelhochdeutscher Dichter und Minnesänger 127
Wartburg 125, 127 ff.
Weimar, Bauhaus > Bauhaus Dessau 109 ff.
Weimar, Weimarer Klassik 97 ff.

Weströmisches Reich > Trier 63 ff.
Wieland, Christoph Martin (1733–1813), deutscher Dichter 97
Wieskirche 4, 47 ff.
Wittelsbach, Clemens August von, Fürstbischof von Köln 57 ff.
Wittenberg, Lutherstadt 121 ff.
Wolfram von Eschenbach (um 1170/80–1220), deutscher Dichter 127
Würzburg, Residenz 13 ff.

Zimmermann, Dominikus (1685–1766), deutscher Stuckator und Baumeister 47 ff.
Zimmermann, Johann Baptist (1680–1758), deutscher Stuckator und Maler 47 ff.
Zisterzienser 7

**Bildquellen**
Sigloch Edition/Bildarchiv
E-Mail: c.falk@sigloch.de
Am Buchberg 8
D-74572 Blaufelden

**Impressum**
© Sigloch Edition, Am Buchberg 8, D-74572 Blaufelden
Redaktionelle Bearbeitung: Friedhelm Messow, Kupferzell
Nachdruck verboten. Alle Rechte vorbehalten. Printed in Latvia
Reproduktion: Otterbach Digital World, Rastatt
Satz: Sigloch Edition, Blaufelden
Druck: Jana Seta, Riga
Papier: 170 g/m² nopaCoat classic matt TCF, Nordland Papier AG, Dörpen
Bindearbeiten: Sigloch Buchbinderei, Blaufelden
ISBN 3-89393-189-9